Earth Rise:

The Case for Studying and Using Earth

in Astrology

Cynthia L.C. Wood

Earth Rise

The Case for Studying and Using Earth in Astrology©

Copyright © 2013 by Cynthia L.C. Wood. All rights reserved. No part of this book shall be reproduced, by any means – electronic, mechanical, photocopying, recording or otherwise – without written permission from the writer.

March 20 2014 ISBN#: 978-0-9899528-2-8 (print)

Printed by Createspace, An Amazon.com company

Available on Kindle and other devices

This book is dedicated to our planet Earth. She gives us life, sustains us, fascinates us, and she does it all with incredible beauty.

Acknowledgements

One of the many oddities of self-publishing is there are very few people to acknowledge. However, I would be remiss indeed, if I didn't thank all my teachers, past and present, astrological or otherwise, and whether they ever knew they were my teachers or not! Thank you to Brenda and Fred Daily, docents at The Dali Museum in Florida (http://www.thedali.org) for their expertise. I owe a debt of gratitude to my dear daughter: Tala K. Wood, an indispensable editor. My heartfelt thanks go also, to my husband Dave for his love, his fantastic tech support, and the many martinis. To my soul-sister Kristine for her content discussions, constructive criticisms, and everlasting encouragement. Lastly, to my parents, Yvonne, Robert, and Bob who are so much a part of who I am, for their patience, guidance, love, and support throughout my life. Thank you all.

Earth Rise
The Case for Studying and Using Earth in Astrology

Annotated TABLE OF CONTENTS

xiii   **Preface**

xiii   The Road to Writing this Book
xiv   Taurus = Earth: The Potential of Planet Earth in Astrology
xvii   An Astrological Crossroads
xviii   A Love Letter to Earth
xix   Why Earth?
xx   Beginning a Discussion
xxi   Technical Note

1   **Chapter 1: The Missing Planet**

1   "The World We Live in" An Astrological Mindset of Earth
3   A Sickness in Earth and Body
4   A (very little) Background
5   Earth and the Astrological Houses, Not Enough of a Good Thing
7   Changing Perspective: Missing Planet, Missing Link?
10   A Remedy for Separation Anxiety and the Copernican Fallout
12   Earth's Place in Astrology
14   Earth and Taurus
16   A Deserving Place

19   **Chapter 2: The Sun/Earth Opposition**
What the permanent Sun/Earth opposition tells us about who we are and why we can't get along with our own planet

19   Looking Back
20   A Planetary Ruler for Humanity

22	The Sun and Humanity
24	The Leo/Aquarius Diametric
25	A Species Apart
28	A Population of Leos
29	The Dark Side of Leo (Five Traits of a Possible Apocalypse?)
29	Self Concern, Self-Aggrandizement, and the Conquerors
32	Pride
35	Greed and Ostentation
37	Passion and Strong Convictions
40	Creativity
43	Handling the Sun Earth Opposition
46	Nature and Nurture
49	Opposing Microcosms: More manifestations of Sun Opposition Earth
53	Our Balancing Act: What does Earth (Taurus) want from Sun (Leo) Anyway?
58	Early Human Habits
60	Going Green: A Taurian Creed
62	The Enlightened Leo: Our Maturing Population
62	From Selfish Would-be Conqueror to Efficient Compassionate Leader
64	Pride…of Place
65	Greed: Time to Value something Besides Stuff
66	Passion and Strong Convictions…For our Mission Here on Earth
66	Creativity: Used with Concern
67	Summary
71	**Chapter 3: Esoteric Earth, Levels of Earth, and the Number 4**
71	The Classical Elements in Astrology and Physics
72	Triplicities of Astrology
73	Modes of Astrology
74	Levels of Existence and the Signs of Astrology
75	The Modes of Astrology and Manifestation
77	Matter and the Three Earth Signs

85	Earth, Astrology and Metaphysics: The Four Fixed Signs, Symbolic Cornerstones of Reality
90	The Four Holy Creatures
93	The Sphinx
95	The Bible and God's Chariot
97	Tarot
101	Earth Symbolism, Science, Physics, and the Unified Field Theory
111	Numerology
112	Number 4 in Tarot
114	Number Symbolism of the Fixed Signs
115	Number 4: The Kabbalah and the Earth
117	The Tetragrammaton
119	More on Number 4
125	Summary

135   Chapter 4: The Element Earth in Astrology and the Natal Chart

135	Living Day to Day with the Symbolic Four Elements
135	The Four Elements in the Astrological Birth Chart
138	Earth Element: Levels of Expression
139	Seasons of Earth
140	Seasons of Earth Signs
146	Individual Personalities: Reflections of the Seasons
150	General Affectations of Earth Signs
152	Levels of Human Population When Influenced by Earth
155	Earth Houses
158	Lack of Earth or Hard Aspects: Problems with the Earth Element in the Natal Chart
161	Female Gender of Earth Signs
162	Transits in Earth Signs
163	Earth on Contrary House Cusps
165	The Challenge of Contrary Elements on the House Wheel
174	Earth the Essential

177   Chapter 5: Saturn: The Surrogate

177	Earth, Where Are You Now?
178	The Astrological Process of Integrating Newly Discovered Planets
180	Saturn: An Illusion of Solidity
183	Saturn and Capricorn: The Highest Level of Earth Energy
186	Capricorn in the Natal Chart
190	Saturn - Theoretical Earth and the Kabbalah
195	Progression of the Earth Signs on the Tree of Life
197	Shifting Saturn's Symbology: Illusions of Earthly Matter?
199	Matter – All Illusion?
200	Subatomic particles and the Particle and Wave Theory
202	Truth, Illusion, Form, and Fear
205	Saturn, Ruler of the Earthly Illusion: Time
210	Saturn and Mythology
213	A Small List of Comparisons
214	A Note on Illusion and Earth
214	New Possibilities of Higher Octave Planets in Astrology
215	Spiritual Earth
217	Changes in the Natal chart
218	More Radical shifts Involving Saturn Likely

226	**Chapter 6: Earth and the body**
226	On Earth and Rabbit Holes
230	Levels of Physical Form
232	Multidimensional Bodies
233	A Sampling: Three Earthly Levels of Incarnation to the Physical Body
238	Earth/Body Consciousness and Our Western Health Crisis

246	**Chapter 7: The Essential Taurus**
246	Taurus the Homeless
246	Foundational Energies
248	Co-rulerships in Astrology

250	The Quincunx or Inconjunct
251	Meanings of Quincunx/Inconjunct in Horary Charts
255	A Taurian Childhood
257	General Taurian Truths in the Human Personality or Natal Chart
260	The Real "Typical" Taurian
264	Digging Deeper
266	The Taurian Salvatore Dali
267	Dali's Childhood
268	Dali and Nature
269	Dali's Quest for Self-Understanding and Self-Expression
273	The City Taurus
274	Taurus and Nature
276	Taurus the sensual
278	Fertility
278	The Stubborn Taurus?
280	Basic not Blasé
281	Value
283	Self-Concern
284	Conservation
288	Willpower and Determination
288	Common Sense
289	Comfort, Luxury and Pleasure
290	Security
292	Taurus: The dark side
294	Security Issues or the Paralysis of Fear - Immovable and Resistant
296	The importance of Understanding and Working with Unique Astrological Signatures
297	Ownership and Hoarding
298	Selfishness and Sensual pleasure
299	Taurian Creativity: The Banker and the Artist
309	**Chapter 8: Taurus, Libra, and Venus**
309	Venus is to Libra…not Taurus
310	Exploring Differences (and *Some* Similarities) of Venus/Libra and Earth/Taurus by Keyword

312	Sign Dynamics of Libra and Taurus
313	Love is in the Air
314	Marriage
314	Partnership
315	Self-Adornment and Self Worth
316	Money
317	Harmony, Gaiety and Happiness
319	Women
319	Art and Creativity
321	Love and companionship
322	Sociality
324	The Light and the Dark side of Libran Shared Experiences
326	Nice-ness
328	Beauty, art and creativity
329	A Few Words about Libran and Taurian Houses
331	Summary

333 Chapter 9: Planet Earth in the Astrological Chart

333	Placing Earth in the Natal Chart
339	Integrating Earth in the Natal Chart
340	Safety and Stability
341	Safety and Stability Affected by Lack of Earth
342	Safety and Stability Affected by Hard Aspects to Earth in the Natal Chart
344	Building and Productivity
345	Building and Productivity Affected by Hard Aspects to Earth or Lack of Earth Element
345	Creativity
346	Creativity Affected by Hard Aspects to Earth or Lack of Earth Element
347	Nature
347	Attitudes of Nature Affected by Hard Aspects to Earth or Lack of Earth Element
348	Quality
349	Quality Affected by Hard Aspects to Earth of Lack of Earth Element
350	Practicality

351	Practicality Affected by Hard Aspects to Earth or Lack of Earth Element
352	Patience and Persistence
352	Patience and Persistence Affected by Hard Aspects to Earth of Lack of Earth Element
353	Sensuality
353	Sensuality Affected by Hard Aspects to Earth or Lack of Earth Element
354	Wealth, Value and Ownership
355	Wealth, Value and Ownership Affected by Hard Aspects to Earth or Lack of Earth Element
356	The Physical Body
356	The Physical Body Affected by Hard Aspects to Earth or Lack of Earth Element
357	Green Living and Ecology
358	Green Living and Ecology Affected by Hard Aspects to Earth or Lack of Earth Element
359	Summary

361 Chapter 10: The Psychology and Physiology of the Sun/Earth Diametric

361	The Opposition
364	More on Earth/Sun Opposition in the Astrological Chart
365	Earth "Signs" of strength and weakness in the body
367	The Aries/Libra Diametric
372	The Taurus/Scorpio Diametric
379	The Gemini /Sagittarius Diametric
384	The Cancer / Capricorn Diametric
390	The Leo/Aquarius Diametric
396	The Virgo/Pisces Diametric
403	Summary

405 Chapter 11 Delineating Earth

406	Astrological Dignities and Debilities of Planet Earth
410	The Influence of Aspects on Earth in Signs
411	The Shadow Earth

411	Planet Earth in Signs
411	Earth in Aries
416	Earth in Taurus (Ruler/Dignity)
420	Earth in Gemini
424	Earth in Cancer (Exaltation)
428	Earth in Leo
433	Earth in Virgo
437	Earth in Libra
442	Earth in Scorpio (Detriment)
449	Earth in Sagittarius
453	Earth in Capricorn (Source Energy of the Element Earth)
458	Earth in Aquarius (Fall)
462	Earth in Pisces
467	Planet Earth in Houses
468	Planet Earth in the 1st house
469	Planet Earth in the 2nd House
470	Planet Earth in the 3rd House
471	Planet Earth in the 4th house
472	Planet Earth in the 5th house
473	Planet Earth in the 6th house
474	Planet Earth in the 7th house
475	Planet Earth in the 8th house
476	Planet Earth in the 9th house
477	Planet Earth in the 10th house
479	Planet Earth in the 11th house
481	Planet Earth in the 12th house
484	Aspects to Earth
484	Conjunctions
485	Sextiles
485	Squares
486	Trines
486	Inconjuncts or Quincunxes
487	Oppositions
488	Transits with Earth
489	Earth in Horary Charts
492	**Chapter 12: Summary**

Earth Rise
The Case for Studying and Using Earth in Astrology

Preface

This astrology book is a little different. It doesn't herald some newly discovered astral body: it covers the one we've overlooked. It's about a planet we're so close to that we don't even see it anymore. A planet we've learned to neglect, but desperately need, to survive. I am speaking, naturally, of Earth. Last time I looked, Earth is a planet and deserves an equal place in astrology.

The Road to Writing this Book

The author of this book is a little different too. As an astrologer, I've had the usual stint as a student, a professional reader, and, finally, a teacher. I've also made some study (and practice) of other metaphysical and physical disciplines that came my way, but I have always come back to astrology: it continues to be first in my heart.

One of the frustrations of studying astrology over time is trying to take that knowledge to a deeper level. There are many "cookbooks" out there, and very good ones at that, but finding a astrology book that really plunges the mind into a subterranean thought level, giving one a real sense of depth when it comes to the meanings of planets, signs, and so-forth are sometimes few and far between. Ironically, the reason for this is the complexity of astrology. When we finally understand something, we tend to hold on tight to it, unwilling to let go of any mental ground gained by adding more details.

Mythology is sometimes used to deepen our delineative capacity, but personally, I find mythology distracting. I am more scientifically inclined, so mythology doesn't always resonate with me. When I apply it to astrology, I also see a certain inconsistency with more contemporary planetary meanings. So, years ago, stuck with a lack of in-depth resources, I just started to sit and contemplate. I would select a particular planetary energy, run the keywords around in my head, and mine for deeper meanings. It is this method of studying that has made me a kind of astrological philosopher, or even a theoretical astrologer.

Taurus = Earth: The Potential of Planet Earth in Astrology

This was probably the start of my sense of loss surrounding the sign of Taurus. While contemplating Venus's energetic signature as the ruler for Taurus, it soon became apparent, to me anyway, that something didn't fit. Libra and Taurus, the signs sharing Venus, have some traits in common, but they are too different in too many significant ways to remain lumped together. More importantly, the signs sharing a ruling planet can never truly come into their own, symbolically, until they have their own planetary match. In casting about for some other planet that better described Taurian traits, it wasn't long before Earth presented itself as an obvious candidate. That idea, when it occurred, shocked me a little, and I suppose it will have a similar effect on others. I never considered reading planet Earth in a natal chart. Yet, the more I perused charts with prominent Earth/Taurian influences and ran charts with Earth included, the more sense it made. The book you hold in your hand is a result of years of fighting with myself over what I knew to be true versus what was accepted in the field of astrology. Finally my instinctual and logical sense won out and I realized that Earth is not only a great fit for Taurus's ruling planet but also reveals an important symbolic addition to astrology itself.

After my acquiescence, the symbolism inherent in this idea, and the meaning we could take from it, began to haunt me. The implantation of the Earth glyph in any astrological chart markedly changes the picture. We move beyond the typical assumption of Earth as only the house wheel. Earth now becomes more than a background template; it becomes an entity and an energy to be reckoned with. It also shifts our personal perspective from subjective to objective, from single earthly experiences to global or planetary awareness.

When Earth is added to a chart, the permanent Sun–Earth opposition is a very unique signature to behold. In the natal chart, this opposition also shifts our attitude to one of dual psychology (body and mind) that coincidentally works well within the dual plane (light/dark, male/female, good/evil, etc.) of existence we find ourselves in. This opposition eventually challenged many of my ideas regarding the way astrology describes the human condition. From a global perspective, the Sun-Earth opposition spoke to me about old and outmoded ideas we may have about our planet in general, and what it may mean to us as members of the human race at this moment in time.

Many questions began to come to the surface. What could the insertion of planet Earth in the astrological chart mean symbolically to our understanding of the earth plane in general? How does this new addition affect our present planetary substitutes for earth energy (like Saturn) in astrology? What changes in rulerships would occur if Earth is now included in astrology? If Earth rules Taurus, then how would that assignment affect Taurus? Where would that leave Venus and Libra? What implications are made when we embrace a permanent Sun-Earth opposition in each and every astrological chart? And lastly: What could all this have to say about our environmental struggles with our own planet and how hard it is for us to live within its parameters?

With the recent additions of so many newly discovered planets and dwarf planets to our solar system, the idea of any signs still sharing a planet seems a bit ridiculous. There is already a campaign afoot for Virgo to be (most likely) reassigned to the planetoid Chiron instead of sharing the planet

Mercury with Gemini. Yet there is no such attempt to separate Libra and Taurus from Venus. Venus may be a nice stepmother stand-in for Taurus, but I don't think she is really in charge. Taurus is a sign (among others) whose characteristics have been over-simplified and she is even more neglected when it comes to the consideration of a rightful ruling planet.

An Astrological Crossroads

Our current technology has given astronomers so many new and exciting discoveries that astrologers are racing to keep up. Conversely, most of the general population today still thinks of astrology as silly, strange, or avant-garde. Inside our profession, I see practitioners scrabbling to compensate for a frustratingly nebulous beginning by becoming security-driven: uptight, conservative, and even somewhat elitist in their behavior. What a way for Uranian-minded[1] people to act! We've become so afraid we won't be taken seriously that we will do almost anything; even turn ourselves into pseudoscientists, just so we can feel like we're on solid ground. It keeps me wondering who we are as professionals at this point in time, and where we are going. We may be at a critical crossroads here and I think trying to prove astrology through only scientific method may do it a great disservice. Astrology does incorporate scientific thought and even some method in many areas of its discipline, yet it also embraces the more mystical and spiritual side of life. I would like to see us stay open to the idea that astrology is capable of translating both sides of life on Earth because it may be the only tool that illustrates how this dual world of science and spirit may work together. The ideas presented in this book are logical in thought and deduction, incorporating ideas from our well-worn astrological field of study, but are also based on spiritual symbolism and (hopefully) serve as an example of the natural balance, or wholeness, astrology has within it.

A Love Letter to Earth

Being a sun-sign Taurus myself, I may be accused of writing a love letter to myself and I will be the first to admit that Taurian energy is more than a little self-involved. Here I must plead patience and offer up the fact that I have Taurus in the 12th house and a stellium in Gemini that includes my Ascendant. Most of my life I have struggled to find what you might call "my Taurus within," or even to find any connection with the earth element itself, as I have only one earth planet in my natal chart. We all specialize in the area of our greatest weakness and there may be a parallel between my interest in Taurus's identity crisis of rulership and my own personal quest for understanding earth. On the other hand, who better to write about Taurian peculiarities than a Taurus? However, if this book is to be a love letter of any sort, I would prefer it be addressed to our incredible home world: planet Earth itself.

Why Earth?

As far as this introduction, Earth needs none: it is the planet that we live on, the environment that sustains us, the ground that supports us, the resource that feeds us, and the raw material we're made of. We use it to construct our homes and grow our communities while its beauty soothes our psyche and inspires our soul. Earth is our home in every sense of the word. This book then asks the question of why, throughout the Western world of astrology, have we tracked, studied, and transited every other planet in our solar system but our own?

It offers suggestions and gives reasons why the Earth glyph should be inserted into astrological charts, addressing such questions as what might have been missed by the exclusion of Earth? Why isn't the fact that we use an earth-based, geocentric zodiac enough to symbolize Earth? Doesn't our own planet deserve a sign to rule? What sign should Earth rule? What does placing Earth in the natal chart really mean to us on an individual basis? What can we learn from the pairing of Earth and the sign of Taurus? How does placing Earth in a chart change our perspective on not only our own lives, but the life of our planet as well? What other planets and their respective symbolism are affected by the addition of Earth to the astrological chart? Does astrology properly address the duality of our earthly existence? Using this new astrological symbolism, who are we, as a species, on this Earth? How and why does all this tie into our current Earth ecological crisis?

Beginning a Discussion

I hope this book is the beginning of a discussion, one that will continue to examine our taken-for-granted procedures, and initiate more questions about the structures and the foundation of our astrological theories. This book introduces a new concept that will seem strange to some. The proposal I make is literally earth-shattering to the astrological way of doing business, but astrologers have traditionally been open to new ideas - we've had to be - because we know from our observations that life isn't stationary and neither is the galaxy. So some new considerations shouldn't be that much of a challenge as long as we can refocus our intentions and remain true to our roots and our progressive, Uranian ruler. Even if I have failed to find the truth here, I feel confident that I have found a truth or at the very least, danced around it.

Some of the information in this book is theoretical of course, because so far, astrologers have not really studied Earth from an outside perspective. Therefore, the content of this book will, and should be, open for debate for some time to come. The interpretations linking Earth and Taurus are based on a "what if" scenario. Be that as it may, the dialogue on what planet should rule Taurus and whether Earth is the likely candidate is long overdue and should be decided as soon as possible. I sincerely hope this book helps precipitate that.

May 12 2010 2:53 pm Revised Feb 14 2011 10:24 am Cocolalla, Idaho

Technical Note

One technical note to impart here involves the capitalization of the word Earth throughout this book. When I refer to our planet Earth it is capitalized and when I am talking about the element earth, it is not.

[1] The planet Uranus is said to be the ruler of astrology

CHAPTER 1

The Missing Planet

"An era can be said to end when its basic illusions are exhausted." ~Arthur Miller

"The World We Live In"[1]
The Astrologer's Mindset of Earth

The Planet Earth has had a long and industrious past. A product of the Big Bang, it started out as a simple gas cloud and turned itself into one of the most beautiful and productive worlds in the known galaxy. It is now home to bounteous plant and animal life, the human population among them.

No one can deny that we are extremely attached to this planet and when we carved out that unique system of study called astrology, we used our Earth as a template, a reference point for all our astrological charts, and then it quietly faded into the background.

Astrology is the effect of planets and points and their positions on our human lives. More than that, astrology is the study of our environment and the particular energy that surrounds each and every one of us. The astrological chart is a lens through which we perceive and understand our reality as human beings. It puts us in touch with the flavors we taste on a daily basis and whether they are bitter, savory or sweet;

telling a constant story of how our environment responds to us and how we respond to it.

From our perch here on Earth, astrologers have contemplated the story of humanity, studying and watching the universal symbols of our lives circle, dance, and spar with each other. Ever on a quest to learn the language that will tell us who we are and give an answer to what we are doing here. Parallel to that has been a longing for a deeper understanding of our plane of existence and how we may truly connect with it. For astrologers, the search for meaning has always been above us in a star-filled sky, the place where the answers come from. Maybe it's time to look down for a moment. For as long as astrology has existed, it has embraced and investigated all particularities of interest in our galaxy, with one exception: Earth. Our planet has never been included among them.

In the beginning of the award-winning documentary "An Inconvenient Truth," Al Gore talks about Christmas Eve 1968, when the Apollo 8 astronauts took what is now a very famous photograph of the Earth coming up over the moon's surface. It was the first picture humanity had ever seen of our Earth taken from somewhere else. It showed this self-contained and fragile world floating alone in the vastness of space, and for the first time in our evolution we could really get a sense of Earth as a whole and separate entity existing apart from its population. It was titled simply: "Earth Rise."

This photograph caused a paradigm shift in human awareness that helped perpetuate the burgeoning ecological movement to heal our now ailing planet.

A Sickness in Earth and Body

Some extraterrestrial might be quick to ask an intelligent species like us: "By the way, why is your planet sick?" One answer to that question is in the way we currently think about our planet. We don't. We have learned to take it for granted as something that is just always here. By excluding Earth in our astrological charts, unwittingly or unconsciously, astrology has perpetuated that.

If we invoke the fractal-like idea of "as above, so below," so often used in astrology to describe its effects, does it follow that if the Earth is sick, we are sick? Every politician, media personality, and health professional today is talking about the health crises in America. As a species, we seem to have lost a way to connect with our own bodies and to balance what we want with what we need. In our relationship with the Earth, the problems are similar.

Hypothetically, inserting Earth in an astrological chart opens up a question or two about our linear thinking in this land of duality. It offers us a better bead on reality, reawakening more potential for earthly creativity and a global perspective we've never been quite able to grasp. The discipline of astrology, at its best, is all about progress, growth, and integrating ever-more complicated ideas about the nature of reality. Truth may be simple, but the journey to it requires having all the crucial data.

Of course, Earth has a representative glyph, but that icon isn't used in any astrological charts in geophysical astrology. In astrology books, Earth is almost never mentioned unless they are discussing the element earth. Needless to say, astrological interpretations for Earth are nonexistent. Astrologically, we know a lot more about our connections to Jupiter, the moon's nodes, and even Antares, than we do about our own planet.

Astrology is a tool and a language that utilizes symbology. This is a book about a missing symbol, what that has meant to our human reality, astrology in general, and whether this omission might have even led us to some errors in our philosophy. Embracing the global, or dare I say, cosmic, species that we have become, we can no longer afford to persist in giving our planet only a cursory glance in our astrological studies.

A (very little) Background

Researching any written history of astrology is an exercise in frustration. Many original writings did not survive the times. Whatever was preserved isn't very accessible to the average astrologer. "Project Hindsight" [2] and the study of Hellenistic astrology has done a lot to help remedy this. Yet, it is still hard to get inside the head of the original astrologers and know what they were thinking. So in the absence of a primer, one may come to the conclusion that if astrologers were standing on Earth when they began to note the movement of the stars and planets, it would certainly never have occurred to them to include the planet under their feet. At the time, we could not see the Earth's placement in space, so what kind of observation, sign, or symbol could we have hoped to take from it anyway? It was a natural thing that Earth be dismissed as not relevant in any chart. Ancient astrologers probably didn't leave Earth out as an intended slight. In our present-day astrological charts, Earth is taken for granted as simply the point from which the planets and points are observed. That place becomes, of course, the houses of the chart, or the astrological wheel.

Earth and the Astrological Houses: Not Enough of a Good Thing

The houses in an astrological chart are the imaginary lines drawn through our planet, creating the 12 divisions of human life. The so-called Angles (1st, 4th, 7th, and 10th houses) of a chart are the horizontal and vertical lines that give us a frame of reference to the place we were born. At the moment (or time) we are born, it is as if we stand at the center of the wheel of houses in our natal chart, facing the east, watching whatever constellation or sign is rising over the horizon of our Earth. This is our Ascendant, or 1st house. Looking down, we see the Imum Coeli (Nadir), or 4th house, of our chart, and this is a picture of what <u>could</u> be observed if we had X-ray vision, and could see through the globe beneath our feet, clear through to the sky at the bottom of the world. We then note what constellation or sign is there. As we turn around, we can see the Descendant, or western horizon, that is the 7th house with its setting constellation (sign), and lastly, looking up at the sky directly over our heads, we see the Medium Coeli (Midheaven), or 10th house cusp, and note what constellation (sign) is on that point. From this standpoint, the Earth is the back-drop in all astrological charts, and when you plot the planets' and points' positions in the sky at birth onto the wheel, it shows where, in the life of that person, place, or thing, those various planetary energies are most easily recognized as operating. The house wheel is the only currently used symbol of our home world. As I live my day-to-day life, it is as if I am mentally moving across the landscape of my natal chart wheel, creating awareness and the resulting physical manifestation of my life. This wheel was laid down as my personal template at the time, day, and place I was born. I absorb or attract a particular sign's energy as I move from my home (4th house) to my friend's house (11th) to my workplace (6th). I resonate with the positions of these signs and planets because they were imprinted on me when I took my first breath. In fact, I may have even chosen them in utero, matching their energy vibrations (for good or ill) with my own as the perfect time to enter this world.

When casting a natal chart, astrologers, in an almost unconscious routine, place the planetary degrees around a divided circle that has long since lost any connection to the separate planet we inhabit. The zodiacal wheel's meaning has come to be pertinent to us only in terms of our own individual daily lives. This wheel and the experiences it relates are completely subjective. The natal, and almost every other astrological chart, leaves out the symbolic or iconic representation of our own world, that is, the Earth glyph, while including all the other planets and points of interest, this is a troubling omission.

Changing Perspective: Missing Planet, Missing Link?

Astrology carries within it an understanding that the closer a planet is to us physically, the more immediate and direct its influence in our everyday life. Right now, as far as understanding the influence of Earth on our psyche, it's the astrological elephant in the room.

If astrology is the study of the mechanics of the universe in relation to ourselves, then what we include in our astrological charts is what we're conscious of. When we cast a chart, the symbolic representations we see on the wheel, reflect back to us everything that is possible to know about our plane of existence. If we agree that the map we hold is truly an accurate representation of our reality on paper, how can we leave our home planet's symbol out of the pattern and not expect our reality to be somewhat skewed?

The lack of an iconic representation means we have no perspective on our own world. Therefore, we have no way to study it from the outside - not even a way of thinking of it in those terms. What does our planet mean to us when it is separate from our single lives, our everyday work-a-day world? The houses may contain (and symbolize) our individual lives, or tell us how we will be treated by society and how we feel about that, but they don't show us what we think about our planet or what our experience of that planet may be. The Earth glyph is different from the house structure in that it symbolically contains all of us at once, every life form. It is the world, the entire planet as a whole. Now we are thinking globally.

If I insert Earth's icon, its planetary symbol, into that astrological wheel, I have symbolically gained distance, or perspective, and acquired an attitude I didn't have before. I am no longer a blind, unconscious, or irremovable part within an environment; I am a separate being who perceives a planet that exists in the Milky Way Galaxy. In this way, placing the icon into a chart is not an act of redundancy. The Earth icon becomes symbolic of Earth with or without us. That is, the planet exists whether we are here or not. Earth is, in reality, an independent entity, the same as Mercury or Jupiter.

This lack of symbolic representation in the charts of astrology is very revealing in how we look at our planet. How are we treating our own planet? Like a non-entity. Every time a new planet or point is discovered, accepted, and added to our astrological charts, we say that we are now psychologically and emotionally ready to embrace and integrate its qualities. Since planet Earth is missing from most of our charts, what does this say about our current struggle to work with and heal the Earth? That we take our planet for granted and are not ready to think about it seriously?

As we might expect, the charts we have been studying do reflect our current attitude quite well. Aldo Leopold, the great conservationist, said: "One of the anomalies of modern ecological thought is that it is the creation of two groups, each of which seems barely aware of the existence of the other. The one studies the human community, almost as if it was a separate entity, and calls its findings sociology, economics, and history. The other studies the plant and animal community and comfortably relegates the hodgepodge of politics to 'the liberal arts.' The inevitable fusion of these two lines of thought will, perhaps, constitute the outstanding advance of the present century." [3]

Our way of thinking in the astrological community puts us in the first group. For the most part, we emphasize humanity and its culture, but astrology isn't just about people and personalities. In order to be truly valid, astrology must reflect the world we live in, too. Astrology must describe the energies that make up the world and show how they operate as well. People are only a microcosm of the macrocosm. The way people experience life and process their thoughts or emotions have very similar recognizable patterns to operations of physics in Earth science. Action and reaction, contraction and expansion: these principles can also be used to describe the human condition. The planet, its processes, its wildlife, and the human species, mimic and reflect one another; we are all interconnected. We are intrinsic, not separate from this world. Now here's the kicker: we are not even separate from the universe at large! For how can we be? Astrology has shown us time and again that even out in the vastness of space, we are touched, and our lives reflected, in the lumbering movements of gigantic bodies of energy thousands of miles away.

A Remedy for Our Separation Anxiety and the Copernican Fallout

In 1543, humanity received a shock. Nicolaus Copernicus published a little book called <u>On the Revolutions of the Celestial Spheres</u>, suggesting that we put the sun, instead of the Earth, into the center of the solar system. This change in perspective resulted in a new understanding of the motions of the planets, and our calculations finally made sense. Thus began the journey to our present western path of scientific thought. The Copernican revolution was a triumph for our intellect and a complete disaster for our psyche.

In his recent book, <u>Cosmos and Psyche,</u> Richard Tarnas had this to say about that moment in time: "The radical displacement of the Earth and humanity from the absolute cosmic center, the stunning transference of the apparent cosmic order from the observed to the observer, the eventual pervasive disenchantment of the material universe was all paradigmatic for the modern mind, and these have now come to epitomize humankind's underlying sense of disorientation and alienation."[4]

Essentially Tarnas is saying that ever since Copernicus came to the conclusion that the sun didn't revolve around the Earth, we were left with the idea that the universe was impersonal and we were not as connected to it as we thought. We were disconnected and disenfranchised from our home; the center of our being was rocked with separation anxiety. Our connection to the center of the universe was shaken and now we felt like it was impersonal and incapable of relating to any human interaction, devoid of feeling.

We were thrown back on ourselves, and we pulled in psychologically. The result was, instead of relating to the

Earth and the universe; we thought we had nothing but ourselves to relate to. As Tarnas explained: "The new universe…was a spiritually empty vastness, impersonal, neutral indifferent to human concerns, governed by random processes devoid of purpose or meaning." [4] We are, in his words: "estranged and decentered."[4]

The simple addition of planet Earth to our astrological charts connects us once again; it gives us something to relate to and shows that we are indeed part of this environment and it is a part of us. Now, with Earth represented, we can find the shamanistic idea of connection, give and take, and cause and effect that we have with the other planets and points in our lives. The Earth once again has great meaning to us, and placing it in the chart allows us to see and study that, maintaining our connection with it.

Earth's Place in Astrology

It doesn't matter whether we think that the stars and planets influence us, or whether we're somehow in control of them. It's all relevant; it's a self-contained system that has evolved to operate using every element within it. Although many of us haven't consciously thought of it in quite this way, our ecosystem includes the sky as well as the Earth. That's what is told to us through astrology.

It isn't hard to understand that we create the human world around us through what we perceive, feel and think -

that is, our attitude. For example, we think war is necessary, so we have war. Whenever time is spent mentally or emotionally on some idea, that idea then manifests into the reality of our physical world. Since we are the dominate species here, our collective attitude has a huge influence on the natural world. The way we think about the Earth dictates our action (or non-action), leading to our current environmental dilemmas.

Those who are less familiar with astrology might ask: "How will studying astrological symbology help us understand our problems with the environment and live in harmony with the Earth?" For astrologers, the symbolism in astrological charts is read as a representation of reality. Charts contain all that it is possible to know on any level, about a person, situation, place, or thing. We can study the chart to better understand the world it represents. When done correctly, it is amazingly accurate.

Symbology is the practice of representing things through pictures, or investing things with a symbolic meaning or character. Pictures possess the ability to have more than one meaning or many related meanings. It is also a way of looking at a concept to study or simplify it well enough for immediate understanding.

A set of symbols, like those used in astrology, stand for a whole entity, whether a person, or a system, or a time or place. It captures all the intricacies, nuances, contradictions, and levels of this thing, and as you can imagine, it is very complex. A chart tells the story of the owner of that chart and lets the reader explain and explore reasons why the owner is what it is. It tells you what is knowable there, and can also show what is not there and the reasons for that, too. What the symbols "say" can be used to get clues or perspective on any person or situation. That is why it is crucial to have everything we know of be represented on that wheel. We can't afford to leave anything out, as this shows a deliberate slight and also has symbolic meaning. When Earth is placed in any chart, it is as if the rug is put back under our feet, physically and psychologically. On a personal level, we gain the other half of our dual existence: the sun, our psychological center, and the Earth, our physical body. On a mass scale, we gain, once again, our planet and our special place in the universe.

Earth and Taurus

Astrologers have spent centuries waiting for the arrival of a planetary order that matches twelve <u>single</u> planets with our twelve signs. Since the dawn of the daily horoscope, we've limped along, with a vital piece of information missing at the very core of our philosophy. Almost half of our astrological signs have had to share planetary rulers at one time or another because of a shortage of known planets. This was always a workable, but unsatisfying, solution. Over the last hundred years, we've witnessed several new planetary discoveries and made additions to our repertoire. We have watched eagerly as the gap between signs and planets narrowed. Now, out of the signs that originally shared planetary rulers, Gemini and Virgo still share Mercury, and both Taurus and Libra come under the rulership of Venus.

With the discovery of Chiron in 1977, it looks as though Virgo may have its own ruler at long last.[5] That still leaves either Taurus or Libra without its own home. The recent planetary additions of Sedna, Eris, and Ceres seem to raise more questions than answers, and the interpretive speculation surrounding these newcomers does not yet address the issue of rulership. As our technological scope continues to expand, I am sure that we will go on discovering ever more planets, comets, and planetoids in the outer reaches of space. However, astrologers continue to overlook a certain logical symmetry in our more local universe: Earth is in need of a sign, and Taurus is in need of a ruling planet. I propose that we consider Earth as the logical choice to rule Taurus. At the very least, this pairing of Earth and Taurus merits the same study we are giving the rest of the solar system, and Taurus deserves the same scrutiny as a possible match for Earth that we are giving to Virgo and Chiron.

When discussing the placement of Earth in our charts, we must also consider the future. We're already living in an era when some of us leave this planet for weeks or months at a time. Someday, a select few may even live off this world entirely. Then, the case for incorporating Earth in the chart will become absolutely essential. As astrologers, we must accept the changing universe, and can't afford to get set in our ways, even when these ways have seemingly endured for eons. There is always more to embrace and understand out there — that's why we love astrology. Humanity is changing too, and some of those changes may be crucial to our very survival, and of course, that too, needs to be reflected in any future astrological charts. The time for a Taurean-Earth consciousness has come.

A Deserving Place

If we continue to use our astrological houses as the only Earth symbol available to us, we will remain too close to the situation to ever see our own planet and the problems that result from that. Incorporating the Earth glyph removes any "forest for the trees" nebulousness when it comes to fixing Earth in our consciousness. I feel that this is important if we, as a species, are ever going to bring an awareness of the importance of Earth to the forefront of our lives.

In addition, the Earth symbol will have a unique position in each and every astrological chart. On a personal level, it will allow an individual to see in what part of their life (what house) they will be aware of the Earth's presence and how they can personally work and connect with it. The

Earth icon would also represent their physical body, how they seek stability, their security issues, and how they would feel about Earth and their reaction to reality in general. It might even be indicative of their unique contributions to the planet.

Considering everything we know to be true about astrological symbols and their reflection of our reality, how can we continue to leave planet Earth out? The idea that this wouldn't have ramifications on our present awareness and attitude makes little sense to me. If we really thought about what this says symbolically in our list of calculated charts, we would all be running to our computers to remedy the situation immediately. For the continued growth of the astrological community, and for the sake of the planet we all love, I offer this book as the start of our own "Earth Rise."

[1] "The World We Live In" is a Life "Special Edition for Young Readers" Book I received from my maternal grandmother and grandfather on my sixth birthday in 1961. It was, and still is, a source of fascination for me: it served to greatly expand my love affair with Earth.

[2] "Definitions and Foundations ." *Project Hindsight*. Project Hindsight , 2008. Web. 13 Jun 2011. <www.projecthindsight.com>.

[3] Hughes, J. Donald. *An Environmental History of the World Humankinds Changing Role in the Community of Life*. N.Y. N.Y.: Routledge Publishing, 2001. 6. Print.

[4] Tarnas, Richard. *Cosmos and Psyche*. N.Y. N.Y.: Penguin Books, 2006. 28. Print

[5] Fairfield, Gail. *Choice Centered Astrology: The Basics*. Smithville, In.: Ramp Creek Publishing, Inc., 1990. 144, 209-214. Print.

Chapter 2
The Sun/Earth Opposition

What the permanent Sun/Earth opposition tells us about who we are and why we can't get along with our own planet

"The earth is like a spaceship that didn't come with an operating manual."
~Buckminster Fuller

"There are no passengers on spaceship earth. We are all crew." ~Marshall McLuhan

AUTHOR'S NOTE: THIS CHAPTER IS A TREATISE ON WHAT LEAVING EARTH OUT OF OUR ASTROLOGICAL EQUATIONS HAS MEANT TO US AND OUR ENVIRONMENT.

Looking Back

One major reason Earth may have been left out of astrological charts could be its awkward aspect to the Sun. The first thing an astrologer notices when placing Earth in an astrological chart is that Earth is in a permanent opposition to the Sun. From our point of view, in Geocentric Astrology, we are always facing the Sun. (That is probably a good thing if we want to stay alive.) The Sun may go down past our horizon every night, but it is still hitting the globe somewhere at all times. We are locked in this position and the astrological chart reflects that.

If an astrologer in antiquity did try and insert Earth into an astrological chart at some point, he might have said: "Earth and Sun are in a permanent aspect. This is wonky from an interpretational point of view, what's the use of that?" (Okay, he probably didn't say "wonky") Confrontation of this oddity probably didn't help any case being made for using the Earth glyph. However, this permanent opposition gives us a symbolism that is as revealing as it is startling. This awkward position of Earth in natal charts for earthlings may be just the key to understanding not only our immediate universe, but our unique connection to it.

A Planetary Ruler for Humanity

When we consider the human race symbolically, what astrological material best represents us? One of the few reference books regarding astrological symbolism, <u>The Rulership Book</u> by Rex Bills, has no listing for humanity in general. He has humanitarianism being ruled (quite correctly, I believe) by Uranus. For "Humanity, one's attitude toward," he has "11th house" in parentheses, meaning he is offering that house as one ruler and suggesting that there may be more. Another listing, "human nature," is linked to Aquarius, again in parentheses, saying he isn't positive. At this time, I have to disagree with this last assessment. I see very little

Aquarius in human nature, at least at this point in our evolution.

If anything, I see us, as a species, trying to get to an Aquarian level, but we aren't there yet. Aquarius does rule communities (eclectic groups of people living together as equals) and perhaps this is indeed the future of humanity, but it is not where we are today. Another keyword that might embrace the idea of humanity is "the public." The symbol for the general attitude of the public is, for me, the Moon. Bills also lists the 10th house under "the public," so it is connected to Saturn as well. With "the public," I personally see the emotionality of the public attributed to the Moon, and the judgment of the public with Saturn and the 10th house. Pluto obviously rules humanity from a generational standpoint. Each time Pluto changes signs, we have a section of the human population that, through their birth, shifts our priorities and reflects those issues that Pluto raises through that sign. Each new generation of humanity puts its own unique stamp on the growth and power of the human race. However, we are looking for a planetary energy that is more basic and constant here. In The Rulership Book, there is nothing listed under "population", another possible word for the concept of humanity, but there are some interesting suggestions under "popularity", including the Moon, Sun, Venus, and the 10th house. This is the first hint of a possible connection with the Sun.

Even though <u>The Rulership Book</u> is highly respected in our field, it is woefully inadequate and Bills is quite aware of that, stating in the foreword: "Serious up-to-date research is vitally needed." Another great book on our very short list of general astrological correspondences is Michael Munkasey's <u>The Astrological Thesaurus</u>. He <u>does</u> list "humanity" and although I have sympathy with his placement of humanity in the 4th house, thereby pulling in the Moon as ruling planet once again, I think of the Moon as more about "popularity" or "the public," which is an emotional temperature reading on groups of people and not the idea of humanity as a species. The Moon might even rule our emotional nature as a whole, but I think of general humanity as an organism, that not only includes our emotional make up, but a species that is described by several other ideas as well: consciousness, body structure, mental acuity, attitude, ongoing evolution or development, and more. Of course, each one of these attributes, if taken alone, has a single planet assigned to them: i.e., mental acuity being Mercury, Mars as action, and so on, but what planet, symbolically, tells us who we are as a species?

The Sun and Humanity

In the 16th century, the Copernican revolution threw humanity on its ear. When the Sun, and not the Earth, was found to be in charge of the solar system, we were stunned and it helped solidify a direction we were already heading in. At that time, Earth's status (never a high priority for us anyway) was lowered further still, becoming just one of many heavenly bodies in the vastness of space. It was easy to become disenfranchised from our own planet as we turned our attention now to the real central power of our universe: the Sun.[1]

It seems to me that, at this point in our development, the human race is living out Leo energy and is ruled by the Sun as a whole. Symbolically, it is the only "planet" the rest of the population (non-astrologers and astronomers) even thinks about. In astrology, the Sun is the life force of each individual, the "I am." In a natal chart, it represents our ego, our will, our essence, and the human center of our being.

The astrological Sun symbolizes a very human energy, the urge we have to actualize ourselves and what is unique and special about us. It is what we are put here to radiate out in this lifetime, but also our inner knowing that leads us to the lessons we need to learn this time around.

When we are living through our Sun energy, we are said to be truly in touch with ourselves, exuding a creative individuality at the highest level. Our Sun, for us, is the touchstone for human self-awareness; in short, our consciousness.

I think this Sun symbolism would have to apply to all humanity as well: the macrocosm of the microcosm.

The Leo/Aquarius Diametric

Conveniently, the opposite of Leo/Sun is Aquarius/Uranus. We are a species symbolically caught in a Leo/Aquarius rulership cycle. Living within the duality of the individual (Leo) versus the masses or the tribe (Aquarius), the importance of our own national tribe versus the whole tribe of humanity, and finally, even caught between the tribe of humankind and the other tribes (animal, vegetable, and mineral) of the whole world. It is an opposition that may fully describe us as a species, one that is moving, consciously or unconsciously, back and forth between these two signs throughout our entire evolution. We began with a primitive Aquarius representing tribal man and moved on to Leo representing modern man. Now, we are spiraling up another evolutionary path, coming full circle to a more evolved, Aquarian attitude. This would indicate that, in the future, we will go from everyone wanting to be king, to everyone having an equal say; from one person having all the power, to everyone having power. It may be that all complex organisms contain this kind of rulership duality inherent in astrological oppositions. This would certainly be reflective of the duality mentioned in metaphysical writings about this Earth plane. We live in a place of opposites - light and dark, negative and positive, male and female - so why wouldn't any sophisticated species reflect that duality in its makeup? Is this why it is difficult to, astrologically and symbolically, pin down general planetary rulerships of more complex organisms, and why lists of astrological correspondences for those organisms don't yet exist?

At any rate, the symbolic attitude of the human race today is definitely much more Leo than Aquarius, and has been for eons. However, I am not proposing that we swap out our Sun-sign dominance for Earth signs in our astrological charts, but what would happen to the imbalances in our collective human consciousness if we incorporated Earth, and our Earth sign, with our Sun Sign as a <u>set</u> to describe who we are at our central base? The duality of our existence - the population versus the planet, the individual versus the population, and the anima/animus (male/female) halves within our own individual personalities - could now be considered as one entity. The Earth would then take up a more central role for us, as well it should, and still the Sun is in its rightful place in the heavens.

A Species Apart

If we agree, at this moment, that the Sun is ruling humanity in general, the permanent opposition between Sun and Earth reveals a lot of interesting information about us. The Sun, in each individual natal chart, represents the native's will (the human center of our being), and to be aware of our Sun means to be in touch with our creative individuality. When we act as individuals (Sun), we are in opposition to all Earth influences.

There are two ways to consider this opposition: within an individual chart, as an individual's psyche, and the more general concept of humanity's interaction and opposition with the physical planet Earth we inhabit. The opposition of humanity (Sun) and the planet Earth would indicate that our current environmental crisis is somewhat natural: a result of simply being a species of the Earth. When one studies this aspect, how astrologically clear our present ecological problems become! Yet we know how to handle an opposition. The solution is balance, and we're currently on a mission to balance our wants and needs with the needs of the Earth so that both may thrive.

When it comes to Earth, with the exception of our very earliest ancestors, we have almost always had a mindless, opposing attitude lurking in the background of our consciousness. We consider ourselves somewhat separate from our planet - Earth's planetary rules really don't apply to us. There is some history in this.

When the Cro-Magnons, or modern homo-sapiens, began to make a go of it on the Earth plane long ago, we were a small tribe with a mindset to match. In his book, <u>Pan Travails</u>, Donald Hughes, in discussing prehistoric societies, states:

"...these people regarded the universe as a sacred realm where everything was alive and conscious, including the earth and sky. They treated themselves not as separate individuals, but as integral members of a tribal community..."[2]

At the start-up of humankind's history we were not separate individuals (here perhaps, is some of that Aquarian seed energy). Astrologically, our collective Suns had not come into their full power as individuals yet. Our sense of being separate from nature hadn't completely kicked in, so we were still able to see an inter-connection to the web of life. Almost as soon as we gained some self-awareness - that is, stepped into our Sun Signs - we began to cross paths with our Earth.

Even as far back as the beginning of recorded time, we couldn't seem to keep ourselves from making a mess of our environment. Hughes goes on to say: "The Paleolithic period [still] had its ecological crises, however. In spite of traditions that taught rudimentary conservation, the hunters and gatherers could not leave nature untouched. Their traditional taboos would never have developed if mistakes had not been made, and in any case traditional teachings are notably resistant to change even when alteration in social, economic, and ecological conditions demands it."[2]

It just went downhill from there.

"In ancient Rome, the statesman Seneca complained about 'the stink, soot and heavy air' in the city. In 1257, when Henry III's wife visited Nottingham, she found the stench of smoke from coal burning so intolerable that she left for fear of her life."[3]

It is absolutely amazing that we had ecological problems before we even knew what an environment was. The whole history of humankind and Earth is one of a perpetual struggle for control. Even though we must be quite aware which side is going to ultimately win here, we continue to wrestle and roll the dice. How can we feel so alienated from, and unconscious or disrespectful of, our own environment? Why do we trivialize our home planet? What is wrong with us anyway?

A Population of Leos

The Sun is, of course, the ruling planet of Leo, so it might be said that the entire human race are all, to some extent, Leos. At least we act like it. Of course, Leo is the sign of individuality, and we have sure used that sense of individuality to separate ourselves from our planet. When we look at Leo's darker side, an interesting picture emerges. My apologies to natal Sun-sign Leos, but we must begin with the unenlightened Leonian traits, because all beginnings are raw, instinctual, and ignorant. Nothing ever emerges full-blown and mature, except in myth, and early humankind was no exception. One must always have time and experience to be wise, and, as a species, we are certainly still learning.

The Dark Side of Leo (Five Traits of a possible Apocalypse?)

We emerged as a species from the evolutionary shadows and began to develop our minds and our consciousness. In came our full Sun (Leo) awareness. Like the complementary Leos we are, we charged ahead, armed with a dangerous idea: that we are not only separate from everything around us, we are special. The instinctual dark side of Leo isn't a good thing in a species that has such power to alter its environment.

Uneducated, unthinking, unilluminated Leos, acting only on instinct, carry certain energetic signatures.

Self-Concern, Self-Aggrandizement, and the Conquerors

Looking out for number one is a prominent trait in all the personal signs (Aries through Virgo) to some degree. In addition, Leo is the sign of "self," so it is obvious that Leo's natural first reaction to anything will be to wonder how it affects them, with little thought given to the other guy or situation. Some self-concern is necessary to any species' survival and even preferable when it comes to that, but if we look at the history of the human race, we see an extremely self-involved species living with a kind of myopia, so ensconced in our own human concerns that it does not even cross our minds to wonder about what may be happening beyond our ken. This leads us to pursue ideas and take actions that do not take into consideration any effects (long term and otherwise) on what is outside our immediate use or environment. As long as we have what we want when we want it, the rest of the planet is not our concern.

    We tend to value, or hold important, only those beings or things that somehow relate to us, and if we think something is of no use to us - too foreign or even unattractive - we will downgrade it, dismiss it, and even try to remove it permanently. I have heard the phrase "what good is this animal or plant to us?" uttered time and again within environmental discussions over issues like protecting endangered species. In general, we don't consider an animal or plant valuable unto itself. With us, the simple idea that every plant, animal, or even mineral, has a right to be here, the same as we do, never seems to stick. However, if we can find (or at least hint) that a plant or animal may be of some use to the human population in the future, we are able to obtain public support for its protection. We have a real public relations problem with the world outside our fancy finite doors. Over millennia, we've had many opportunities to make it worse. Now, more than ever, we struggle to relate to a natural world we don't feel part of, developing lifestyles that take us farther and farther away from our root source. We live behind impenetrable walls of our own construction and work in glass and steel office buildings. We get our meat, vegetables, and fruit in boxes delivered to the grocery store: cut, prepackaged, or even precooked in plastic dishes. We travel in fiberglass vehicles that roll over asphalt roads that have run roughshod over every part of the land. It looks to us as if the Earth is merely background, some nice scenery passing by on our way to a destination. Many people don't even see something as basic as a tree on a daily basis. We have managed to, superficially at least, contain and control most of our environment; living on the Earth and not a part of it. We might be asking: "Earth; what Earth?" This is very indicative of the missing glyph in our charts. Without constant exposure to natural earthly processes, we've developed short-term memory loss, losing track of the fact that, despite appearances, we are still an integral part of this landscape and that everything we do really does affect the lives of all other life-forms on this planet.

    Historically, we have always wanted to be the important ones: to come out on top, to be the conqueror. The land and sea was something to be bested or claimed. If we have conquered, then we are in charge, in control, and we are assured of getting everything we want. The only problem is that we now rule over a sick land, dirty air and polluted water. What went wrong?

Pride: Pride is a way of thinking well of ourselves. Taken in moderation, it is a good thing to feel worthy. Pride is the thing that helps us get out of bed in the morning and comb our hair. However, in the shadow of pride rides arrogance and egotism, an insatiable need for the confirmation of one's distinctions, begetting an obsession for flattery and deference. With an unevolved Leonian group of people, we have beings that think they are better, or more worthy than, anyone or anything else on the planet, even better than the planet itself. In darkest Leo, the sign of humanity tends to think that they are the only thing that counts.

If we feel we are too special to consider any other species, we will act as if what we do is in the best interest of all, and will feel that our numbers, our species, are the only ones that really count, giving us a go-ahead for unlimited population growth. After all, we are the best species, why not make more? In many ways, we are obsessed with having babies and raising our children (another Leo trait). Unlike the rest of the animal world, we make a very conscious (Sun) choice to have them. Human children are among the species that spend the longest time with their parents. We orchestrate their every move, acting like they are only an extension of ourselves (Leo again), instead of the separate citizen they are trying to become.

If we want to start a war against some animal or other life form on Earth, just let it look like it is trying to hurt our young. Although surely we are not the only species protective of its young, no other species has moved into every habitat on Earth and now has the power to wipe out an entire species based on a threat. Every time a mountain lion or bear hurts or threatens someone, especially someone young, instead of thinking that the animal has a right to its instincts and its home, we start a terrible drama, wanting it shot and the species itself wiped away from that region. With our species living in every area on Earth, just where are these animals supposed to go? No other animal has the mind we do to understand a wild thing's instincts and keep themselves and their children out of harm's way the way we do. We don't seem to want to take that responsibility. The fact that many of us don't think it is right to stop, or at least slow down, our procreation has lead to overpopulation, the biggest and most devastating effect on the planet's ecosystem to date.

According to Chew Sing, the author of <u>World Ecological Degradation Accumulation, Urbanization, and Deforestation 3000 B.C. - A.D. 2000,</u> "The growth of [our] population has had an exhaustive impact on nature...This is especially the case when the economic and cultural lifestyles foster productive and consumptive levels that are extremely macro-parasitic in nature."[4] It follows here that when we are operating from the dark side, we do not want to feel less important by stooping down to any "lower levels" of life on earth. We may ask ourselves: "Why should we care if we take all the resources and leave none for other, far inferior, life forms?" The smaller, uglier, or less-aware life forms bear the brunt of our scorn. So, we feel able to change/destroy their habitat, manipulate their lives, or even kill, those insects, animals, and plants that, in our opinion, don't count, with very little thought to the matter.

When we manipulate or make life-or-death decisions about our fellow species, we are being one part narcissistic and one part god. Coincidentally, we even began most religions making God in our image, and now many of us even say that God is within. (How Leo can we get?) Narcissism is another part of pride; it explains that one sees the world only as a reflection of oneself. With narcissism, if a species looks alright to us (read: pretty or pleasing), or behaves like we do, or how we think it should behave according to human laws, then we can accept or even love it. Woe to anything though, that not only doesn't look or behave like we want it too, but has the audacity to thwart or threaten us.

I find it fascinating that we are so uncomfortable with the idea that we are animals. We do not acknowledge our affiliation with them, and are somewhat embarrassed by this connection. It may be time, with an acceptance of Earth in astrology, to get practical and earthy here. After all, we <u>are</u>

one of the animals of the Earth, whether we like it or not. Perhaps our denial stems from the fact that we think of animals as so inferior. If we held animals in higher esteem (to use a Leo phrase), we might not feel so bad about being included in that group. We might see them as fellow creatures that have their own unique talents with lives to live, same as us. Other species have a moral right to be here the same as we do and we have a moral obligation to make sure we are not so selfish in our living as to threaten their existence. We must find a way to live and let live because every species deserves life on Earth.

Greed and Ostentation

It all started with our early ancestors and the intrinsic part of us that ran out to gather ever more nuts and berries in order to live a better life. Then we just ran amuck.

Leos also like to do things in a big way, so human genes seem to carry a certain lack of restraint that breeds excess in the way we do business. Wanting and having more made our species a successful one. In our early days, craving excess helped us to have enough to eat, enough firewood to keep warm, and if we found a better shelter, by god, we moved. Today it has simply become rote: when we have enough to afford better, we buy it; a better house, we move.

In Leonian fashion, people also have a built-in need to show off, to attract notice, and feel important and superior.

It not only became part of flaunting our success, it is part of our creative expression. Our culture places great value on fame, the ultimate goal of a show-off. We revere those who are in the spotlight. Getting constant recognition by others of our kind helps us to feel that we are rich and successful. We want to be the best we can be (or at least look like it). When we pursue this idea in a negative, unconscious manner, it is warped into greed and ostentation. Then we want at all costs: fancier items, prettier clothes, and all the glitz available, so as to be the envy of everyone around us. The more money we can make, the more we can own, the more stable and secure we feel at our base of operations. It is how "keeping up with the Joneses" was invented.

Leo/humanity's fondness for fun and recreation is also getting in our way of trying to curb our enthusiasm for gluttonous ideas. Who, in their emotional right mind, wants discipline (a Saturn, and perhaps even an Earth, quality) that reins in our collecting, buying, and using resources instead of play? Our western lifestyle has evolved over centuries and we are in love with it. We enjoy going away on trips, eating out, decorating the house, and shopping. So who wants to hear that our present way of life is using up all our natural resources, keeping us distracted and disengaged from our natural roots and the very source of our sustenance?

"Ecological degradation is a consequence of cultural lifestyles and economic organizing principles. However, over world history, it seems that when social systems reach a level of complexity and differentiation, their relationship with nature turns degradative. Time (Saturn) is the key factor in ecological crisis and degradation. Nature has its rhythms and rejuvenates itself through cycles of regeneration. Ecological degradation and crises emerge when cultural transformations of nature occur too rapidly. Leaving little time for nature to regenerate itself or during historical epochs when the technology and practice employed modifies the intrinsic character of the constitution and diversity of nature. This latter alteration is the most drastic, and is dependent on the cultural values (Taurus/Earth) of the utilization of knowledge (Capricorn/Saturn) and technologies."[4]

In our present state of mind, we never give the natural world a chance to catch up with our apparently insatiable appetite. Heck: we don't even think about the natural world <u>needing</u> to catch up with us; we are perpetually at play, childishly expecting or hoping that nature will always provide for us all the toys we want. Our present lifestyles and even our pastimes, the very sources of our recreation, have become the activities that most threaten our planet.

Passion and Strong convictions

Passionate is a word for Leo and for the human race. Passion isn't just the fiery and romantic notion expressed by people in love. It is a powerful way of feeling and expressing one's ideals, period. A way of feeling focused, excited, and enthusiastic about anything. Passion manifests when we are feeling totally engaged on all levels (physically, emotionally, and mentally) with something that has touched us where we live. It also occurs when we feel sure and certain about some idea or theory, for example: when we think we have discovered some truth. We can make a strong physical and emotional connection with something in our minds and, through passion, we acquire conviction. A conviction, in turn, generates belief and a deep adherence or loyalty (Leo) to that belief once it is acquired. As a result, we become stubborn or fixed in our beliefs, and because of our passionate nature, change and adaptability, in many areas of our lives, are really hard for us. We doggedly and determinedly follow a course until it kills us (or presumably, the planet). Perversely, we also fear criticism and when we feel we aren't being supported, we become terribly defensive and overbearing in our zeal to convince everyone that we are right. We need to feel right in order to feel okay about ourselves. "The human force of will (Leo) is amazing and when in a dark place we forget all about everything but getting the upper hand."[5]

    This is one of the ways we lose objectivity: identifying so strongly, so passionately, with what we have come to believe, it becomes part of who we are. Then, we feel that we cannot change our beliefs, because in addition to our belief, we will lose our identity. This is a very dangerous and limiting trait for us, not only for the future wellbeing of our environment, but for any work toward that elusive prospect of world peace.

We may abhor criticism, but learning to be self-critical is an important step toward objectivity (Aquarius). We must learn how to distance ourselves (Aquarius) from what we believe and not take things so personally (Leo). Objectivity: the understanding that, as strong as we feel about something, it still isn't who we are. This gives us the room we need to change beliefs at the appropriate time. Perhaps, given our passionate natures, we should consider moving completely away from "believing" in general and only entertain possibilities or ideas (a very Aquarian way of thinking). Then we have total freedom to keep learning and changing and moving beyond where we are, entering a progressive (Aquarian) state. Until we embrace objectivity (Aquarius), and feel okay about ourselves, regardless of our strong emotional investments in things that may ultimately fail us, we will never be free to make changes, and we will never be a mature species.

Speaking of passion, I am sure that many people reading this already take exception, and even feel passionately insulted and consequently resistant, to some of the content in my above paragraphs. Please bear with me, as I am trying to show how ingrained these traits appear to be in

ALL of us. When we grasp this and gain some perspective, we will find the freedom to choose a new and better way to proceed onward as a species.

Creativity

Much like curiosity and the cat, creativity gets the human race into a lot of trouble. The Leonian trait of creativity means that human beings are very imaginative. This is not a bad thing in itself, but wedded with passion, pride, and self-concern, it carries us right away.

Other ways human beings feel important or unique is through self-expression. Whether an artist, writer, scientist, or business person, we want to have a noticeable place in the world; to be recognized as someone who is distinct and unmistakable from the rest. We are so fascinated with ourselves that we want to duplicate who we are through our work. We want to see ourselves reflected in everything we do and the things we do carry our stamp on them. We then feel powerful and special. This is the root of most creativity. Over millennia, we have developed that propensity in ourselves into a highly-skilled and technologically-advanced group of beings. We really are amazing. Our creativity is a gift that has handed us the ability to survive and thrive through many of Earth's changes (some of which we brought on ourselves), and we have been very successful. We have also taken it a bit too far, as per usual.

"[Historically] Humans have [always] made major changes in their environments. Then they have had to adapt to the changes made, by altering the patterns of their societies, or to disappear. This has happened in every historical period and in every part of the inhabited earth."[6]

This is especially true when we notice a potential benefit for humankind in some Earthly resource. Our modus operandi has been to tinker with it, make it more powerful or longer lasting, or just make it more specialized and suitable to our needs. From herbs to drugs, wood to paper, oil to plastic, minerals to chemicals, and even Uranium to the A-bomb. These things may be helpful to us, but due to our creative distillation, they sometimes end up becoming foreign substances to the Earth. The planet has a lot of trouble breaking them down and reabsorbing them back into the ecosystem. Many times, they become a toxin or pollution.

When a little of something is effective, more will be better! This is our philosophy and it gets us into terrible trouble. We alter nature with frightening frequency and with a speed and casualness, giving almost no thought to future ramifications. One of the reasons we don't seem to see the Earthly impact of what we are doing, ironically, pertains to our level of skill.

Our unique talent for survival and invention has isolated us from the rest of life on Earth, even to the point of losing our memory of what the land is providing for us. Our insular lifestyle has a surface look and feel that does not seem to depend on anything from this planet for its survival. Even if we know that isn't true, on some level we have no immediate and tangible proof of it.

Yet, "[H]istorical explanations must take account of the fact that the human species is part of ecological systems. What has happened to human societies, and continues to happen to them, is in many important ways an ecological process. The distinction first made by the ancient Greeks, between 'nature' (*physis,* what exists and grows of itself) and 'culture' (*nomos,* what human societies create) is not an absolute one; in an important sense, culture is part of nature because culture is the product of a species of animal, the human species."[7]

The characteristics of the human race, these Leonian or Sun-dominated traits, taken together, have created a culture, that Alfred Kroeber and Clyde Kluckhohn describe in their book: <u>Culture: A Critical Review of Concepts and Definitions</u>, as "an integrated pattern of human knowledge belief, and behavior that depends upon the capacity for symbolic thought and social learning" together with a "set of shared attitudes, values, goals, and practices."[8] That has led us, as people, to a mind-set that is constantly dividing us from our environment (Earth/Taurus) and yet still has a profound impact on it.

"The idea of environment as something separate from the human and offering merely a setting for human history, is misleading. Whatever humans have done to the rest of the [Earthly] community has inevitably affected themselves."[9]

This is the story of our species' tenure on Earth, a tale of ignorance, arrogance, and error, but also survival, skill, and (hopefully) enlightenment. We are growing and learning and trying to find a better way to live on this planet. Learning to live in total harmony with our bodies and our environment is probably the biggest challenge a species like us will ever face. To do this, we will have to change not only the way we live, but also the way we feel and think about our lives and, ultimately, our planet! It certainly won't be easy, but all environmental indicators say we must. Now, we can use all the help we can get.

Handling the Sun-Earth Opposition

The Sun's opposition to Earth in astrology gives us plenty of solid information as to what Leonian traits in our human arsenal need to be modified, and in what way.

As astrologers, we know how to handle oppositions. The solution is always the balancing of the two opposing energies, favoring neither one nor the other, but working equally with both. Coincidentally, humanity's current mission <u>is</u> to balance our wants and needs with the needs of the Earth so that both may thrive.

So if Taurus is now linked to Earth, we need to consider and compare what Taurus/Earth and Leo/Sun share, and most especially, how they differ. In the astrological chart, the signs of Taurus and Leo form a 90 degree "square," a challenging aspect. However, in a chart, the planets that rule those signs have a 180 degree, or oppositional relationship. The opposition aspect is also challenging, but carries within it a significant advantage over the square; the two opposing forces have some shared characteristics.

Leo and Taurus do share a fixed (consistent) nature, but while Leo is fixed fire, Taurus is fixed earth. As one may suppose, fire is all about enthusiasm and action, so Leo is consistent in its fiery drive. Leo is about energy and will. Fire, when taken symbolically and metaphysically, is an intangible essence that moves, motivates, pushes, resists, consumes, and strives to affect whatever it touches. Leo embodies the concentration of these traits, keeping them flowing at a certain sustained level. Taurus seeks consistency too, but with Taurus (and Earth) the concentration is more focused on creating concrete or material things. Taurus (and to some extent all the earth signs), cultivates stability, reliability, value, and sustainability.

Leo and Taurus are personal signs, self-concerned and sometimes even selfish, and this particular flow of energy says, in essence: there is no difference between me and the rest of the world; the world and I are one: "I AM the world." Yet Leo always has the tendency to want more or (at least) feel superior to whatever is around them. Feeling that way allows them to have the right to dominate and manipulate what is theirs; i.e., the world. We can follow this to a certain recognizable conclusion: "The world belongs to me because I am the world, I know what's best for the world, and I will change the world to be more what I would like it to be."

Taurus is another personal sign that falls into the "I am the world" syndrome, but with a difference. Taurus never feels superior; it has the humility that Leo is lacking. When it comes to relating self to everything else around them, their tendency is to feel kinship, not kingship. This would include their environment. Taurus might say: "My environment belongs to me, so I will protect it so that it may serve me well. I take care of the things that belong to me because this preserves their value." It is still selfishness; it just happens to be more in favor of whatever Taurus attaches to. Taurus's tendency to be realistic really helps offset the selfishness of its sign too; it doesn't lose sight of the basic limitations in any situation.

Taurus is looking for connections that bring in an amount of productivity or profit, but also peace and serenity. Taurus isn't a fire sign; it isn't out there to start anything or 'fire' things up. It's looking for slow, steady progress and calm, centered action with an outcome of ease, or even luxury. Leo is looking for excitement and leadership (maybe even a drama with themselves in a starring role), resulting in admiration for their brilliance and a job well done.

Taurus and Leo both want things to be under their control and do their bidding. If we consider the Earth symbolically as an entity, and humanity as another whole entity, then we can picture two separate and self-concerned beings living side-by-side, each having their own set of wants and needs. Like roommates, perhaps, that get more and more distant from each other, living their own separate lives, wanting their own separate outcomes. Roommates, but with a significant difference: we need our roommate Earth to stay alive, and Earth doesn't need us.

Nature and Nurture

The distance humanity has traveled from Earth's natural world can be seen in the way most people view nature today. We might comment on a pretty sunset, or how cute some animal is, but the man/woman on the street almost never talks about how important, how vital, the pure products of nature are to our survival. We perpetually put everything else ahead of it, especially economics. While it's true that when we can't make money we can't make a living, it doesn't mean we <u>cannot</u> live. The things that sustain us (air, water, and soil) are still available to us. We can have a strong economy, make a lot of money, and still die of asphyxiation.

Like the 19th century Cree Indian saying: "Only when the last tree has died and the last river has been poisoned and the last fish has been caught will we realize that we cannot eat money."

There is even mistrust among our species of the natural world as something dark and brooding that lies in wait for us. "Don't go into the woods!" still haunts our collective unconscious. How many times have I heard the lament that nature is so impersonal, harsh, brutal, and deadly? The fact that Earth has a "predator and prey" system is hard to accept sometimes, but nature doesn't do anything underhandedly or meanly. Predators, we included, need to eat, that is all.

Nature also has a kind, caring, and gentle side. Many animals show affection not only for their own kind, but for other species as well. Countless news reports and even online videos show animals of all kinds caring for a different species' offspring. The plant kingdom too, has its own way of reaching out to others of its kind. Sick trees have been found to send warning signals to the other trees in the woods to shore up their defenses against the insects that are attacking them. Ian Baldwin, a biologist and director of the Molecule Ecology department at the Max Planck Institute for chemical ecology in Jena, Germany, has discovered that trees are able to communicate with each other. "Specifically, Dartmouth biologist Jack Schultz and Baldwin's experiments seemed to confirm a hypothesis put forth by University of Washington researcher David Rhoades: that if a tree is attacked by bugs, it somehow alerts nearby trees, which in turn take defensive action by increasing the level of phenols—digestion-inhibiting chemicals—in their leaves. Rhoades at first thought that trees might communicate via chemicals released through their roots (in effect, by playing footsie)—but the experimenters now suspect the communicating agent is a chemical released in the air by damaged leaves."[10]

This doesn't seem impersonal to me. The more we learn and understand about the natural world, the more we will see it as a place of kinship; relating with us, and all species of the Earth.

At present, we overemphasize the left hemisphere of our brain, always looking for facts and logic to forward our ambitions and forgetting how to stand back, relax, and feel our connection with everything around us. A more shamanistic view of the world could be a great addition to our empiricism. Shamanism is the idea that there is no disparity between any animal, any plant, any rock, and any human. Not only are we not more important, but we are a part of the whole and the environment is a reflection of us. We are equal to everything we see. We are made of the same stuff and all have certain gifts or talents. Beyond equality, Shamanism says that the environment and its creatures are actually aware of us and communicate with us on many levels. There is constant connection and interplay between us and everything around us, if we would only notice. This is a very foreign idea to many people.

Opposing Microcosms: More manifestations of Sun opposition Earth

So, we've established that for us humans, the opposition of Sun and Earth in an astrological chart indicates a need to integrate two separate entities, but there is more at odds here then just a planet and its people. This is also a conflict between interior ideas of the human personality and exterior reality of those other things that would be ruled by Earth in astrology. We have imbalances everywhere.

Our plane of existence is all about duality. Everywhere we look, we see opposites - light/dark, good/bad, male/female - and we're not very good at integration. We tend to live on one side of a philosophy for a couple millennia, and then the other, swinging back and forth, pendulum-like: matriarchal versus patriarchal, tribe or individual, science versus spirit, and when one side of this dual reality is emphasized, the other side is always trivialized, downgraded, or dismissed.

In Western culture, we've been living this century and the last with an outgoing, progressive, technological, and developmental mindset, so we've trivialized and downgraded interior experiences. That is, we stopped placing value on improving our personalities with self-education, culture, art, or spiritual enlightenment in favor of power and ownership.

When we meet each other or read about one another, the first thing we want to know about them is what they have accomplished on a physical level? We want to know what they do, what they own, where they live, how much money they make, and maybe where they've been. When we greet each other on the street, we aren't going to ask: "How's that problem with fear coming along?" or "Did you make any headway on your integrity issues?"

Instead of internal progress on mental acuity, philosophical enlightenment, psychological balance, or proficiency in math, music, or art, we revere the outward and superficial qualities of the external: career advancement, monetary achievement, athletic ability, and beauty. It isn't who you <u>are</u> that counts, but what you do or look like. No one can argue that we haven't made great strides with our inventions, machines, and medicines, but along the way, we lost a lot of our internal compass.

This has sent many of us to counselors, doctors, psychiatrists, and astrologers for our developing health problems related to frustration and stress. Finally, some of us end up on drugs or alcohol for relief or an escape. When you don't have a compass, you can get pretty stressed. You forget how to live, or why you are living, and are always searching for meaning. Since the 1960s, we have witnessed an increased interest in personal growth, and many are considering it a worthwhile pastime once again. Even when these internal ideas are embraced, we still carry the "one side or the other" mentality and feel that when we develop character we have to give up our outward ambitions and technology.

Another symbolic illustration of external earthly manifestation versus our internal human consciousness is the conflict between our body and our inner spirit. The human body is also symbolized, in my opinion, by the planet Earth. So besides the war between what we want and what our planet needs, the schism between our outward achievements and inner peace, we also have our bodies versus our selves. This is most prominent in the Western world where almost all women, and some men, are dissatisfied with, or even hate, their bodies. This is due to an outward, glamorized, and idealized (Leonian) idea about how our bodies should look, behave, or operate.

Here we have a creature of the Earth that is losing its ability to work within the parameters of its own body. We have unrealistic ideas about how our physical body should look, and more importantly, we don't want to deal with what our bodies need. Our inability to "get real" (Earth) with our body is one of the greatest challenges facing our health and well-being today. We seem to live from the neck up; paying little attention to the rest of the corporeal vehicle that takes us where we want to go. Part of the population wants to be thinner than is practical, so they are starving themselves to death. The other half eats way too much of all the wrong things and never gets any exercise. We all like to eat what tastes the best. We even work at inventing more foods that tickle our taste buds but savage our hearts and digestive systems.

We've developed a plethora of diseases that are increasing all the time, specifically traceable to these learned, out-of-balance, bad habits: diabetes, anorexia, obesity, heart disease, and colon cancer, just to name a few. So, instead of getting reacquainted with what our bodies need and adjusting our behavior to some happy medium, we staple our stomachs and pop any pill that will allow us to go on living in our imbalance. These microcosms, or patterns, are part of the macrocosmic problem of people opposing (whether they mean to or not) planet Earth, or the Sun opposing Earth. They are not going to be solved by giving up one for the other, but in the balancing of both.

Noticing a problem, and then searching charts in astrology for patterns that symbolize that problem, means we can study how the owner(s) of a chart are using that interplay of problematic energy. Like natal chart readings for individuals, studying astrological symbolism for a people and then applying it to their general mindset helps us all to see what we might be denying as a population. When we have in our hands something as impersonal as a chart, which looks more like a mathematical equation than a personal affront, we can talk intelligently and think rationally about it.

Astrology always gives us a safe, emotional distance from our blockages or problems and allows us to understand how our attitudes are influencing them. It helps us to understand what we are doing, why we are doing it, and with that understanding comes acceptance. Only then can a problem be acted upon. Astrological symbolism not only shows us a problem, it shows us the solution. If we embrace a new philosophy that includes balancing Earthly resources with human needs, then we will gain stewardship over our bodies as well as the Earth. Learning how to balance one Sun/Earth opposition will give us the key to balancing it all.

Our Balancing Act

What does the Earth (Taurus) want from Sun (Leo) anyway?

Taurus, when attached to the Earth, would ask this of the Sun people: to accept reality. This means embracing a true and deep understanding of the parameters and limitations of the natural world before we try imposing our ideas and will on everything that grows, walks, or flies. The world is the way it is, and not necessarily the way we want it. When we face Earth's true makeup and its limitations, we won't be a burden to it. We will always be able to anticipate and understand the outcome of anything we might do.

Simply being realistic may seem obvious, but the average human being has gotten so out of touch with the natural world that we have lost track of what is out there, why it is there, and how it works. Nature has its own rules or limitations, the same as we do. In human-land nature's rules are called things like biology or physics. When we do things that are contrary to nature's biology, we get trouble, tragedy, or mayhem. The Earth behaves according to its needs and boundaries. Animals and insects have their own lifestyles, and when we get in the middle of their domain with no thought of them or their rules, that's when we get ourselves hurt or killed.

As far as our knack for improving Earth goes, this does not mean that we should just give up our ideas in that area. However, it does mean that we should begin all our ideas for improvements with a firm grasp on how the Earth really works and what our side effects on it will be.

Taurus is never interested in Leo's penchant for instant gratification, in how fast or how flashy something is done, but how well it is done and how long it will last.

Taurus isn't so much into taking action as they are looking for something to invest in, to align themselves with, or lend their energies to, that would be meaningful and worthwhile.

If they do decide to put forth energy and work on something, they want to see good, stable results; a sound, material product of their labor. They are unimpressed with how good something looks: they want to know what it is made of and what its guarantees are. Taurus is like someone who always looks for "the catch" in a reward. Leo just looks for the reward.

Security is important to Taurus, and they want the security of something that has definition and boundaries; something they can understand and that is concrete and consistent. Consistency means reliability. When things are reliable, they are operating to the best of their ability; they are healthy and will perform at a top level. This means that Taurus can continue to safely rely on it. When someone or something is safe, and in a zone that is comfortable, it has the endurance to continue on for as long as is necessary.

Taurus is patient and willing to make the sacrifices necessary for quality. Taurus asks Leo to slow down and take in all the ramifications of what it is about to do, to look realistically at any results of an action and ask what the true value of any endeavor will be. In other words, facing the full reality of an action one must always ask: Is this worth it? How will this action add value to ALL concerned? (The "all" being everything and everybody involved) Taurus tells Leo that creating or making something jazzier doesn't necessarily make it better, whispering that old expression "All that glitters is not gold."

Taurus sticks to the basics in thought and problem solving: what makes the most sense, what is necessary for the preservation of the whole. Things that have worked well in the past are important, too. Taurus keeps alive the thread that leads to the center of creation, supporting a continuation of the pattern and coming back to the basics whenever there is confusion and things are in danger of spinning out of control. Deep in our gut, we have lost our connecting thread to Earth; it is completely missing from our planning and our actions. We need our thread to nature restored and a reinstatement of our heart connection to our own planet.

When it can't think something through, Taurus relies on gut instinct, feeling what is right on a visceral level. Leo would fall back on what is popular, what the crowd would support, applaud, or approve of. We do that, don't we? We feel better and more confident of our place if everyone agrees with us, so we tend to make decisions based on a consensus or agreement, not necessarily on what is true or right. We are consistently too frightened of the rejection of our tribe to strike out and forge ahead with an idea whose time may have come, but requires some shift in thought or action. We do ourselves great damage through denial and procrastination, waiting for everyone to feel okay before we move to make things better. Because of this, most of our history includes last-minute decisions and last-ditch attempts to right what is wrong before it's too late. We've been lucky that this "wait 'till there is a crisis and it will force us to act" attitude hasn't had any long-term effects. That is, until now. No one really knows if we have time enough to heal the planet now or not, and we have barely started.

In spite of being a personal sign, Taurus's humility never lets their personal zeal overtake their sense. They are willing to admit when they don't know something, and submit to whatever is smarter or in greater authority. Though they have a reverence and respect for power, they don't really want to be all-powerful, as many Leos dream. To be the one in charge is too much pressure, too much trouble, but if things are not being run in a way that makes Taurus feel secure, they will be only too glad to step in with the idea that, when all is fixed, they will step down again. A signature Taurian trait is always a blend of wanting ease, but not being afraid of hard work and sacrifice when the times require it.

Taurus is a collector of things, people, or ideas, so naturally they don't ignore or discount anything that looks like it could be utilized. They are always sizing things up to see if they have value, and they are also good at assigning value, knowing what something is worth. This, coupled with a slower and more deliberate pace, means that it is rare for Taurus to leave something out, cast anything aside, pass over, or forget about anything of importance. Taurus includes, because anything can be valuable down the road, even if today isn't the day. Taurus asks Leo to be vigilant for value. It isn't always necessary to make something new, or have the latest toy, or have an item look nice. Taurus asks Leo to recognize that even cast-offs and old, used items can be useful again. Recycle, or as the old Depression era saying goes: "use it up, wear it out, or go without."

Early Human Habits

At some point in our early development, humanity began to store food and live together in one location. It was a lot safer, not to mention convenient, to have your neighbor watching your back for predators. They were proactive, Leo people who began to erect buildings for shelter and fences to create towns. In those days, we were not in control of our environment but we wanted to be. Naturally, there was fear of the woods: too many things could be hiding there that could spell doom, or at least pain. We were highly suspicious and violently distrustful of the natural world, and we had a right to be. It was dark in the forest, and we hadn't a clue as to what was living there. There were so many unknown factors, the safest thing to do was to cut down all the trees around our homes and clear the bushes out too, right down to the grass. Having a clear view all around our living quarters was a great idea: nothing would ever sneak up on us again. We still do that today, in the form of our lawns. We really are creatures entrenched in habit. With this simple exercise, we realized that we had gained some power over our own lives. Now, what else could we do?

As soon as we were safe, we wanted more. More area cleared, more buildings built, walls erected. Leo is about moving forward with the ultimate creative leaps and attention-getting enhancements. How far could we go here? How elaborate or fancy could we get? After making the land all around us ours, we took great pride in our accomplishment. Then we had to defend it when other tribes got envious and wanted to take our land for their own. After all that work, we sure weren't going to give it up.

There is no doubt that our Leo-ness has served us well. In fact, we probably wouldn't have been such a startlingly successful species without it. Yet here we are, hundreds of years later, and in many ways we still live in almost the same way. We mow our lawns and worry about cougars getting our kids, when the cougar hasn't much of a chance against us anymore. We know exactly what is in the woodland now, how to safeguard ourselves, and have practically eliminated anything threatening us in almost every area of the globe.

We've become entrenched, mentally and physically, in an old, outmoded way of life, even when the scariest thing out there today is <u>us</u>. We're still cutting down the trees as if there are more unexplored and vastly productive lands somewhere to our west, instead of Los Angeles. The wild isn't wild anymore.

We've done an excellent job at surviving using our old ways, but if we stay this course, we're going to go the wrong way. Instead of helping us to live, these ancient ideas will ultimately kill us and just about everything else on the planet, too.

As a species, we need a sea change. It's time to see ourselves as what we've become, let go of old attitudes, and adjust to the changing circumstances we now find ourselves in. We need to be realistic and practical. We need to incorporate some Taurian common sense into our Leo drive and flamboyance. Taurus is about basic survival. Are we ready to go back to basics and re-learn how to live our lives in conjunction <u>with</u> the planet instead of in competition with it?

Going green: A Taurian creed.

One hopeful campaign that is spearheading our way for infusing Taurian qualities into our Leonian mindset is the Green Movement. "Green" living is finally catching on, and about time, too. This philosophy, and subsequent lifestyle, is based on the idea that we can not only clean up what we have soiled, but change our way of living to prevent future destruction. "Green" ideas challenge us to be mindful of the impact our every action has on our environment, and to adjust our action to a more workable, more common sense approach in order to keep our home clean, healthy, and running smoothly. "Green" living is also showing us that despite our habitual leanings, we can change and we understand that better choices are available.

A fear of change (that fixed nature) in our species creates a lot of missed opportunities to handle things in a timely manner. One of the fears holding us back from going "green" has been that our economy will suffer some fatal blow. If businesses or companies make changes for the environment, they will not be as successful. This fear is not based on reality.

Holland has shown the world that "green" living and a strong economy are not mutually exclusive at all. Their program and the radical changes they made as a country were featured in Outside magazine the summer of 2003.[11] They surprised the globe by not only making their businesses clean, sustainable, and profitable, but in record time as well.

Even here, there is some need for caution. We must be careful that in our Leonian zeal, we don't take "green" too far, as is our usual inclination. We have seen that whatever we decide to do, we do with Leonian abandon, that is, to excess. If there is anything to take away from this chapter, let it be a shift away from the insular, Leo, ego-driven, what-about-me attitude of humanity to the open-ended question of: what can we do together, as a team, working with all creatures/plants/soil of Earth, to improve life for all inhabitants? (Taurus)

So, before we plaster every hilltop with wind turbines and/or some other good idea that, in our hands, has the potential to run amuck, we must take stock of the situation. Is anyone studying the effects that thousands of turbines are having on the creatures living in the vicinity? We must find balance in the Green Movement, too. Whatever idea we have, whatever plan we make, whatever action we take, let us keep the balance between passionate Leo and practical Taurus. Leo creativity combined with Taurian grounding is the very best path for a better future, not only for humanity, but the rest of the world as well. With balance achieved, Leo, and humanity, is free to move beyond any negative aspects of its sign.

The Enlightened Leo: Our Maturing Population

While the negative traits of Leo illustrate what we have done wrong, the positive side of Leo can save us from our own destruction. We take our cues for our, and Earth's, salvation once again from the Sun rulership of Leo and humanity.

From Selfish Would-be Conqueror to Efficient Compassionate Leader

As a species, we have a lot of initiative and energy. It

is natural that humankind wants to be important; a true leader of all the other species in the world. However, we must understand that leadership is a position of trust. Leo leadership, when balanced with an awareness of how their followers feel and what they need to thrive, becomes the very best kind of leader.

A true leader isn't a tyrant who barks orders and expects everything to be under his control. Instead, a leader is the one in charge, who oversees all situations and tries to do the best job he can with what he has to work with, for the betterment of all concerned. He looks at each of his followers and discerns who would be right for what job, position, and office, and then makes assignments, delegates authority, and coordinates all actions of the group. Like a conductor of a symphony, he feels the responsibility of his position keenly. If the group, or in this case, planet, is in jeopardy it is in some way the leader's fault. The status or safety of a group always reflects the leadership involved. When we are comfortable in our leadership role, when everything is going well, we, as Leos, will become very magnanimous and generous. We have that capacity. Here's where leadership becomes stewardship. Humanity's role, and best destiny, will always be as stewards of the Earth.

Instead of looking to conquer nature, we can now be the conquerors of pollution and waste. We'll declare war, and fight the most important battles of our lives and the lives around us. If we do this, the glory we crave will be ours. We are perfectly suited to this. Our brains are computer problem-solvers: we can think through problems and yet still have heart; the compassion and ability to put ourselves in another's place, even when that other is another species altogether. We've spent years studying Earth and her plants and animals. We know how to do this. All we have to do is stop living for ourselves alone, and we will be an unbelievable force of positive change for healing the entire planet.

Pride... of Place

When I lived in Connecticut, there was something there referred to as "pride of place." This meant that the yard or grounds of any household were well-tended, healthy, and impeccably neat. People living at that address loved their patch of ground, worked it, and were proud of their surroundings. We could easily transfer our propensity for pride, into any job well done, and this includes cleaning up the planet. Beyond that, what if, besides our yard, we had pride of place for the entire Earth? That everywhere we went we felt involved and invested in what was around us? Wouldn't we stop and pick up that beer can, or better yet, never trash up our "yard" again? The way the Earth looks, and the vitality of it, is a direct reflection of us and the way we treat it, so where is our dignity and pride in this matter? Why can't we have pride in our planet?

Greed: Time to value something besides stuff

At the moment, we have a terrible economic system in the United States. It is based on buying stuff we really don't need. We have become addicted to shopping, and the natural resources we must use to make these things, are not something the Earth can sustain.

When we feel connected and a part of something greater than ourselves, we aren't going to feel that we need so many things to make us happy. Greed and hoarding is a human impulse that occurs when we feel deprived, undernourished, unloved, or empty. Our empty lifestyles are making us unhappy. We aren't grounded (Taurus) and we don't feel we belong to anything very impressive (Leo). In spite of, or actually as a result of, our selfishness, we don't even feel especially powerful because we lack largess. We lost our sense of value (Taurus/Earth) in non-material things. Yet, there are plenty of grand ideas out there, enriching personal habits to acquire, culture to develop, good causes to join, communities to support, and friends to make. When we slog through our lives not feeling we have any real purpose, we go buy a bunch of stuff to cheer ourselves up. Let us choose to change our value system from external to internal accomplishments and we will soon have the satisfaction that has eluded us. Once we feel "full," we will be willing to share what we have. We won't need so many things and we'll share the planet's resources with the rest of the life here.

Passion and Strong Convictions… for Our Mission Here on Earth

When we apply our intensity and enthusiasm (Leo) to changing our values (Taurus), we can invest our energies in ideas and projects we can really believe in, with startling results. The human force of will (Leo) is amazing, and because of our strong convictions, we have dedication that will see us through the work that must be done. We can apply our passion to saving the Earth and her inhabitants, and go on to make this planet, our home, a vital and vibrant entity.

Creativity: Used with Concern

Our Leo creativity is the stuff of legends, literally. I am convinced that there is nothing we couldn't solve and improve through our incredible and most human way of inventing and creating. Creativity, when applied with a global perspective, environmental consciousness, and a little forbearance, could lead us out of any predicament in no time at all. Our self-expression could lend itself to creating a virtual Disneyland of "green" living and developing the highest human ideals.

When working on the positive side, Leos are in their full glory. Leo's chin is always up and they're looking at the stars. Whatever road Leo travels, it can easily become the high road, not debasing themselves, or anyone around them, with impurities in thought, word, or deed. This means living with a higher purpose in mind at all times and searching for something much more important than simple self-gratification.

If we are truly moving into the "Age of Aquarius," perhaps this can be the time when we can shift our present Leo paradigm to embrace humanity's opposing and more rightful ruling sign of Aquarius. Finding another balance in the oppositional axis of Leo and Aquarius can also bestow on us an attitude of tolerance, equality, mutual respect for all life forms, and allow us to begin sharing everything with every life form on Earth. I will address this in more depth in Chapter 10.

Summary

When considered in literal terms, the Sun-Earth opposition (and the Leo/Taurus square) is the story of us, our human history, and the arc of our tenure here on Earth: why we are the way we have turned out to be, and how we got into the current environmental mayhem we find ourselves in. The more we study, talk, write, and teach about this astrological opposition between ourselves and the Earth, the more understanding and progress will be gained. I believe in us, I believe in the nobility of humankind and how this world could easily reflect the best we have to offer. All we have to do is decide, with Leo joy and with Leo playfulness, that we can create a whole new way of life that is not only beautiful, but completely healthy and sustainable for all concerned. We'll begin, or continue, this journey by including Earth in our astrological philosophy and by adding the planet Earth to all our astrological charts.

[1] Tarnas, Richard. *Cosmos and Psyche*. 1st Ed. New York, N.Y.: Penguin Group, 2006. 28. Print.

[2] Hughes, J. Donald. *Pan's Travail Environmental Problems of the Ancient Greeks and Romans* . Johns Hopkins paperbacks edition. Baltimore, Md. : Johns Hopkins University Press, 1994. 25. Print.

[3] Lomborg, Bjorn. "Take a deep breath... air quality is getting better." *Guardian* 15 Aug 2001: 1. Web. 25 Mar 2011.

<http://www.guardian.co.uk/environment/2001/aug/15/physicalsciences.globalwarming>.

[4] Sing, Chew. *World Ecological Degradation Accumulation, Urbanization, and Deforestation 3000 B.C. - A.D. 2000*. Lanham, MD: AltaMira Press, 2001. 3. Print.

[5] Diamonnd, Jared. *The Third Chimpanzee*. First. New York, N.Y.: HarperCollins, 1992. Print.

[6] Hughes, J. Donald. *An Environmental History of the World.* 2nd. New York, N.Y.: Routledge, 2009. 1. Print.

[7] Hughes, J. Donald. *An Environmental History of the World.* 2nd. New York, N.Y.: Routledge, 2009. 5-6. Print.

[8] According to Wikipedia: Culture (from the Latin cultura stemming from colere, meaning "to cultivate") is difficult to define. For
example, in 1952, Alfred Kroeber and Clyde Kluckhohn compiled a list of
164 definitions of "culture" in Culture: A Critical Review of Concepts
and Definitions. However, the word "culture" is most commonly used in three basic senses:
* Excellence of taste in the fine arts and humanities
*An integrated pattern of human knowledge, belief, and behavior that
depends upon the capacity for symbolic thought and social learning
* The set of shared attitudes, values, goals, and practices that characterizes an institution, organization or group.

http://en.wikipedia.org/wiki/Culture#cite_note-1

The Book:

Kroeber, Albert. *Culture: A Critical Review of Concepts and Definitions.* Cambridge, Mass.: Harvard University Print Office, 1952. Print.

[9] Hughes, J. Donald. *An Environmental History of the World*. 2nd. New York, N.Y.: Routledge, 2009. 6. Print.

[10] People Magazine Jul 18 1983 vol 20 number 3

Also see Volatile Signaling in Plant-Plant Interactions: "Talking Trees" in the Genomics Era Ian T. Baldwin Science Magazine 10 February 2006: http://www.sciencemag.org/cgi/content/abstract/311/5762/812

Discover Magazine April 2002

http://discovermagazine.com/2002/apr/featplants

[11] Williams, Florence. "How Green Is My Polder." *Outside Magazine online* June 2006: 1-6. Web. 25 Mar 2011. <http://outsideonline.com/outside/features/200306/200306_how_green_1.html>.

CHAPTER 3
Esoteric Earth, Levels of Earth, and the Number 4

*"This world was once a fluid haze of light,
Till toward the center set the starry tides,
And eddied into Suns, that wheeling cast
The Planets."* ~Alfred Lord Tennyson

"We don't see things as they are, we see them as we are." ~Anais Nin

"[Man] does not see the real world. The real world is hidden from him by the wall of imagination." ~George Gurdjieff (1874-1949), Russian mystic, author

The Classical Elements in Astrology and Physics

In addition to a planet, earth is one of the classical elements that make up our world. The others are of course: air, fire, and water. The classical elements are a set of energies used historically to explain patterns in nature. They were the physics of the ancient world. On a scientific level, physics today is a far more complicated and refined matter; elements are defined by the number of protons a pure substance possesses.

However, astrology is a mythical and symbolic language that attempts to describe a state of being in more immediate and philosophic terms.

On the symbolic level, or metaphysically, the four original elements are still used and they are easily recognizable as states of being or existence in our world. I pair the elements with the four forms of matter as labeled by physicists:

EARTH/SOLID: The particles of a solid are tightly packed together and have definite shape and volume.

WATER/LIQUID: The particles of liquids are tightly packed, but far enough apart to slide over one another and have definite shape and volume.

AIR/GAS: The particles of gases are very far apart and move freely and have indefinite shape and volume.

FIRE/PLASMA OR ENERGY: The particles of plasma are conductors of electricity and are affected by magnetic fields. They move past each other with a great deal of free space and so have indefinite shape and volume.

Triplicities of Astrology

When organizing astrological signs, astrologers group signs in the same element together and these are called Triplicities. The name sometimes confuses students of astrology because there are four elements. The "triple" part is the three signs that fall under each of the four elements. When studied together as a group within their element, Triplicities offer another layer of understanding about the character of a sign, and, consequently, the person, place, or thing that has that sign's elemental influence in their chart.

Modes of Astrology

The modes in astrology are yet another level of organization for understanding astrological signs. They describe the action of a sign, its mode of operation. In this case, there are three modes: Cardinal, Fixed, and Mutable. There are four signs under each of the three modes.

The three modes, or cycles of energy, are called:

CARDINAL:

Their type of action is: initiating; driven, energetic. This is a mode that helps gets things moving.

The cardinal signs are: Aries, Cancer, Libra, and Capricorn.

MUTABLE:

Their type of action is: alternating; connecting, adaptable, flexible. This is a mode that helps things shift, change, or adjust.

The mutable signs are: Gemini, Virgo, Sagittarius, and Pisces.

FIXED:

Their type of action is: persisting; stable, concentrating. A mode that helps to get things done or holds things steady.

The fixed signs are: Taurus, Leo, Scorpio, and Aquarius.

Levels of Existence and the signs of Astrology

In esoteric or metaphysical schools of thought, it is believed that everything on Earth has an energetic counterpart in the ethers. That is, the solid matter we see all around us is brought into being by an energy emanation from some source (some call this source god), and has an energetic counterparts on other levels. Many masters or theosophists also feel there is not just one level of existence, but several beyond the solid (Earth) level we can conceive. They teach that matter, or reality as we know it, comes into being through levels or dimensions that start with (or even before) something as intangible as thought, and that the field of energy gets progressively denser until finally we have solid matter or the earth plane.

The term "earth plane" is a way of labeling our physical reality within these terms. This is the name for the dimension we are living in, a place of solid matter. The original source of the word "plane" in this context is the late Neoplatonist Proclus, who refers to *to platos*, or "breadth", which was the equivalent of the 19th century theosophical use. Thinking of solid objects here on Earth as having an energetic double, or signatures elsewhere, makes perfect sense in astrology. This is what astrology is about, the labeling and tracking of energetic signatures of the manifested reality all around us, whether it is an object, a person, or an event.

The subsequent planes of existence in metaphysics may have more layers than three, but when I consider the triplicities in astrology, I think of the three matching signs of any element as existing on certain graduating levels, similar, but not equal to, the planes of existence in metaphysics.

The Modes of Astrology and Manifestation

When we read a chart, we almost always read the house motion counter-clock-wise. Therefore, the order we see, time and again, for the modes of astrology is usually cardinal, fixed, and mutable, with mutable helping to make the transition to the next cardinal sign in the next element.

However, if we go clock-wise on the house wheel of the zodiac, we get the order of cardinal, mutable, and then fixed, producing a different spin on the order of the signs. Concentrating on the elements of the signs, each mode of a sign in an element would have three levels.

1) CARDINAL
SOURCE OR INITIATING ESSENCE, LEVEL WITH THE SPIRITUAL PLANE

Starting with cardinal signs (Aries, Capricorn, Cancer, and Libra), we see their respective elements at the highest level symbolically; they are the signs that carry the most abstract ideas or the purest essence of that element. The cardinal signs represent the wellspring of any element, the highest ideal or theory of the elements' energy. On this level, they exist in an unfiltered and dynamic form. The energy level is high because it must initiate the element.

2) MUTABLE

VIBRATIONAL ESSENCE, FILTERING AND ADAPTING, LEVEL WITH THE ASTRAL OR ETHERIC PLANE

The mutable signs (Sagittarius, Virgo, Pisces, and Gemini) are the signs that symbolically represent the energy that is helping to make the transition from an essence to a solid. Through these signs, the energy grows denser and is filtered through, or shaped by, frequencies or vibration in the subatomic particles with intent to facilitate the creation of a resulting form. They "ask" what type of form is being created. What color, what shape, will it be? The sign's element here is ethereal, or between the worlds of spirit and matter. Mutable is the binding, marrying, or merging principle of the universe. The energy level is moderate.

3) FIXED

GROUNDED OR ESTABLISHED SOLID, FORM, THE PHYSICAL PLANE

Lastly, and most dense, are the fixed signs (Leo/fire, Taurus/earth, Scorpio/water, and Aquarius/air), or the elements as we recognize them. They are the saturated essence: tangible, focused, deep, stable, consistent, steady, and established. A fixed sign is the symbolic representative of the concrete element, fully manifested, formed, rooted, and integrated into the earth plane. The energy level is low because the requirement for these signs is to hold together that which has been created, and to simply maintain it. The strength of these signs lies in inertia, the ability to not move or change. This kind of energy is vitally important for the earth plane.

Matter and the Three Earth Signs

With the earth signs especially, we get an easy-to-follow, symbolic path to the physical reality of the earth plane. The universe consists of:

IDEA/ESSENCE

Capricorn = fundamental particles

ENERGY

Virgo = vibrational frequency

(Vibrational frequency determines the form or solid matter)

Taurus = manifested things, mass.

1) CARDINAL CAPRICORN

Cardinal is the beginning of any element of a sign in astrology. The cardinal sign of Capricorn, being an earth sign, begins with the <u>idea</u> of organizing energy for manifesting form. It rules *theoretical earth*, the conceptual, abstract, fundamental, or initiating earth: what makes Earth, earth? Capricorn also represents form at its most elemental level, basic data and material. This level of earth exists but we can't sense it.

In Capricorn and its ruling planet Saturn, are found the theory, fundamentals, and principles of matter and form;

the blueprint, the road map to our reality. Capricorn is the earth principle that leads to an idea or an essence that helps form manifest. It initiates the possibility that there may be consistency, stability, and subsequently a use for all things. "I Use": the concept of usability.

Capricorn carries the concept of something being able to have a form.

This category includes the invisible realm of the physical, the subatomic fundamental particles that make up our world such as fermions, quarks, bosons, neutrons, etc. Subatomic particles are the raw materials of form, where matter is perceived to get organized and sorted. Once organized by vibration (Virgo), they can begin to set barriers and boundaries for each completed form, be it a person, a garden gate, or a rose.

It would seem to be a contradiction to include subatomic particles with theory and abstract principles, but everything we know, or more accurately, don't know, about these particles, tell us that although they exist, we don't know how, or in what way they exist.

At the subatomic level, there are no objects, no forms that one can trace, or keep track of.

On the quantum level, particles get even less predictable and stable.

"According to quantum theory, particles act as waves rather than point masses on very small scales. This has dozens of bizarre consequences: it is impossible to know a particle's exact position and velocity through space, yet it is possible for the same particle to be doing two contradictory things simultaneously. Through a phenomenon known as 'superposition' a particle can be moving and stationary at the same time — at least until an outside force acts on it. Then it instantly chooses one of the two contradictory positions."[1] Only through observation at that particular time and place does a particle really define itself.

There is something very intangible and mysterious about this type and level of matter. There is no real world of form on the subatomic level, there is, however, an idea of form, a beginning of earth principles, and the basic building blocks of form, that I call theoretical earth.

Here, also, are theories involving earth that we have yet to see, touch, know, or understand in the physical sense. This theoretical earth category consists of what we have not yet discovered about earth, what we don't know about earth, or have incorrect ideas about, including any illusion we have around earthly reality, i.e., what works here or seems to work on this plane, but isn't really part of the particle base - that is, not composed of substantive pieces or real solid form, for example: time. We don't yet know what time is or if it is truly relevant or just a human construct.

Also represented in this theoretical earth category is how to go beyond our concepts of earth or how we can apply our earthly knowledge beyond Earth (in space, for example) when, or if, it comes to that.

A WORD ON MUTABLE SIGN ORDER IN THE ZODIAC

One of the translations I give for the action of mutable signs is connecting one thing with another. Mutable signs, in the human personality, are the most open, allowing, and accepting of different kinds of attitudes or energies.

The standard order and position of mutable signs in the zodiac (cardinal, fixed, mutable) loosens up the fixed sign concentration of an element, so that the energy of the universe may progress into a new element. Another way of looking at this order of cardinal, fixed, and mutable is to read it backward on the zodiacal wheel. Since we are talking about manifesting something out if its essence on the astral planes, we would start with the Earthly essence or source, Capricorn and the 10th house. The 10th house is at the top of the chart and usually corresponds, in the placidus house system, with the Medium Coeli or MC.

Now you get the order of: cardinal, mutable, and fixed. Read this way, mutable now connects cardinal to fixed, connecting the essence (cardinal) of an element or sign with its manifested physical form (fixed).

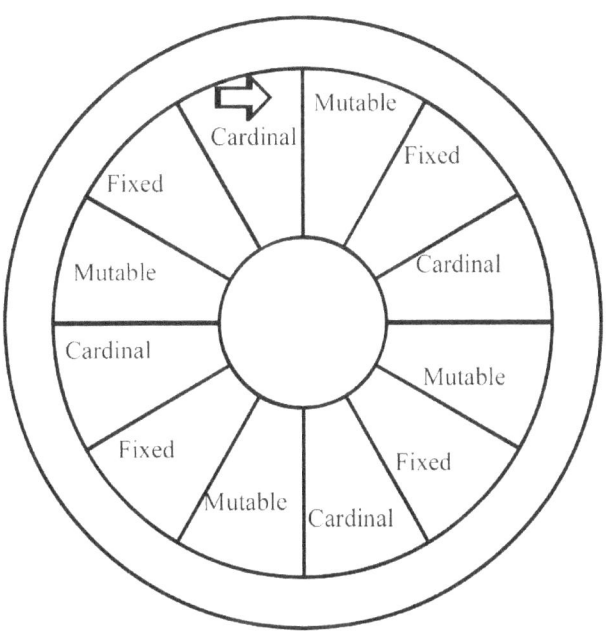

Cardinal, mutable, fixed, cardinal

2) MUTABLE VIRGO

With the mutable sign of Virgo, we have the representation or 'ruler' of functional or *vibrational earth,* earth at its most flexible.

Here we have earth energy that is closer in physicality to the world of form, but still not dense enough to manifest. It is similar to thought in that it is flexible and changeable. Mutable earth is an energy that is astral/etheric, even intuitional in nature, an energetic interface between essence and manifestation or form. Decisions at this level are still being made about the outcome, the solid form of this manifestation.

Virgo is an enabler for Capricorn. Virgo is vibration, the motion of subatomic particles. It is the rate of vibration of the particles (frequency or sound) that creates different kinds of matter. Essence, or matter and energy together, create form. It is the movement or vibration of the matter that begins to differentiate one piece of matter from another, shaping the atoms into what form they will take.

Virgo also shifts matter once it has formed, like the atoms of a human being. Although the human body holds the same general shape throughout its life, the form ages, gains weight, or gets sick, depending on the attitude or action of the being, so there are changes within the shape.

Capricorn is the intent or intention of manifesting; Virgo is the act of manifesting. Virgo is a filter for potential form. Virgo (mutable) is the working and crafting of the earth element; a "decision" of sorts is reached through a sifting of what will work in the manifestation and what won't. "I analyze" is Virgo's creed. Virgo analyzes the action of earthly particles, carrying earth operations out, arranging them into their many forms.

The astral/etheric plane is thought to be the last higher sub-plane before the solid earth plane. This plane of existence is closest to the physical plane and carries the data, signature, or the energetic imprint of all physical incarnate form. The aura is here. In human beings, the astral/etheric body reflects the physical body formed and vice versa.

If we are out of balance, ill at ease, or sick on this level then we will soon be sick in the physical body as well. The energy of the earth sign Virgo has the ability to tap into what is just beyond the physical. Virgo people in general have an innate understanding of what comes before, or what is leading to, physical manifestation. This is what makes Virgo people excellent healers. They sense, or "read" the earth body as an energy body and are then able to manipulate the body on that energy level and create a different physical result, such as wellness out of illness.

Virgo, and its newly proposed planet, Chiron, is also about the daily operation of life or life cycles; the health and wholeness of an organism; proper procedures where E/earth is concerned; rules, manners, systems, integration of the actions of Earth or earth element; and working, regulating, fixing and/or tweaking the earth element.

Virgo, with its discerning qualities, hones earth energy and is always perfecting what is working and pushing away what isn't. Natural selection and evolution fall under the rulership of Virgo, as does the idea of connectedness and wholeness of spirit between all earth life and forms, i.e., Shamanism.

3) FIXED TAURUS

Now we fall to the densest level of earthly reality: *manifested earth,* or form, solid objects, and the physical bodies of living beings.

The fixed earth sign Taurus represents or rules basic earth: the grounding, manifesting, deepening, and maintaining the shape of whatever has been conceived, selected, and energized for the final physical outcome of the arrangement of atoms, et al. on the subatomic level. Taurus is the end result. Its concern is with the manifested parts, resources, tools, and basic objects/materials of existence that is our earthly reality as we know it. What is solid, or creating and promoting, solidity with a material result? The act of manifesting and re-manifesting; Taurus is the builder, taking those items that have material corporality and creating something tangible and valuable, something _more_ than they were before, something that will last or live on. Taurus says "I have."

Tremendous creativity is latent in Taurus. With a great understanding of how the physical world is structured, the nuts and bolts of it, so to speak, they know how to put the pieces together to make something useful and/or pleasing. They understand not only how earth operates, the action of earth, or the way earthly reality behaves under many different scenarios, but also how symmetry and balance work within that reality or structure to create harmony and beauty. They know what will work on the physical plane and what isn't likely to hold together. Taurus rules anything in a solid, corporeal state. In the most general terms, this is all forms of matter, or the furniture of our reality. This includes everything from the bodies that spirit lives in, to the structures they create: landscapes, trees, rocks, buildings, roads, and books.

Taurus is also all about resources, including an understanding of the limitations of manifested earth and its resources. Taurus is physical limitation, not only of what an object or form can do or sustain, but how long it can last and why. With this inherent knowledge, Taurus is understandably known as a cautious, conservative, or prudent sign.

Earth, Astrology, and Metaphysics: The Four Fixed Signs, Symbolic Cornerstones of Reality

In metaphysical disciplines, the element earth, or that which is more consistent, solid, or stable, aptly describes the most recognizable feature of our Earth. But when we consider the qualities, or states of being (cardinal, mutable and fixed in astrology), it is the fixed temperament that exemplifies planet Earth best because when we say a sign is fixed, we mean that its quality is the epitome of stability and solidity. So, even though a sign's element may be air, if it is fixed air, it is the most stable of the air signs. Air has different qualities: think about this in terms of weather. What would solid and stable air be like? One answer is a clear, quiet day when the air is certainly present, but doesn't move around. Solid and stable fire is fire burning with consistent heat, like the sun, or in one place, like a fire pit. Water that is frozen is, of course, solid and stable, but that isn't in its purest form, which is liquid, so water can also be fixed as a deep pond or lake that was formed eons ago. It can also refer to a stagnant pool.

As you might imagine, earth that is fixed is the most stable of all. It is almost immovable and unchangeable, like rock embedded in a hillside (Earth does move, of course, but most of the time we aren't able to perceive it).

Each of the four elements in astrology has a fixed sign:

- Aquarius is fixed air
- Leo is fixed fire
- Scorpio is fixed water
- Taurus is fixed earth

I like to say that the fixed signs are determined and consistent. So, in an astrological natal chart, Taurus would be determined and consistent in a physical or earthly way; Scorpio, determined and consistent in an emotional way; Leo, determined and consistent in an energetic/active way; and Aquarius, determined and consistent in an intellectual or mindful way.

The four fixed signs, when taken alone and outside any chart, describe in archetypal, metaphysical terms our plane of existence because they encompass all four classical elements with a quality or nature that is fixed - reliable, stable, and consistent. The sum total of these fixed signs symbolically sit, pooling their energy, creating a framework for form, much like particles or atoms work to hold our world together.

The Greek philosopher Empedocles, "the first philosopher to give a detailed explanation of the mechanism by which we perceive things," [2] is credited with the idea that the four classic elements were the root of all existing matter. Because they represent the most stable form of the four elements, these four signs (Taurus, Leo, Scorpio, and Aquarius) are, in my opinion, the cornerstones, the astrological or symbolic representative of, the building blocks for life on Earth.

The energy of fixed signs is self-contained. They give off energy but that energy still stays within a kind of orbit or framework and continues to feed and sustain itself. It makes fixed signs strong, consistent, and powerful.

Leo, ruled by the Sun, is fixed fire and masculine in nature, or outward and pursuing. Leo is fire energy that is stable and consistent in its outward flow. Energy is within all life as vibrancy or motion. It is used to power life forms, to run the machinery of each life form. It is contained within the life form, but moves dynamically around like a contained and focused electrical-type current that runs our bodies. When describing the human body in action, we use fire-centered analogies, like "we are burning calories." Within our hearts, we say we "burn" for things, we get "fired up" or "charged up" about things. Our drives, our desires, are the things that push us to get up in the morning and get going. Our action is driven by our fire. When we have done too much, we become "burned out".

Besides energy, fire is also heat, generated by friction or chemical reactions within a human body or even a planetary body. The Sun is the planetary body we most associate with energy and heat. The Sun is the most necessary "planet" for life on Earth.

Aquarius/Uranus is fixed air and masculine. Fixed air has movement, yet is held within an area the way our air is held to the planet in a bubble known as the atmosphere. Air must be present in the form of this atmosphere (consisting of various gases) for life to sustain itself. Within this framework, air moves freely and sometimes quite dramatically, yet we know how it will behave in any given circumstances, therefore it is predictable in that respect. Aquarian air allows us to think our most profound thoughts, to cast our intellectual net ever wider, and to solve our most complex problems. It is the energy that gives us enough mental distance to understand anything on the deepest, truest level and not be hampered by attachment.

Scorpio/Pluto is fixed water and feminine, or water that is absorbing, inward, and attracting. All of Earth's plant and creature life depend on water, or at least moisture, to survive. We drink it, it provides lubrication that allows process and movement, it runs in the veins of every plant and animal species, nourishing and sustaining us. Stable water is a breeding ground; it holds within it the seed of life itself. It is where all life began.

Scorpio's symbolism is complex because it rules both reproductive aspects: sex and procreation, but also the destroying aspects of life: death and decay. This indicates that in some way, symbolically, birth and death are the same. Scorpio/Pluto rules transition and a birth is certainly that, also the line between life and death at the birth of anything can be very tenuous. This may be contemplated as simply the nature of birth, something coming from a place of nothing, of death, and coming into life.

Scorpio is the opposite sign of Taurus, so appropriately, death (Scorpio/Pluto) is on the other side of life (Taurus/Earth). Life, when symbolized by Taurus, is the everyday, noticeable part of life. Life, when symbolized by Scorpio, becomes the release of that life unto death. Taurus is the stability of the predictable routine of living and Scorpio is release, the cycle of life and death. Scorpio is also the process of rebirth, another vulnerable and vacillating moment between life and death. Even as we live, we live with the aspect of death within us: age. Then, at the conclusion of life, there is Scorpio and death once again. The duality of our level of existence is never better illustrated than with the opposition between Taurus and Scorpio. Scorpio allows us to feel at the deepest levels of our being what it means to be alive, but also to understand that we will die. With that knowledge, we look for what is real and true and powerful, and we discard triviality.

Taurus is the fixed Earth sign and feminine in nature, inward/attracting in its functionality. It is life as we prefer to know it: stable and everlasting. It is the planet Earth itself; the ground we walk on, the soil and rocks on which we build our homes and grow our food. It provides place, the foundation that is the basis of our ability to go anywhere and do anything. Taurus allows us to create and build upon what is given to us in this life; to embrace permanence even when we know we are not permanent.

The Four Holy Creatures

Another representation of these four fixed signs of astrology has been portrayed in the mystical writings of the Kabbalah and the Bible. Many metaphysical writings talk of the Mercabah, the chariot of God and its Holy Creatures as seen in a vision by Ezekiel. When Ezekiel saw God, he noted that God was sitting in a chariot on a throne and there were four beings with him, creatures that looked like a bull, a lion, a human, and an eagle.

3

The Mercabah, also known as the Mercy Seat, is from the vision of Ezekiel. He sees the seat of God upon wheels and the angels with four faces, that of an eagle, an ox, a lion, and a man.

The first time I saw a picture of these animals I immediately thought of the four fixed signs of astrology and the animals that are their symbols:

The bull, which is the symbolic animal of Taurus,
The lion, the animal representative of Leo,
A human, easily matched to Aquarius,
And the eagle: Scorpio.

The eagle may be confusing to some because Scorpio's most recognizable animal is, of course, the scorpion, but the sign actually has two other creatures associated with it: the lizard (or snake) and the eagle. Again, Scorpio is complex. The three animals symbolize the three vibrational levels Scorpio can operate from. The lowest level (base, crude, and cruel) being the scorpion, the middle level (instinctual, barely conscious), the lizard/snake, and the highest vibrational level is the eagle, which flies above the Earth (rising above base instincts with vision and aspiration).

Aside from being described in metaphysical and biblical texts, these four holy creatures are depicted in religious paintings, pictured in books, and on cathedral walls all over the world.[4] I have personally observed their likeness sitting right over the altar in many of the churches I have visited here in the U.S. and in France.

5

The Sphinx

The four creatures can sometimes be found represented in the Sphinx. The oldest known sphinx was found in Gobekli Tepe, Turkey and is dated to 9,500 B.C.[6] The most recognizable sphinx today is in Egypt and dates back over two thousand years ago. Many Sphinxes have the face of a man or woman, the wings of an eagle-like bird, the body of a lion, and the tail of an ox. Once again, the four fixed signs are represented. For the Egyptian royalty of old, the lion was symbolic of the sun, ruling planet of Leo.[7]

There is speculation on where the label "sphinx" for this statue came from. One interpretation is said to come from the Egyptian name "shesepankh," which meant "living image."[8] Explanations are given as to what is meant by "living image," such as carved from "living" stone; that is, rock that was not moved from the site. This is not a very satisfying answer, so I will try my own. The sphinx became a symbol of mystery, power, guardianship, and even fear in the ancient world. If we take the idea that, in some cases, the sphinx was a statue that had all four classic elements represented as one creature, then this would be a symbol of great power indeed! It could be that this statue is an "image" representative of the "living" world. If any one person could understand and harness all four elements, the very building blocks of life, in ancient times, this would make them very knowledgeable and confer power on them as well. A powerful person with great, and perhaps secret, knowledge is sometimes a person that inspires fear.

    The sphinx image also has been adopted into Masonic architecture as a watcher or portal that stands between the initiated and uninitiated in the quest for higher knowledge, sometimes standing at the door of Masonic temples. This idea was probably adapted from the legends out of ancient Egypt that the Sphinx guarded the road to Thebes and asked the famous riddle: "Which is the animal that has four feet in the morning, two feet at noon, and three in the evening?" The answer was a human being, who, when born in the morning of life, crawled on all fours, when mature, (noon) walked on two feet, and finally in old age, or evening, used a cane. The Sphinx only allowed those with the answer (or those having knowledge) to pass on, thus making the Sphinx a gatekeeper.[9]

When looked at from this angle, the sphinx becomes a symbol for the opening, or gateway to, the road to understanding the great, metaphysical or otherwise, mysteries of life, which involve the four elements, air, fire, water, and earth.

The Bible and God's Chariot

The four animal symbols - lion, human, bull or ox, and eagle - are found under Ezekiel in the Bible. They were part of his vision of God. Since they were the wheels of God's Chariot, it seems as if they are what power the vehicle of the Mercabah.[10] Could this be symbolic of the power of the four fixed signs (and their animal representation of the elements) that run the earth plane? "The spirit of the beings was in the wheels"[11]

The Mercabah is described as a "divine light vehicle used by the Masters to probe and reach the faithful in the many dimensions of the Divine Mind".[12] To probe: to find others worthy of the knowledge, perhaps, and to reach the faithful, or find those that can be entrusted with it?

The lion, the bull, the human, and the eagle turned the wheels of Jehovah's chariot like the fuel that powers creation. God decrees and the beasts take God's energy and distribute it. This makes sense metaphysically; matter is composed of one, two, three, or all of the four elements. The four holy animals were considered helpful creatures to God.

Conversely, they could also be detrimental in reaching the spirit world; a barrier one could be up against in trying to reach God. Presumably, that barrier would have to do with "right" knowledge or "right" use of the power of the earth plane.

I look at the four holy animals as a biblical mystery, a reference that leaves me with the impression that these animals are nothing less than the four guardians of the world, appropriately representing the four fixed signs in astrology, who represent, in turn, the four classic elements that make up our world.

Ancient biblical scholars left us with four holy animal symbols to represent God's creative force; a force that produces not only us, but everything around us. Our existence and these animals perfectly correspond to the fixed signs of astrology: Leo, Taurus, Aquarius, and Scorpio.

Tarot

The four holy animals turn up once again on Tarot cards. Although no one knows for certain the origin of Tarot, there is a legend around the cards that appears to be backed by historical fact. The story goes that when the Christian church authorities became powerful enough to dictate policy for society, they found the knowledge of other belief systems, most notably occult or metaphysical knowledge, threatening to their power and began a campaign to obliterate it. It had to be hidden away or it would be destroyed and lost. Individuals stepped forward to protect the knowledge, but they could be persecuted or even killed were they found to be in possession of it. The Tarot developed as a way to preserve metaphysical knowledge. Put into a symbolic picture code, this knowledge became a deck of cards that could be disguised as a game. The Tarot is really a book that explains the way the world works on a physical and energetic level. Each card is a page of that book. In this way, hard-won ancient knowledge was passed on. Now, using the cards, an explanation, or maybe even the secrets, of life on this earth plane can be contemplated symbolically and perhaps understood once again.[14]

The Tarot card "Wheel of Fortune" in classic decks such as the Rider-Waite almost always have the four holy animals (and a sphinx) depicted on the card, right on the wheel itself. The wheel in the card is a symbol of Earth and Earth's cycles.

[15]

One interpretation for the Wheel of Fortune is: Earth and its seductions of the material plane. We're at the mercy of the earth plane and one can get caught in an endless cycle of habitual personality traits and thoughtless routines that can hamper our ability to grow, inhibiting progress with your life. In other words, one cannot find God if one is too distracted with, or too ensconced in, earthly energy.

In the Rider-Waite Tarot deck, the animals are also found on the last card of the deck: "The World."

"The World card depicts a young nude girl centered surrounded by an elliptic garland and the four living creatures of the Apocalypse. The garland symbolizes all sensible things which surround sentient man. The girl, as though dancing, is symbolic of the swirl of the sensitive life, of sense intoxication."[16] This is a nod to the Wheel of Fortune card, but even this supposed Earthly paradise is guarded by higher knowledge and an outer presence. This knowledge of the *mystery* of fire, air, water, and earth, the combination of which, the transmutation of which, creates all that is. "Success has come to him who understands evolution in its deepest sense; the evolution of inner man as symbolized by the four creatures in the World card.

"The head of the man indicates both intelligence and intuition (male and female)

[AIR OR AQUARIUS]

"…the eagle signifies sex energy which is used to lift one to lofty goals and heights and reality. [WATER OR SCORPIO]

"The bull represents the fructifying agent of will...

[EARTH OR TAURUS]

"The lion denotes that moral courage which is necessary to true success and which comes from the proper use of sexual energy." (i.e., *love*) [17]

[FIRE OR LEO]

These are considered the four egos of man. Man is the microcosm of the macrocosm of the earth plane.

The interpretation or description of The World card can be read as "everything in the material world is available to you, success or self-mastery."

"The World" shows Earth symbolically, and this card seems to show that these animals hold, or at least guard, humankind's key to all its power. Perhaps telling us that if we can plumb the depths of what these animals represent, we, too, can be in control of our own destiny on Earth.

In some Christian traditions, the four holy creatures are also connected with the canonical gospels in the following way:

Matthew: Human (the humanity of Christ)

Mark: Lion (courage and for action)

Luke: Bull or Ox (strength and perseverance)

John: Eagle (clarity of sight and divinity)

The four holy living creatures have also been described as the cherubim at the throne of God or the four guardians of the world. These creatures show up again in the

Bible, Revelation: 4 through 6. When Jesus breaks the seals one through four, it is they who release the four horses of the apocalypse, bringing the end of Earth's days. Does this mean that if we don't master what these animals represent, we shall destroy the Earth as we know it?

Connecting the four fixed signs and the four holy creatures with these chapters in the Bible could be the source of much speculation and more symbolic interpretation than there is room for here, and will only serve to take us too far off the point of this particular volume.

Still, it seems to me that there is a wealth of intriguing information here and the choice of these four particular animals as laid out in the Bible and what they could represent symbolically is just a little too coincidental. Biblical references are trying to tell us something about the way the God energy works on Earth and these four animals that just happen to equal the fixed signs in astrology make more than a tidy representation of that idea. This is especially true when considering another very different area of our Earthly life.

Earth Symbolism, Science, Physics, and the Unified Field Theory

On the science side of things, particle physics is attempting to describe all the fundamental forces of our world and the relationships between elementary particles in terms of a single theoretical framework.

The theory that describes all four forces of our world and all of matter within a single, all-encompassing framework was named the Unified Field Theory by Albert Einstein.

Called the Holy Grail of Physics, it, when completed, will be a distillation or simplification of our reality, marrying the particles that make up our earth plane into one single equation, function, or explanation. Right now, there are, tentatively, four basic categories that will (it is believed) be found to fit into one another, making one single unit a single particle description of our universe.

Physicists are fairly certain that they have three of the four fundamental forces (or interactions) of the theory established, and they are:

1) The Weak Nuclear force
2) The Strong Nuclear force
3) Electromagnetism.

The fourth force, Gravity, is the accepted last component of the Unified Theory, but physicists have not yet discovered its hypothesized mediator, or force carrier: the gravity particle to be called the graviton. There is certainty in that community though (especially with the new Hadron Collider up and running), that time will come very soon.

Here we have a group of professionals again attempting to give a description of our reality, this time through scientific means, with four conspicuous categories. If we look at these four forces symbolically, we might see a pattern emerging:

1) THE WEAK FORCE allows for the releasing of energy and governs the decay of subatomic particles, allowing them to shift and change into other particles, in turn, changing the surrounding space.

The weak force is without discernible mass and its actions are so subtle and indirect that it is still somewhat of a mystery to scientists. As it drifts around and bumps into other matter, its slowness or subtleties allow it to infiltrate or interact with other particles, causing them to change into totally different particles. This force precipitates, for example, a neutron change into a proton or an electron. It is the only force that governs change.

"The weak force is involved in everything from nuclear beta decay and muon decay to high energy collisions of neutrinos with other particles of matter. The details and final products may vary but migration is always at the heart of it and identity changes are common."[18]

The weak force is an invisible force that insinuates itself into other particles and causes change or transformation.

The traits of the Weak Force could be symbolically represented by the sign of Scorpio and its ruling planet Pluto. In astrology, Scorpio/Pluto presides over those parts of our world that are subtle and hidden, things that, by their nature, are more comfortable in the dark.

Its ruling planet Pluto presides over death and decay. At the same time, Scorpio is about the ability to transform an object or a landscape into something radically different. Death is one form of change. Sometimes a piece, or all, of something has to die so that something new can take its place.

Psychologically, or in human terms, Scorpio is the energy that infiltrates and manipulates human psychology. It is a subtle and yet insistent energy that asks us to change and transform ourselves. Scorpio keeps humanity's secrets, or what we tend to hide or push away, not wanting to see or acknowledge.

2) THE STRONG NUCLEAR FORCE, on the other hand, holds the universe together. It weaves webs of energy that hold atomic particles together.

"The strong nuclear force, also known as the strong interaction, is one of the strongest forces in the universe…

"The strong force does not actually occur directly between protons and neutrons in the nucleus, but in the smaller quarks making them up. The force is mediated by fundamental particles called gluons, named for the way they glue quarks together. Each proton or neutron is composed of three quarks.

"The strong force has a property called asymptotic freedom, meaning as quarks get closer together, the force diminishes in strength, asymptotically approaching zero. Conversely, as the quarks get further apart, the force gets stronger. Failure to find free quarks has been taken to mean that no phenomena in the universe, except perhaps for black holes, are capable of ripping quarks apart from one another.

"The strong nuclear force is what is liberated during nuclear reactions, of the sort that take place in the Sun, nuclear power plants, and nuclear bombs."[19]

The traits of the Strong Force could be symbolically represented by the sign of Leo and its ruling planet the Sun. Leo is the fixed fire sign.

Fire is a chain reaction of heat applied to two objects: oxygen and some sort of fuel, creating a chemical reaction. It also has to do with the right balance of oxygen and fuel. Things will burn depending on how much of each part of the equation (heat, oxygen, fuel) is there.

Fire also sustains itself.

"A side effect of these chemical reactions (that cause fire) is a lot of heat. The fact that the chemical reactions in a fire generate a lot of new heat is what sustains the fire. The dangerous thing about the chemical reactions in fire is the fact that they are *self-perpetuating.* The heat of the flame itself keeps the fuel at the ignition temperature, so it continues to burn as long as there is fuel and oxygen around it. The flame heats any surrounding fuel so it releases gases as well. When the flame ignites the gases, the fire spreads."[20]

Psychologically, or in human terms, Leo is the most passionate sign energy. Love is the most binding, psychological force of the human species. Leo is in charge of love. Leo is about the fixity of fire in the heart or in our desire. With Leo energy, we are able to be inspired and enthusiastically stick to something to see it through. People with Leo burn steadily in their desire for things and have the energy to make them happen.

3) ELECTROMAGNETISM is a seamless fusion of electricity and magnetism. It was realized by Michael Faraday. Magnetism is actually produced by electric currents. "When electricity passed through a wire, a magnetic field is created around the wire. Connecting a wire to a battery and placing a compass near the wire can demonstrate a magnetic field. When the current is turned on, the compass-needle will move. If you reverse the direction of the current, the needle will move in the opposite direction.[21]

"Electromagnetism speaks to electric fields and the relationship between magnetic fields and moving electric fields. Electromagnetism is also light. The light need not be visible light. Heat, infrared radiation, UV (ultraviolet radiation), gamma rays, microwaves, radio waves - all of these are examples of light."[22]

The traits of Electromagnetism could be symbolically represented by the sign of Aquarius and its ruling planet Uranus.

Aquarius is an air sign whose ruling planet governs electricity and lightning. There is a fire aspect to both of these things but lightning and electricity are generated by friction between positive protons and negative electrons that jump from one object's atoms to another's through the air. Static electricity is a condition that exists when electrons are displaced and remain so. They build up until a release and redistribution through the air is necessary. Lightning is one example of static electricity. Magnetic fields are created by electricity and electricity creates magnetic fields existing and traveling through space or air.

Psychologically, or in human terms, Aquarius is that thing that allows ideas. When we have an idea, our minds (mentality is connected to air) "flash" to something new. Inventiveness and the advanced mind are governed by Aquarius. The computer is an example of an invention that extends the mind and its learning process. Computers are under Uranus/Aquarius jurisdiction. Aquarius also includes any or all information and recognizes that every thought, just like every kind of human, has something to contribute to the whole process. Aquarius puts its energy to lifting the greater whole of humanity up to see truth and then light will come into the human mind, allowing us to live together as equals.

4) GRAVITY

The last fundamental force or interaction, gravity and the particle we assume will be a graviton, lends a natural affinity to Taurus and its proposed ruling planet Earth.

"Gravity is a force of attraction that exists between any two masses, any two bodies, and any two particles. Gravity is not just the attraction between objects and the Earth. It is an attraction that exists between all objects, everywhere in the universe."[23]

"Gravity pulls together all matter (which is anything you can physically touch). The more matter, the more gravity, so things that have a lot of matter such as planets and moons and stars pull more strongly.

"Mass is how we measure the amount of matter in something. The more massive something is, the more of a gravitational pull it exerts. As we walk on the surface of the Earth, it pulls on us, and we pull back. But since the Earth is so much more massive than we are, the pull from us is not strong enough to move the Earth, while the pull from the Earth can make us fall flat on our faces.

"In addition to depending on the amount of mass, gravity also depends on how far you are from something. This is why we are stuck to the surface of the Earth instead of being pulled off into the Sun, which has many more times the gravity of the Earth."[24]

We know that gravity also assisted in forming the universe. Without it, nothing could have held together long enough to create mass.

Traits of gravity, in part, belong somewhat to the symbolism of the planet Venus, leftover vestiges that Taurus will carry for who knows how long, even after Earth is officially assigned to Taurus as her ruling planet. Venus, the planet governing attraction, has always lent Taurus her "come hither" ability. Beyond Venus though, Taurus fits here because we are also talking about mass. Gravity is a property of matter and space. The more mass, the more the space around the mass is warped and the more gravity is generated. Having mass or having substance comes back to Taurus's jurisdiction and consequently planet Earth, because in astrology, earth symbolism has to do with things that have mass and weight, things we can touch and therefore know exist.

Psychologically, or in human terms, Taurus is the energy that craves the security of solid things. It wants to see solid results or proof that the world exists. Taurus presides over things we can depend on.

Solidity and consistency gives us, as human beings, the confidence that the world is real and we are safely in it. We are then able to produce our own reality or manifest our own solid or lasting things

The comparisons I make of human psychology and mythology to particle physics may seem like a stretch to some. I think it is important to begin the attempt to take scientific evidence of the world we live in and connect it to mythological, astrological, or psychological symbolism, as this process will lead us to a place in the future where science and spirit can become one explanation of existence. Science and religion (or as I prefer to call it: spirit) each explain the world in their own way and yet we are all still talking about the very same thing. I entertain the belief that only when we are able to fully draw the parallels of both of these (apparently diverse) halves together will we have one complete picture of our universe. We will have a different kind of unified field theory.

NOTE ON EARTH AND METAPHYSICS

Metaphysics tries to explain God and our existence. It also tries to show how things work, just as science does, but instead of physical properties, it explores the abstract, symbolic, or philosophical level. Many aspects of metaphysics are not well known to the general public and this was partly by design, as occultists were renowned for shrouding their knowledge in various layers of secrecy and that made people nervous. Occult is a word in itself that used to scare people, but occult simply means "hidden." The knowledge that falls under metaphysics was hidden due to paranoia and elitism. The paranoia might have been well-founded, for in the past, having this knowledge might have meant persecution or death. Elitism came from the ego of those who, upon risking their lives for it, started to feel superior for having another kind of information about life that other people did not have. They set up secret societies to guard their knowledge (and their lives) and would only teach those they thought were ready to receive it. Some of these teachers sincerely thought people who weren't ready to know would do themselves harm. It all boils down to energy and that energy can be manipulated by us. The energy around us, the atmosphere, is influenced by our emotions and our attitudes. I think we all know by now that on some level, we create our own surroundings or reality, and in essence, that is an application of so-called occult knowledge.

Numerology

In numerology, the number 4 is usually associated with earth. Four of almost anything easily makes a square. Mathematically, a square, by definition, is a "plane figure having four equal sides" and it makes a very stable geometric shape. It is easy to place even numbered objects at regular intervals with even distribution, allowing any weight placed on the top of that object to be evenly placed as well, creating a secure and durable situation. Our buildings are usually squares or rectangles for that reason. A single number equivalent of Earth should be reflective of a stable form.

The even-numbered astrological houses on the chart wheel match the earth and water signs, the signs that are connected to the ground. In astrology, signs in earth and water have the most energetic sympathy with each other. The other category of sympathetic signs, air and fire, relate more to sky. Starting with Taurus (earth) as number 2, and doubling that to four takes us right to the sign of Cancer (water), and so on around. The planets, the signs, and the houses all have twelve components and can be divided by 4.

Number 4 in Tarot

There are four kingdoms of the minor arcana, representing the four elements:

1) Cups = water

2) Wands = fire

3) Swords = air

4) Pentacles = earth

The cards are numbered from one to ten.

In the minor arcana, the fours of these kingdoms usually involve manifesting. "The fours often show people who are taking steps and actively creating what they've planned."[25]

In other words, the fours are manifesting. "Things that were previously imagined now become real."[24] Four in the minor arcana is a perfect match for Earth.

However, with the major arcana, the number four is "The Emperor" and that card is usually attributed to Aries, not Taurus. The explanation resembles Earth at times with Theodor Laurence's explanation in How the Tarot speaks to Modern Man: "Realization of the power that has lain dormant within man,"[26] the idea that humankind can master and finally control his domain, both inside and outside of himself in a positive and life-affirming way. Other descriptions of "The Emperor" explain that this card is symbolic of that moment when someone goes from an unconscious, unthinking creature to a fully realized individual, no longer part of the pack. That sounds like Aries to me. Yet the picture of "The Emperor" on his very solid and square throne made of stone certainly gives a reader an earthy feeling of permanence. Joseph Campbell calls this card "the manifest world"[27] and the scepter the emperor holds is symbolic of the four seasons and the four points of the compass.

The very next card of the major arcana is "The Hierophant." The number five card (unfortunately for any kind of Earth/Taurus uniformity here) is the one usually associated with the sign of Taurus. Five, or the Hierophant card symbolizes humankind according to Joseph Campbell in his book: Tarot Revelations. Four plus one equals five, so this card moves from the four of earth, adds a component, and is now five: humankind appears. The five card symbolizes humankind. We are, in essence, one number past manifesting. In the Aleister Crowley Tarot deck, the Hierophant card has (one more time!) the four holy animals surrounding the Hierophant figure. The Hierophant is about consciousness and the power of choice. The energy described by this card is the point reached in the consciousness of a single person when they start to recognize they are part of a society and how, by their working to improve that society, all are benefited. It is interesting to note, however, that when you add the (Taurian) number 5 card (The Hierophant) to the number 21 card (The World), you get the number 26.

Number Symbolism of the Four Fixed Signs

- The fixed signs are the 2nd, 5th, 8th, and 11th signs in the zodiac
- Add the numbers and you get 26.
- Ezekiel is the 26th book in the Bible.
- By Gematria, (a system assigning numerical value to a word or phrase) the value of GOD (7 + 15 + 4) is 26, and there are 26 letters in the English alphabet.
- By Hebrew Gematria, as used in the Kabbalah, the value of "God" is also 26. IHVH (Yahweh) is $10 + 5 + 6 + 5 = 26$

Number 4: The Kabbalah and the Earth

Like astrology and Tarot, the Kabbalah, once again, has symbology to contribute with ties to the number four. The Tree of Life in the Kabbalah includes God and the 11 Sephiroths (emanations): Kether, Binah, Chokhmah, Daat (usually not shown), Geburah, Chesed, Tipareth, Hod, Netzach, Yesod, and Malkuth, with four worlds dividing it.

The Four Worlds are:

1) Atziluth or Asiluth, the highest world, the spiritual plane or the divine world of the Sephiroth. It is a boundless world, the plane of the life force, the world of emanation from whence everything flows. It contains the three top Sephiroths: Kether, Binah, Chokmah and sometimes Daat. Here is the element of fire.

2) Briah or Beriah, the mental plane. It is the world of formation or creation associated with intuition and the element of water. It contains the Sephiroths: Geburah, Chesed, and Tipareth. (The Big Bang would fall into this category.)

3) Yetzirah or Yesirah, the Astral plane, the world of the heavenly spheres. It is the world of formation associated with intellect, consciousness, and mental perception. It contains the Sephiroths: Hod, Netzach, and Yesod and is the element of air.

4) Assiah or Asiyyah, the physical plane, the world of manifestation, matter, and the elemental world of animal

instinct and substances. A world of action, here is the sphere of the four elements. The last plane contains the Sephiroth: Malkuth and is connected to the element of earth.

God/Goddess is not on the Tree, so we start with the top Sephiroth, Kether, numbered one. The Sephiroth, numbered four, is called Chesed. Chesed is the first Sephiroth you come to after you leave the first world (Azilut) of the divine or the spiritual and enter the second world (Beriah) of formation. It is also the first time a Sephiroth is split into the duality of male/female. According to Rachel Pollack in her book, The Kabbalah Tree, Chesed is like the first day of creation, when God separated the light from the darkness.

The bottom Sephiroth, numbered ten, represents the earth plane or the level called Malkuth. Malkuth is often shown divided into four. It contains the four complete worlds or levels the whole tree was divided into. The names of the worlds are repeated here in Malkuth as a microcosm to the macrocosm (the Tree), showing that there is a repeating pattern in all existence. In the Kabbalah, Earth is not only included, it is quite essential in the Tree of Life.

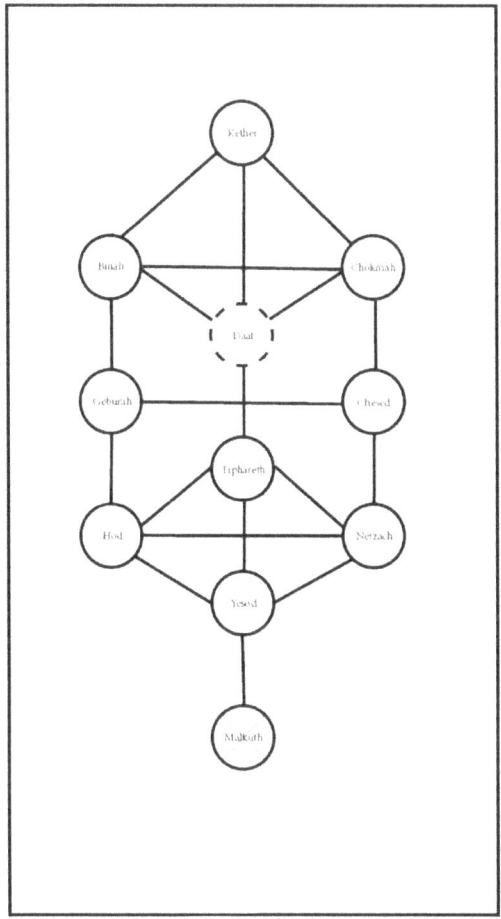

28

The four elements in the world of Assiah refer to the four aspects of God's name, or the Tetragrammaton.

The Tetragrammaton

The name of each of the four worlds, in turn, spells out the name of God in four letters. This is called the Tetragrammaton, "tetra" meaning four and "grammaton" meaning grammar or letter. The words "grammar" and "gravity" share the same root.

The Tetragrammaton also falls under the jurisdiction of the Jewish faith and is intimately connected to the Kabbalah. The prefix "tetra" means four. The four letters are Hebrew and Hebrew is considered not only a sacred language, but a living one. This is another mystery that is covered in other publications. The Tetragrammaton, or name of God, is overlaid on the Kabalistic Tree of Life just as the worlds are. The letters, properly read from right to left, in Biblical Hebrew, are:

Hebrew Letter / Name

    י   Yodh

    ה   He

    ו   Waw

    ה   He

Many people are familiar with the pronunciation of the four letters YHWH: Yod Hey Vay Hey or Yahweh.

The first letter is for force. The force is the active principle in our world. The second is pattern and form. The letters repeat, meaning that we have repeating themes and energies in our world.

All these references to four and their symbolical meanings are just to show how consistent the number is when it comes to explaining our earthly reality. The number four and its repetition seem to be the important factors in creating a stable existence.

More on Number Four

Continuing with the idea that the building blocks of life on Earth are symbolized by the number four in biology, we have Deoxyribonucleic Acid, or DNA. DNA is referred to as the building blocks of life. Life as we know it could not exist without DNA.

There are four components to DNA:

1) A, or Adenine,

2) G, or Guanine,

3) T, or Thymine,

4) C, or Cytosine.

Coincidentally, or perhaps not, RNA has four chemical components as well:

1) Adenine,2) Guanine, 3) Uracil, and 4) Cytosine.

There were four humours in medieval science referred to as Hippocrates medical theory of bodily systems and temperaments.

"The Theory of the Four Humours was an important development in medical knowledge which originated in the works of Aristotle. The Greeks believed that the body was made up of four main components or Four Humours. These

Four Humours needed to remain balanced in order for people to remain healthy.

The Four Humours were liquids within the body.

1) Blood

2) Phlegm

3) Yellow bile

4) Black bile

These could be connected to the four seasons of the year: Yellow Bile with summer, black bile with autumn, phlegm with winter and blood with spring." [29]

These humours can also be matched to the four elements:

1) Earth: black bile

2) Air: blood

3) Fire: yellow bile

4) Water: phlegm.

Other examples of the number four:

The Archangels: 1) Michael, 2) Gabriel, 3) Raphael, and 4) Uriel.

The Four Cosmic Pillars

These are referred to in many folk tales and legends on different continents. A quick glance at the internet turned up stories from Asia, Greece, and The British Isles. Here are two:

Greek

"KRIOS (or Crius) was one of the elder Titan gods, sons of Ouranos (the Sky) and Gaia (the Earth). Led by Kronos, the brothers conspired against their father and prepared an ambush for him as he descended to lie with Earth. Krios, Koios, Hyperion and Iapetos were posted at the four corners of the world where they seized hold of the Sky-god and held him firm, while Kronos, hidden in the centre, castrated him with a sickle.

In this myth the four brothers probably represent the four cosmic pillars found in near-Eastern cosmogonies which separated heaven and earth. In this case, Krios was surely the Titan of the pillar of the south, while his brothers Koios, Iapetos, and Hyperion were gods of the pillars of the north, east and west respectively. Krios' connection with the south is found both in his name and family connections--he is "the Ram," the constellation Aries, whose springtime rising in the south marked the start of the Greek year; his eldest son is Astraios, god of the stars; and his wife is Eurybia, a daughter of the sea." [30]

The British Isles

"The Celts may thus have possessed the Heaven and Earth myth, but all trace of it has perished. There are, however, remnants of myths showing how the sky is supported by trees, a mountain, or by pillars. A high mountain near the sources of the Rhone was called "the column of the sun," and was so lofty as to hide the sun from the people of the south. It may have been regarded as supporting the sky, while the sun moved round it. In an old Irish hymn and its gloss, Brigit and Patrick are compared to the two pillars of the world, probably alluding to some old myth of sky or earth resting on pillars. Traces of this also exist in folk-belief, as in the accounts of islands resting on four pillars, or as in the legend of the church of Kernitou which rests on four pillars on a congealed sea and which will be submerged when the sea liquefies--a combination of the cosmogonic myth with that of a great inundation." [31]

For people of an earlier time, to imagine that the Earth was supported by four pillars or four Gods, creates an imagery that must have seemed stable and soothing.

Dimensions

The four dimensions commonly used by mathematicians and physicists are a human concept, invented to simplify mathematical descriptions of the physical world. Customarily we use three dimensions:
1) Length, or back-and-forth (where back is just negative forth)
2) Width, or side-to-side (left is just negative right)
3) Height, or up-and-down (down is just negative up).
4) Time (Time is theoretically the fourth dimension)

Animals need (humans included):
1) food (earth), 2) water, 3) air, and 4) warmth (fire).

Cells need:
1) elimination, 2) nutrients, 3) water, and 4) temperature.

Plants need:
1) food/soil (earth), 2) water, 3) oxygen (air), and 4) warmth/light (fire).

The four winds are:
1) Boreas (north), 2) Notus (south), 3) Eurus (east), and 4) Zephyrus (west).

The four seasons are:
1) spring, 2) summer, 3) fall, and 4) winter.

The four directions are:
1) East, 2) South, 3) West, and 4) North.

The four elements are:
1) earth, 2) air, 3) fire, and 4) water.

There are four levels of reality in physics:
1) time, 2) space, 3) energy, and 4) mass.

Life cycles consist of:
1) egg, 2) caterpillar, 3) pupae, and 4) butterfly, OR
1) birth, 2) growth, 3) maturity, and 4) death.

The four planes of existence, manifestation, or reality, are:
1) spiritual, 2) mental, 3) astral, and 4) physical.

There are four laws of correspondence for magickal working. It is a law in occultism that says everything above corresponds to everything below ("as above, so below"), so when working with magick, you call in the four directions. Everything in the world can be matched to or associated with those states or directions, repeating the idea of "four" having power.

There are four categories that all creatures can be sorted into as acknowledged by the Native Americans:
1) Winged ones (birds and bats)
2) Four-leggeds (most animals)
3) Crawlers and swimmers (snakes, insects, and fish)
4) Two-leggeds (human)

The four sublime states of Buddhism are:
1) loving kindness, 2) compassion, 3) sympathetic joy or joyousness, and 4) equanimity.

Summary

Four of anything can be placed equal distances apart, creating a stable shape or structure. It is the basis for a steady and fixed energy or structure that has come to mean manifestation, or Earth, the place of manifestation.

Esoterically, the number four symbolizes our earthly reality with representations of everything from elements to atomic particles to biblical history, leaving behind us a tantalizing trail with explanations both philosophical and physical that endeavor to explain the building blocks and functionality of our Earth. The repetition of these four levels across such diverse and seemingly unrelated fields may, when taken together, begin to explain how our world works, incorporating both science and spirit. From science to philosophy to religion, we think and talk about the world we live in in terms of four. There are four energies, four principles, or four ideas that together make up the world we live in. For astrologers, these four principles just scream for a match-up with the four fixed signs of the zodiac. They are our own symbols of reality and manifestation.

The bull, found in so many symbolic and religious documents along with her three fellow animals, the lion, the eagle, and the human, is obviously Taurus. Taurus needs a true home, a ruling planet, her own place of power.

If there is a ruling planet for three of these four fixed signs of life on Earth, isn't it imperative that there should be a ruling planet for the fourth forthwith? These four energies are so basic to life on Earth, and yet on the astrological level we continue to flounder around with a shared planet for something as essential as Taurian energy! Should we be looking outside our own solar system for a planet this basic, as some have suggested, or consider Ceres or even Vulcan? Not in lieu of the imagery laid out here. The very symmetry in these equations demands that Taurus (the bull) belongs not only to earth the element, but planet Earth. It does not even necessitate a leap of faith. The evidence is compelling. The energy of Taurus is part of the basic building blocks of life here on Earth.

    And finally, Earth Day is the day we have chosen to think about our environment and to recognize and celebrate our planet. It was founded on April 22, 1970.[32] The astrological charts I cast for that time were located in Madison, Wisconsin and Washington, D.C., since the Wisconsin Senator Gaylord Nelson is credited with the idea. The chart for the first Earth Day is, as you'd expect, very dynamically Taurian. The Sun, Saturn, Sedna, Mercury, Venus, and Anti-Vertex were all in Taurus. Planets Earth, Moon, and Jupiter as well as the Vertex were all in the opposing sign of Scorpio. Every year on April 22, at one minute past midnight, the Sun Sign heralding Earth Day is Taurus.

[1] Brumfiel, Geoff. "Scientists supersize quantum mechanics." Nature International Journal of Science. 2012 Nature Publishing Group, a division of Macmillan Publishers Limited. , 17 March 2010. Web. 19 Jul 2012. <http://www.nature.com/news/2010/100317/full/news.2010.130.html>

[2] Campbell, Gordon. "Empedocles (c.492—432 BCE)." *Internet Encyclopedia of Philosophy*. National University of Ireland, Maynooth, 11 Jul 2005. Web. 16 May 2011. <http://www.iep.utm.edu/empedocl/>.

Kosmix Staff, . "Empedocles (Philosopher)." *Kosmix*. N.p., 2007-2011. Web. 16 May 2011. <http://www.kosmix.com/topic/empedocles>.

[3]Mekabah Pic Unknown, . Tetramorph. Fresco, Meteora.. 16th century. Fresco. Wikimedia CommonsWeb. 23 Jul 2013. <http://en.wikipedia.org/wiki/File:Tetramorph_meteora.jpg>.

PD-1923{{Information |Description=Tetramorph Fresco, Meteora |Source=http://wwwnsadru/indexphp?issue=48§ion=10019&article=1062 |Date=XVI c |Author=unknoen |Permission= |other_versions= }} Category:Tetramorph Category:Meteora <--{{ImageUpload|b, see Unknown http://en.wikipedia.org/wiki/File:Tetramorph_meteora.jpg

[4] Four holy animals

http://catholicresources.org/Art/Evangelists_Symbols.htm Mar 4 2011

"Symbols of the Four Evangelists in Christian Art." *Sacred Destinations*. N.p., n.d. Web. 16 May 2011. <http://www.sacred-destinations.com/reference/symbols-of-four-evangelists>.

McGough, Richard. "Fulfillment of Ezekiel's Prophecy of the Wheels." *The Bible Wheel*. N.p., 1995-2011. Web. 16 May 2011 <http://www.biblewheel.com/wheel/ezekiel_wheels.asp>

[5] Sphinx Illustration Vector Illustrations (by Roverto) canstockphoto.com csp10236284 Used by permission/purchase

[6] Birch, Nicholas. "7,000 years older than Stonehenge: the site that stunned archaeologists." *Guardian.co.uk*. The Guardian Newspaper, Wednesday 23 April 2008. Web. 16 May 2011. <http://www.guardian.co.uk/science/2008/apr/23/archaeology.turkey>.

[7] Werness, Hope. *The Continuum encyclopedia of animal symbolism in art*. N.Y. N.Y.: Continuuim International Publishing Group, 2003. 255. Print.

[8] Wikipedia What names their builders gave to these statues is not known. At the Great Sphinx site, the inscription on a stele erected a thousand years later, by Thutmose IV in 1400 BCE, lists the names of three aspects of the local sun

deity of that period, *Khepera - Rê - Atum*. The inclusion of these figures in tomb and temple complexes quickly became traditional and many pharaohs had their heads carved atop the guardian statues for their tombs to show their close relationship with the powerful solar deity, Sekhmet, a lioness

The historian Susan Wise Bauer suggests that the word "sphinx" was a Greek corruption of the Egyptian name "shesepankh," which meant "living image," and referred rather to the *statue* of the sphinx, which was carved out of "living rock" (rock that was present at the construction site, not harvested and brought from another location), than to the beast itself.[http://en.wikipedia.org/wiki/Sphinx#cite_note-0]

From : "The History of the Ancient World: From the Earliest Accounts to the Fall of Rome" Page 110-112

W.W .Norton and Co.

[8] "Sphinx." *Wikipedia*. N.p., n.d. Web. 16 May 2011. <http://en.wikipedia.org/wiki/Sphinx>

[9] Aldington, Richard. *Larousse Encyclopedia of Mythology*. Prometheus Press, 1959. 207. Print.

[10] New World translation of the Holy Scriptures Page 1057 Ezekiel 1:5 19 to 21

[11] Tyndale, . *The Living Bible*. 16th ed. . Wheaton, Il. : Tyndale House Pub. , 1971. 633. Print. (Ezekiel Chapter 1 Paragraph 19, 20 and 21)

[12]Hurtak, J.J. *The Keys of Enoch*. 3rd ed. Los Gatos, Ca. : The Academy for Future Science, 1973. 590. Print. (Glossary)

[13]Copy by unknown artist after illustration by Matthaeus (Matthäus) Merian the elder (1593-1650), . Engraved illustration of the "chariot vision" of the Biblical book of Ezekiel, chapter 1, after an earlier illustration by Matthaeus (Matthäus) Merian (1593-1650), for his "Icones Biblicae" (a.k.a. "Iconum Biblicarum").. 1670. Photograph. Wikimedia CommonsWeb. 25 Jul 2013. <http://en.wikipedia.org/wiki/File:Ezekiel's_vision.jpg>.

{{Information |Description= Ezekiel's vision/ From "L'Histoire du Vieux et du Nouveau Testament", Nicolas Fontaine (author) Call Number at Pitts Theology Library: 1670Font |Source=http://wwwbiblical-artcom/artworkasp?id_artwork=26660&showmode=Fullhttp://wwwbiblical-artcom/artworkasp?id_artwork=26660&showmode=Full From "L'Histoire du Vieux et du Nouveau Testament", Nicolas Fontaine (author) Call Number at Pitts Theology Library: 1670Font, {{PD-1923}}

[14]One source: Hasbrouck, Muriel. *Tarot and Astrology*. N.Y. N.Y.: Destiny Books, 1986. 193-194. Print

[15] Smith , Pamela Coleman. Illustrations from the Rider-Waite Tarot Deck®, known also as the Rider Tarot and the Waite Tarot, reproduced by permission of U.S. Games

Systems, Inc.Wheel of Fortune Tarot card. 1909. Graphic. Wikipedia/U.S. Games Stamford, CT 06902 USA. Web. 26 Jul 2013.
<https://en.wikipedia.org/wiki/File:RWS_Tarot_10_Wheel_of_Fortune.jpg>.

Illustrations from the Rider-Waite Tarot Deck®, known also as the Rider Tarot and the Waite Tarot, reproduced by permission of US Games Systems, Inc, Stamford, CT 06902 USA Copyright ©1971 by US Games Systems, Inc Further reproduction prohibited The Rider-Waite Tarot Deck® is a registered trademark of US Games Systems, Inc.

[16]Laurence, Theodor. *How the Tarot Speaks to Modern Man*. N.Y. N.Y.: Bell Pub. Co., 1972. 82. Print

[17] Laurence, Theodor. *How the Tarot Speaks to Modern Man*. N.Y. N.Y.: Bell Pub. Co., 1972. 82-83. Print

[18]Tuzo, J. E. "What is the Weak Force?." *Starpulls Theory of Quantum Gravity*. N.p., 2003-2011. Web. 16 May 2011. <http://www.starpulls.com/Weak.htm>.

[19] Anissimov, Michael. "What is the Strong Nuclear Force?." *WiseGeek*. N.p., 22 April 2011. Web. 16 May 2011. <http://www.wisegeek.com/what-is-the-strong-nuclear-force.htm>.

[20] Harris, Tom. "How Fire Works." *How Stuff Works*. N.p., 1998-2011. Web. 16 May 2011.

<http://science.howstuffworks.com/environmental/earth/geophysics/fire1.htm>.

[21]Kurtus, Ron. "Electromagnetism." *Ron Kurtus' School for Champions*. N.p., 3 April 2005. Web. 16 May 2011. <http://www.school-for-champions.com/Science/electromagnetism.htm>.

[22]Wiki , . "What is electromagnetism?." *Answers.com*. Wiki Answers, 2011. Web. 16 May 2011. <http://wiki.answers.com/Q/What_is_electromagnetism>.

[23] Dejoie, Truelove , Joyce, Elizabeth. "What is gravity?." *StarChild Question of the Month for February 2001*. High Energy Astrophysics Science Archive Research Center (HEASARC), Dr. Alan Smale (Director), within the Astrophysics Science Division (ASD) at NASA/ GSFC., Feb 2001. Web. 16 May 2011. <http://starchild.gsfc.nasa.gov/docs/StarChild/questions/question30.html>.

[24]Qualitative Reasoning Group Northwestern University, . "What is Gravity?." *Space Environment*. Qualitative Reasoning Group Northwestern University, Evanston, IL, n.d. Web. 16 May 2011. <http://www.qrg.northwestern.edu/projects/vss/docs/space-environment/1-what-is-gravity.html>.

[25] Fairfield, Gail. *Choice Centered Tarot*. 2nd ed. Iowa City, Iowa: Iowa City Womens Press, 1982. 52. Print.

[26]Laurence, Theodor. *How the Tarot Speaks to Modern Man*. N.Y. N.Y.: Bell Pub. Co., 1972. 38. Print

[27]Campbell, Joseph. *Tarot Revelations*. 3rd. ed. San Anselmo, Ca.: Vernal Equinox Press, 1987. 88. Print.

[28 PIC] Wood, Tala K.K. Kabbalah with Four Worlds. 2013. Graphic. n.p. Print. Author's own work

[29] Boylan, Michael. "Hippocrates (c.450—c.380 BCE)." Internet Encyclopedia of Philosophy. Marymount University, July 5, 2005. Web. 28 Jul 2012. <http://www.iep.utm.edu/hippocra/>.

[30] Atsma, Aaron. "Krios." Theoi Greek Mythology. Theoi Project Copyright, 2000-2011. Web. 1 Aug 2012. <http://www.theoi.com/Titan/TitanKrios.html>.

[31] MacCulloch, John Arnott. "CHAPTER XV COSMOGONY." THE RELIGION OF THE ANCIENT CELTS. Scanned at sacred-texts.com, February, 2004. John Bruno Hare, redactor Public Domain., October 1911. Web. 1 Aug 2012. <http://www.sacred-texts.com/neu/celt/rac/rac18.htm>.

[32] "Earth Day: The History of A Movement." Earth Day Network. N.p., n.d. Web. 16 May 2011. <http://www.earthday.org/earth-day-history-movement>.

Additional Reading:

Site of Interest for Numbers and their meanings on the net NumberQuest.

http://www.numberquest.com/knowledge_number_meaning.php

Chapter 4
The Element Earth in Astrology and the Natal Chart

"Reality is that which refuses to go away when I stop believing in it." ~Phillip K. Dick

Living Day to Day with the Symbolic Four Elements

As stated in the previous chapter with esoteric Earth and metaphysics in general, the classical elements slide easily into representations of certain qualities, actions, or principles of human personalities. Indeed, everything on Earth can be divided symbolically into these ancient categories.

AIR, when used symbolically, is usually associated with ease of movement, changeability, transfers of energy, adaptability, connection, and energy exchanges.

FIRE is symbolic of energy of all types, movement, strength, force, and will.

WATER is used to describe processes that carry, flow, surround, dissolve, nurture, heal, decay, or infiltrate.

EARTH rules things that are forming or manifesting and are stable, solid, predictable, dependable, and enduring.

The Four Elements in the Astrological Birth Chart

The characteristics of the elements, when attached to an astrological sign, can also very aptly describe human temperament. In the astrological natal chart, the four elements become human characteristics.

AIR is the element that bestows flexibility on the native. A lot of air signs in a natal chart give people a light touch, with the easy ability to change anything, from their ideas to their relationships, in any area of the chart where air signs are found. They are tolerant, accepting, and curious on a mental level. For a human being, air is all about the mind, the thinking processes, and communication. The more air in the chart, the more the native enjoys mental exercises and discussion. The air signs are Gemini, Libra, and Aquarius.

FIRE is the element that bestows drive, passion, and energy on the native. Fire governs desire and people with a lot of fire in their natal chart are energetic, always questing after their heart's desire. They can't stand to be idle, and need to engage their bodies with the world around them and feel the movement that tells them they are alive. They want to feel contact/connection with, have an effect on, or have interaction with, people or with life itself. The fire signs are Aries, Leo, and Sagittarius.

Water is the element that bestows integrational abilities and receptivity on the native. These people are even somewhat absorbing of people's feelings/moods and the vibes of places and things on a very personal level. Their penchant for forming attachments allows them to explore the world through the inner world of feelings. A lot of water signs in a natal chart produce people who want to embrace and nurture something and know that they have made an emotional connection and/or difference, either with others or with the world. They rely on their feelings to process the world around them and this gives them great intuition. They want to share or exchange emotional expressions. The water signs are Cancer, Scorpio, and Pisces.

    EARTH, in the human personality, is the element that contributes to reliability and common sense. A lot of earth signs in the natal chart not only give natives practicality, but also an ability to understand on a gut level what ideas or actions will work or operate successfully on our physical level of existence. They are interested in things taking form through procedures that make sense and can be repeated to affect the same results. Another area of interest is the manifestation of ideas, to "bring down to Earth" ideas and create or build a working model of them so they may be utilized in the physical world. They want to work with something real and solid that yields results everyone can count on. The earth signs are Taurus, Virgo, and Capricorn.

    No matter what Sun Sign you are, you have a certain individual proportion of these four elemental influences in your astrological chart. You may have a lot more of one element than another. The 12 houses of the astrological chart represent the 12 areas of human life and everyone has the earth signs (Taurus, Virgo, and Capricorn) in at least 3 of those areas or houses (There may be more depending on the house system you use). In other words, everyone uses earth energy somewhere in their life. More significantly, some of the other planets in a chart could also be in earth signs and that would give any native an extra dose of earth, the know-how attitude.

Earth Element: Levels of expression

I use the phrase "the earth plane" a lot, and what I mean by that is our earthly level of existence. This level has sets of laws or rules of operation. These laws are not human laws, but we certainly live within them. We can't levitate or see through matter and if we want to make something happen, we always need a basic understanding of the way things are done according to the natural laws here on Earth. There are procedures we must start with or certain steps that have to be taken that will lead us to the place we want to go. We invented science to study and explain Earth's rules to ourselves and because of this, we have learned what works and what doesn't work here. We have certainly tried to alter the framework we've been given, with everything from the invention of the airplane to biological cloning, but we are still (as far as we know) bound by it to a certain extent.

Some of the laws and rules of a culture or a society evolve from these natural laws. They began as simple common sense: how to keep our food plentiful or wholesome, for instance, or not wanting people killing us whenever they feel like it and ruining our plans. Remembering these rules were (and still are) a key to our peace of mind as well as our survival. Rules also become expectations among a group of people, giving them a "normal" way to proceed through life and all their ideas about "normal," period. Deviation by anyone of what is then considered "normal" is perceived as a threat to survival whether it really is or not.

Earth plane energy has to do with all the levels of these rules, structures, and procedures, from the Earthly laws of physics to the expectations of people we live with. The earth element in an astrological chart deals with these issues.

Seasons of Earth

Seasons are also a reflection of the Sun's sign (influence) on our Earth and our orientation; our attitude toward it. For us, it's the earthly "weather" around us. Astrology was developed in the northern hemisphere and so the seasonal correspondences were marked and studied in that part of the world, making the symbolism in astrology forever connected to those seasons. This is an inconvenience for people in the southern hemisphere, as the symbolism is backward.

Seasons of the Earth Signs

MAY/TAURUS

Of course, during the time the Sun is in earth signs we have particular seasons. In May, the Sun, for the most part, stands in the sign of Taurus and the Earth is just past the first hurdle of spring.

The progression of spring starts in February:

- The stirring of life underground in February (Aquarius)
- The snow melt and warming skies of March (Pisces)
- The waking plants and animals from their winter sleep in April (Aries)

The warmer and longer days of April/Aries have prepared the ground for birth and the seeds have reacted by springing up with the tremendous energy (Aries/Mars) it takes to be born. Now comes Taurus's month: May. Taurus is a fixed sign. It has a solid, stable, and sometimes stagnant energy. In May, the Earth is in the process of solidifying spring and bringing it to summer. What April and Aries brought forth, Taurus must ground further, making it ever more real and tangible (In the southern hemisphere, Taurus stabilizes and solidifies autumn). With tenacity, against the odds of the weakening winter winds, Taurus hangs on stubbornly and says to winter: "You will not take back this season of spring. I will continue against these odds and get the deepest and hardest grip I can on warmer weather and the life that depends on it. Winter is finished. I lay the ground out ever warmer and richer, safe from frost so that all seeds may be planted and plants may leaf out and bloom. I tap the hibernating animals on the shoulder and say it is safe to come out and live again."

In May, insects begin their herculean labor of building hives or other homes, gathering legs full of pollen, eating mouthfuls of leaves to keep up their energy.

The plants are full-speed ahead in their growth and within this fecundity the animals begin to have their young, knowing there will be lots of food available. At this time of year, everyone is building some den or nest. When the green shoots open into flowers this month, Taurus delights in the creativity of each species, all the color and patterns that nature allows. Taurus wants to fill the Earth with the heady scent of their perfume. Taurus holds the warming season in trust so that all life may reproduce and continue. The richness of life is a delight to the senses and a treasure to Taurus. We plant gardens in May: digging in the dirt, fertilizing and weeding, setting out seedlings with great anticipation for what we hope will be the tastiest vegetables or the sweetest flowers around. We rebuild and repair things that are winter-worn. We take on projects that were halted last fall and really get something done, now that weather is good.

Taurus builds on that growth with determination, fortitude, and creativity, laying the groundwork for a prolific, bountiful, and beautiful summer to come.

VIRGO/SEPTEMBER

Virgo is a mutable sign, making it the most flexible of the earth signs. It's a connecting or socially interactive type of energy.

Virgo's month is most of September. Earthly growth, having run high all summer, begins to wind down as the heat mellows out. The nights are getting longer. The Earth's processes are steadily changing and moving into a colder cycle, but soil and rock still hold the Sun's warmth. Leaves slow their production of chlorophyll, as this is a time for resetting their calendar. Virgo asks life on Earth to pull in and take stock of how much growth was accomplished and how much vitality was stored to create reserves for the harsher days that are coming.

The growth of vegetation is at its peak in August. Now, September asks that plants set their seeds, holding over their DNA for the next growing season. Animal life begins shedding summer coats to start their winter coverings. Insects turn themselves into cocoons and birds rally for the big southern migration. Life on Earth is on the edge of being overripe.

With plants in a tangle and vegetables sitting low on the vine, the time is late. We must once again rebuild and repair items now from overuse during the summer months. This time we get them ready to winter-over. Many chores and tasks must be done at once; there is no rest if we want to stay in step with the seasonal changes. We want to be prepared for what is to come. The amount of work could easily be overwhelming, so in order to know where to start, we must discern what jobs cannot wait, prioritize our work, and develop systems that give us the greatest benefit from the least amount of effort. Being exact in our thinking and timing will assure us of not only our success, but eventual peace of mind.

For humanity and its tribe, centuries of autumn harvests peak in this month. In September, we harvest whatever we planted in May (Taurus). Harvest was/is a time when the growth of summer is inventoried, assessed, and put up for storage for winter. Much work must be done to be ready for the eventuality of winter. Traditionally, we had to be careful to select the best fruit and vegetables, ones that would not spoil too soon and would hold through the winter. Decisions had to be made about our domesticated animals: which beasts were strong enough to make it through the winter? How many animals could we keep alive over the winter? Wild beasts were shot and preserved. It was time to judge the quantity and quality of the meat to be had and the produce to store. County fairs were started for this purpose. They called the community together to assess everyone's work, production, and creativity, with the best results selected to be honored. Only after all the work was done did we have the harvest party to thank the Earth for its bounty and reward ourselves for all our hard work.

This was, and still is, a practical and important time to be precise with what was/is to become our sustenance for the remainder of the year. We still take stock in September, although now more on a mental or emotional level, rather than the physical level that at one time was so important to our survival. We still feel the need to prepare and store up. Also, let's not forget that school starts in September, giving us all subliminal messages of preparation, psyching us up for harder work schedules, forwarding our ambitions.

JANUARY/CAPRICORN

Capricorn is a cardinal sign, ambitious, outgoing, and dynamic in its energy output. Capricorn's month is mostly January. Here we have the darkest time of the year in the north. The Sun has no warmth or even much light. The land is locked in cold and ice, life has retreated and has either died or is in hibernation waiting for spring. This month is traditionally a very difficult time. It's the dead of winter in the northern hemisphere and the middle of summer in the southern hemisphere. In either season, the temperature and precipitation is extreme and fairly intense. Here in the north, the weather is brutal and cold.

Stripped down to the basics of life, here we see Earth and the life on it in a holding pattern. Earth has become a complex storage system, holding itself internally away from a surface world that has gotten less than friendly. Capricorn doesn't shirk or shy away from such a harsh reality; it even expects it. Cap says: "I tend to my duty, which is to keep the life I hold in trust throughout any adversity." There is acceptance, no whining about better times. Winter is a test. It is life despite the weather or death. For those left out in the cold, much energy is spent looking for a better way to stay safe, warm, and fed, while dealing with whatever the ice and snow trashes today. The soil during January/ Capricorn uses this period to cleanse itself, going into a rest period. The ground freezes, growth slows to a stop, and the land lies fallow. The season is as dynamic as survival itself.

For humans, historically, there was never much to eat at this time, at least not fresh food, and even then, certainly no bounty. Our ancestors had to decide how to *use* (a Capricorn word) what we grew in May/Taurus and what was preserved, harvested, and stored in September/Virgo. Building was confined to fires in the hearth, but sometimes the power of the snow or wind meant emergency repairs were needed. The temperatures and conditions meant building was quite a challenge. Smart people were well prepared for such eventualities.

We had to be wise and organized now or we would not survive the winter. The way we used everything during this time became of the utmost importance. Resources - buildings, fuel, food, clothing, all material things - had to last till spring. Timing was crucial; what we didn't attend to promptly could cause great discomfort or even death. Life was serious. There wasn't time to be original. What worked last winter was good enough for this one. Extensive knowledge of how things worked and practical application of all resources meant the difference between life at its most comfortable or complete failure.

Studying the seasons and how we behave within them give clues and information about the astrological signs attached to the months involved. The weather and the way we've reacted to it offer great analogies to the way a sign's energy works.

Individual Personalities: Reflections of the Seasons

Seasonal actions when the Sun is in earth signs are, for the human world, a practical, grounding, or deepening time. People born during these seasonal times reflect many of the qualities of that season.

TAURUS

Spring people born during Taurus are as creative and artistic as the season. They create because making something beautiful is thrilling to their senses. They love to have their senses stimulated. Taurus is in charge of the five senses and the senses are what link us to reality. To hear a note of music sung or played is truly wonderful, but being able to do it yourself gives the Taurean ownership of that exciting beauty. The same holds true for painting, sculpting, or any other art form. To be able to call that skill up so that they may listen to that music or enjoy that vision whenever they want is part of their ownership tendencies.

Taurus people also enjoy the process of creating or building because to construct something is to take that which is intangible, existing only in the airy region of the mind, and manifest it into something solid. When this is done, they have created stability. This means that some experience or some thing is sustained in their immediate environment.

Many Tauruses have the reputation of being "Earth Mothers." This is because living any part of a homesteading style of life involves acquiring the knowledge and know-how to make or grow whatever people need to survive, be it gardening, carpentry, soap-making, or animal husbandry. They feel the "safety of substance," knowing they can do what needs to be done and can handle whatever life throws their way, giving them security and peace of mind.

Tauruses always want more of everything, to the point of saturation. They like "feeling full." One definition of luxury (a keyword associated with Taurus) is to be overly full. This craving for luxury mirrors the fecundity of the season of spring. Taurus people always have treasures they will not part with. Like the month of May, they are tenacious in their endeavors. Once they have made up their minds, you cannot stop them.

Taurus always prefers to build on what has come before. Just as Aries thaws the frozen ground in April and pushes the seed to sprout, Taurus/May follows after, blooming the flowers in its seasonal turn. To take something that has been thought out, to actualize it, and even expand or improve on it, is one of the better uses of Taurian energy. They would rather follow this process than start from scratch.

VIRGO

Autumn people, born in September, are careful and exact. They use their powers of discernment to know what (and who) to invest their time in, when to store something, and when to leave it alone altogether. This mimics the fall harvest scenario. They are always in preservation mode, looking to invest in some effort for future benefits. Like any earth sign, they are willing to do what it takes, and if it takes time to do something of quality, they are willing to spend it. Gleaning or making the best use of what is available is one of the best uses of Virgo energy.

Their powers of healing come from their sense of perfection. They always know when something isn't right because their consciousness is all about the health, or rather the wholeness, present in anything. They know "What's wrong with this picture?" before anyone else.

CAPRICORN

Those born in the dead of winter (January) are realists. They never expect life to be easy. They carry within them a sense of lack or limitation, a feeling that there will never be enough, so they don't squander anything. They are disciplined and traditional people who look for the most judicious use of anything that comes their way (A good attitude makes a difference in the middle of winter). This time of year makes for motivated people; they are up for a challenge and keep going through great adversity until their goals are met. Ever practical and organized in all applications, they know how to work with Earth's resources and use what is available for the best results possible. They are also born with a great sense of duty that encourages them take their obligations (and life) seriously. This comes from the idea that they hold something in trust. In January, the land holds the life dependent on it in trust and Capricorn people instinctually carry that through to their every-day life and the people in it. They subconsciously ask themselves: "What am I being asked to do here?" and they are always response-able.

Anyone born under earth signs (Sun or other planets in Taurus, Virgo, and Capricorn), or wherever (house) someone has earth in their natal chart, work with earth energy and manifestation on that level. Capricorn is perhaps the most efficient in that area. For them, it is pure instinct, this understanding of the Earth's processes. They know how to get things done, how to get from point A to point B, and to work within a realistic framework in the most efficient way. They know how to manifest their desires (or anyone else's) into something that will last a lifetime. At the same time, they understand any limitations of such a system. They don't waste time or anything else. They do what is necessary without question or complaint.

General Affectations of Earth Signs

Earth signs in astrology are the constellations that exude and symbolize earth element energy for us, whether in a chart or in the sky. This occurs when a planet is in an earth sign (or constellation) from our point of view for any length of time. The type and duration of the energy expression depends on what planet is holding an earth sign within it.

The Sun, when observed in the sky and found in a certain sign (and element), is an overlay of directional attitude and/or feeling for us (as we read in the seasonal paragraphs) functioning within a complicated pattern of planetary energy that includes the signs the other planets are in. Together, all the planets in their signs dictate what type of energy human society will recognize for that month. It's what we will most likely notice, understand, and experience for that monthly time period on Earth. If the Sun is in an air or water element, then that type of energy will overlay our senses, influencing our perception and our world.

When the Sun in our sky is in one of the earth signs, i.e., Taurus, Virgo, or Capricorn, then our general experience of life, as a population, is overlaid with an earth emphasis. Since the earth element is about solidity, endurance, and having to do with the Earth itself, we would expect that, globally, things around us would reflect that. In addition to the seasonal expectations during a month of earth rulership, the stories in our newspapers under various headings might read:

(Earth-related words are italicized)

GLOBAL: Lava aftermath of a major volcano is cooling and *hardening* into *rock* or a *rock* slide destroys a town.

POLITICAL: A new bill in Congress is signed into law. (Relaying *Permanence and manifestation*)

HEALTH: An *old stand-by* of a drug shows new potential in relief for *chronic* medical conditions.

BUSINESS: A *multimillion dollar* company is still looking for a more *cost-effective* way or *system* for doing *business.*

SCIENTIFIC: Emus: the newest animal *domesticated* for human consumption. (Shows *use of* animal)

ECONOMIC: How to keep your credit card spending *under control.* (Money is ruled by earth)

LAW: The *original* judgment of a criminal's appeal was *upheld.*

ART: *Practical* art: an artist is painting some of their best work on *furniture*.

LITERATURE: The book "*Organizing* your Life" hits the New York Times Bestseller List.

PERSONAL INTEREST: *Creative crafts* for your *garden*.

Levels of Human Population When Influenced by Earth

IF A GOVERNMENT IS RULED BY EARTH

A government, when influenced or ruled by earth signs symbolically, would tend to be a bit of dictatorship or a totalitarian affair because the people in charge want simplicity. By allowing everyone to have their say (as in a democracy), ruling gets messy and cumbersome. This gets down to the basics of: "I am in charge and this is what I think is for the best." Leaders with this attitude don't want to deal with petty details or encounter obstacles to those basic ideas.

IF A SOCIETY IS RULED BY EARTH

A culture or society, when under a heavy influence of earth signs, is against risky propositions. They also don't accept oddities or aberrant behavior well. They are frugal and protective of their resources. This culture would encourage and admire success and wealth, but downgrade what they would deem "frivolous" activities, that is, things that don't contribute to physical or material gain. This society would also want its ideas and systems of government to produce concrete results that stand the test of time.

EARTH PEOPLE

In general, people whose Suns are in earth signs or have a lot of the earth element in their astrological charts are hard-working, practical, serious, trustworthy, reliable, loyal, careful, cultivating, resourceful, value conscious, frugal, natural, creative, organized, and have a good fund of common sense. However, everyone has some earth in their chart. The houses of the individual natal chart must be consulted to see what areas of a native's life are earth-orientated and the aspects should be considered to see if they have challenges to those houses

THE INDIVIDUAL

Individually, people born with many earth signs in their astrological chart, providing they are in easy aspects (or relationships) to other planets, would live life with an agenda or goal in mind and probably a list or two showing them how to get there. Their approach would always be one of common sense and practicality. This would be on any level: mental, physical, or emotional.

Thinking would be done in a rational, concrete, linear, and logical way. They would most often follow proven lines of thought or embrace ideas based on the groundwork laid by other trusted thinkers in their culture. They would be very good at expounding or expanding what has worked before and lousy at originality, innovation, and invention. New ideas are accepted by them when they can be proven to work and to stand the test of time. A new idea would most impress them when it ultimately leads to the manifestation of something that makes a solid difference in the world.

On the physical level, prominent earth sign people would not take risks with their body. Their attitude would be: life is short enough, why speed things up? They are not up for adrenaline highs. If they embrace physical activity at all, they would go in for tests of strength, stamina, and endurance; the kind a long distance run would provide. They will crave the comfort food they ate as a child and go to conventional doctors when they are ill. Too much movement or moving too fast upsets their equilibrium, so they tend to be the most sedentary of the signs.

Emotionally, earth signs are, of course, traditional. It is natural for them to perpetuate or stay within the emotional norms they have been taught or have witnessed in a family or cultural setting. More than any other level of life experience, emotional allegiance is one we are least likely to question and earth signs least of all. The way their country or their family feels about something is usually adopted. It isn't that earth signs cannot be creative or even original, but there must be a logical reason to go to that trouble. Change is almost always an uncomfortable affair and earth signs like their comfort because that is their security. The way people around them felt about things when they were growing up is what now feels right and normal to them. Earth signs revel in that feeling of normality. The feeling of knowing well the path they tread, the feeling of living within accepted parameters, provides them with the safety and stability to face an uncertain world.

Spiritually, earth signs would be inclined to stay within the faith of their family. To follow in the footsteps of those that came before them gives them continuity. They enjoy preserving the link between one generation and the next. They might even feel it is an honor and/or a duty.

Earth Houses

CAPRICORN/SATURN AND THE 10TH HOUSE

Capricorn rules society and the 10th house. Societies are never basic; they are complex, multi-leveled organisms, vastly different in attitude and action one from another. Societies preserve a way of life even when individuals threaten to undermine it. They are a stabilizing entity. Societies are like an archive, a storage of all that went into the creation of this group of people, and how it is perpetuated over a certain time period.

From an individual perspective, the 10th house ruler in the natal chart presides over reputation and social standing. It is also the place of our individual position in society, our contribution to it; in other words, the career. It shows the native what their society and culture thinks of them and what that society will accept from them as an individual. Conversely, we, as individuals, are also a reflection of our society. We are a product of where (and how) we grew up. Our brain is even hard-wired by what we were exposed to at an early age. Society is a human construct: a banding together of what we decided to do years ago for safety's sake, the sharing of a work load in the quest for food, and maybe some company. Society soon became its own entity, one that we now find ourselves caught up in. At this point, who we are and what we're up to has become practically everyone else's business.

Yet, most of the time, we are not our 10th house reputation. A reputation is hear-say, gossip, what things look like, or the interpretation of our actions by others who live outside of the native's home or sphere. What it tells us about the native is not who the native really is, but how they seem. It is not reality, it is an illusion.

VIRGO/CHIRON (MERCURY) AND THE 6TH HOUSE

Virgo's house is the 6th, the house of daily life, health, and work. Day-to-day life is a dance of mundane happenings that involves chores and affects health.

The work here is not inspired or the kind you aspire to. It isn't a career or necessarily goal-orientated work. It consists of routine jobs that must be attended to in order to keep one's life at a certain standard, a certain style, or a certain level of functionality. Every day we have to cook meals, sweep floors, pay bills, pick up the kids from ballet, etc. To get everything done right and on time we need to be organized. We need to understand the best way to accomplish tasks so we may have some downtime and rest (Recreation or play is not found in this house or area of life). To describe what our life looks and feels like at a basic level, this house is always (to use a modern phrase) streaming in real time, up to the minute and in our face. This is the house that asks us to be vigilant as to what might be ready to go wrong or wreck on us, whether the faucet leaks or a deadline for the mortgage payment is due. We must head off any crisis that may throw our life off its track and affect our health. Health, good or bad, is a reflection of these day-to-day dealings. Do we eat right and exercise or sit around eating donuts every day? Does our lifestyle fit who we are so that we live hour by hour, calm and sedate, or are we uncomfortable and stressed? The routines we have in place will determine how well our body will cope with our choices and ultimately function.

TAURUS/EARTH AND THE 2ND HOUSE

One step away from the 1st house ruling the native's attitude, first impressions, and immediate surroundings, the 2nd house is the native's resources and what they value as well as the textbook "money and possessions" interpretation. Taurus's processing of all the sensory impressions in our bodies always bring us back to the basics of the 2nd house.

Taurus and the 2nd house are in charge of basic resources and raw materials. This includes the acknowledgement, use, and outcome of the native's talents and abilities. What do they know instinctually? What are they good at doing? This house, therefore, rules the care and ownership of objects that are built or collected using those talents or abilities.

What is the ultimate *resource* that each individual has? Here we have, symbolically, the Earth and all its provisions laid out for us and we must decide what to place *value* on and to care for, so that we always have it to draw from. What we place value on becomes our greatest wealth and our greatest treasure. The planetary ruler of the 2nd house should be Earth, our most basic resource, and, appropriately residing in Taurus's house, the very first earth sign we encounter on the zodiacal wheel.

Taurus's house (2nd) is the raw materials/building blocks of our life, describing the items/resources we have or will utilize to make our life. Virgo's house (6th) is the life style we've created and maintained, plus our body's ability to live with it. Capricorn's house (10th) is what our life looks like to outsiders and where we are going with it. These are the earth houses.

Lack of Earth or Hard Aspects: Problems with the Earth element in the Natal Chart

People who are born with little to no earth element in their chart do not understand earth energy. It is as if they are missing a key piece of information about life that others are simply born with and take for granted. They are handicapped in some way.

Another problem that can occur with the understanding and use of earth energy in the individual is through difficult aspects in the natal chart, that is, hard angles/difficult relationships of their earth planets to the other planets in their chart. An earth planet is a planet in an earth sign (Capricorn, Virgo, and Taurus). It is also a planet in an earth house (10th 6th, and 2nd). With difficult aspects to these areas, a resistance to earth energy develops because the native continually encounters earth-related problems, creating earth-type issues (physical and psychological) that they must deal with or work around throughout their life.

Whether earth problems stem from a lack of earth element planets or by way of hard aspects to the earth element planets they *do* have, from an early age they are set upon by an outside world continually asking them to "get real" with their plans: first parents, then teachers, bosses, and finally, by society at large. They are naturally impractical. There just isn't an innate understanding of step-by-step processes or practical considerations as part of their planning process, if they even plan anything. They will be taken to task, either by circumstances around them or people having power over them. Authority figures or "an authority of some kind" continually challenges them. Time and time again, they find out just where they went wrong in their logic of thinking or action. Earthly adjustments, in regards to rules, laws of physics, or procedure, must be made if they want to succeed or just plain stay out of trouble. Keeping finances healthy and planning ahead properly are arduous tasks. Many difficult and frustrating times ensue for them. Finding out what makes an idea or a thing work is a task they must master. Even something as simple as knowing what step to take and when, a process that is always going to take a lot longer than they thought, are lifelong barriers to their success.

In summation, a lack of earth hampers someone because they:

- Don't understand proper steps or procedures
- Don't understand how things work in a situation
- Can't spot potential problems
- Don't know how to plan
- Don't know how to organize
- Don't have advantageous connections
- Don't have the money or resources
- Don't have the knowledge or education
- Don't have the time or place available
- Don't want to work for it, practice it, or earn it

For those who happen to lack a birth-given understanding of earth, success means a lot more hard work and a little less frivolity in their life. It may not be a happy-go-lucky fun time, but it can be very satisfying or rewarding. When faced with projects that require earthly talents or abilities, there is nothing for them to do but suck it up, slow down, and learn what is required on the earth plane in order to achieve. Once they do, they will reap the benefits, big-time. We tend to specialize in the area of our greatest weakness, and so, many times these people become even more successful than others who have had the advantage of easy earth energy because they weren't motivated enough to carry it out. It all depends on the natural drive and inclination of an individual.

Female Gender of Earth Signs

It is interesting to note that all earth signs are female in gender. Female energy is that which is attracting, internal, absorbing, and solidifying in nature. Characteristics include those that preserve and protect what is established, rather than exploring new areas and inventing new techniques. While male energy seeks and explores, female energy provides a place, fertile ground so to speak, for the growing of ideas into projects and projects into manifested reality. Male and female are the difference between "force" and "form". Female is also about reproduction, preservation, and birthing. Well, after all, we do have that phrase: "Mother Earth".

Transits in Earth Signs

Individually, during any earth sign transit, people will be thinking about and doing things that are practical and fundamental in whatever area of life (house) is impacted by that transit. They will make plans and lists and organize that area. They will study to understand how to create their own success or how to invest for the future. They will look for ways to bring ideas down to Earth and to make something concrete of them. They will want tangible results now, in that section of life, nothing else will do. They will work with discipline and diligence toward a planned goal, willing to take steps in the proper order and set aside the time it takes to get there. They want to manifest something that will have lasting impact on their life or environment. In addition, whatever they have earned in this manner in the past will come to fruition now. This goes along with seeking completion, or at least resolution and reward, for a job well done in that area of life.

If you lack the element earth in your chart, have difficult aspects to the planet earth, and/or the other earthy planets, you have challenges relating to earth in your chart and in your life. In this case, an earth transit will be more difficult to deal with. Being forced to face realities that normally wouldn't intrude in your life, you will be taught the hard way that you aren't using earth properly in your equations. Things cannot happen or work out the way you wish until you embrace one or more of the earth traits listed above.

Transits are an assignment to get to know and use the earth energy correctly, and although it can be frustrating and painful, life will be better for the time and energy you spent understanding how to work with earth when the transit is over. When the transiting planet moves out of your earth house, hopefully your homework is done and all is in good order and much improved.

Earth on Contrary House Cusps in the Natal Chart

You will also have support or challenges to face with earth signs on the cusps of the houses given to you at birth. Check to see what areas of your life you must use earth energy by looking at what houses in your natal chart have the signs of Taurus, Virgo, and Capricorn.

When it comes to the astrology chart or houses of astrology, we have what we call a natural chart configuration. The natural chart is a template that shows what signs naturally fall into what houses without an applied birth time shifting it. There is a natural match-up of each sign element to each house activity:

> The Fire sign Aries naturally belongs to, or matches the energy of, the 1st house

- Earth sign Taurus naturally belongs to the the 2nd house
- Air sign Gemini naturally belongs to the 3rd house
- Water sign Cancer naturally belongs to the 4th house
- Fire sign Leo naturally belongs to the 5th house
- Earth sign Virgo naturally belongs to the 6th house
- Air sign Libra naturally belongs to the 7th house
- Water sign Scorpio naturally belongs to the 8th house
- Fire sign Sagittarius naturally belongs to the 9th house
- Earth sign Capricorn naturally belongs to the 10th house
- Air sign Aquarius naturally belongs to the 11th house
- Water sign Pisces naturally belongs to the 12th house

When a chart is cast, signs get rearranged according to the time of birth or event and end up in houses that may or may not get along with each other. Considering the elements of the signs is a fast way to determine if the new sign on or in the house is going to help or hurt the owner of the chart.

As you may imagine, the elements earth and water are very sympatico. So, earth signs on water houses or water signs on earth houses work well together. Air and fire signs are also complementary, so air on fire houses and fire on air houses work well. Adding air to water/earth or fire to earth/water is more of a challenge.

The Challenge of Contrary Elements on the House Wheel

NOTE: The following is not intended as a chart reading of any individual. Personalities are quite complex and have many layers to consider. When I refer to an earth sign on a house cusp, it is being considered in a pure state for clarification and with no consideration of any other elements, planets, or aspects in a natal chart.

THE ELEMENT EARTH ON FIRE HOUSE CUSPS

Fire is the element that encourages (notice another "fire" word: "courage" in "encourage") the native to have lofty ideals and desires that push the native to seek, go out, explore, and do. The 1st, 5th, and 9th, or fire houses naturally ask the native to be outgoing in some way, using great energy to achieve.

1ST HOUSE

The 1st house pushes the native to be an outgoing person, to fearlessly explore the outside world. An earth element sign here has the tendency to pull in, reserving their strength, and uncomfortable with that kind of full-on exposure and pressure. They would like people to come to them, not the other way around. Earth on the 1st does give one a steady, practical outlook on life, with an organized approach to accomplish their tasks, and that is not necessarily a bad thing. They just miss the opportunity boat here and there.

5TH HOUSE

The 5th house asks that the native reproduce him or herself, either through creativity, love, recreation, or procreation. This is an act of confidence that doesn't come easily to earth signs. They are, by nature, shy and modest, not comfortable with being pushed into anything, including the push to create. Creating artistically is just a bit too show-off-y and threatening to them, an exposure of some private part of themselves to others, no matter what the medium, unless it just flows easily from the native like a natural talent. It isn't that these earth-element/5th-house people (or any other element for that matter) don't have or don't want children. All the elements do a fine job of child-rearing. One of the reasons that earth is considered an "off" sign for raising kids is their propensity for traditional ideas and slow growth. Tradition is fine if one was raised well themselves, then repeating a cycle would be a positive thing, but not so otherwise. Children require energy and a sense of adventure, an ability to enter into their world really understanding who they are and where they are trying to go. If you're always worried about sticking to the rules, you aren't going to do that. Earth signs don't adjust to change quickly and children change year to year, sometimes faster! Earth-on-the-5th-house people are not flamboyant in their romantic areas either. They may be very attractive, but they usually have no special flair in winning a heart and they don't wish to compete for a loved one. Don't look for "Don Juan" in the bedroom, but they are kind and loyal and attentive and that is attraction enough for many.

9TH HOUSE

The 9th house asks that the native seek beyond his or her comfort zone to new thoughts, ideas, or places. Earth signs, by their very nature, prefer their surroundings familiar, well-trod, and safe, so we can see how well this pairing works out. Earth signs, as a rule, are not great travelers; it's inconvenient (you can't find your favorite toothpaste in those foreign stores) and who wants to go to sleep (a very vulnerable activity) in strange surroundings? They also won't see a great need to get what is known as a "well-rounded education". Their thinking would be: "Why would I want to learn French or understand ancient history when I am working as a plumber or a business analyst?" They would gravitate toward a trade school situation, learning just what they need to know and how to apply it. They just want to make a living and are not interested in symbolic meanings and lofty ideas: that is extra and, in the end (in their opinion), not very useable.

THE ELEMENT EARTH ON AIR HOUSE CUSPS

The air houses, 3rd, 7th, and 11th, ask the native to connect with other people, either individually or as a group. Earth signs have a tendency to keep to themselves. They aren't easily moved by what others think or do and play their hands "close to the vest". They aren't into risk either, outward risk (as in the fire element) or inward mental risk (air element). Naturally, they enjoy friends, but they prefer uncomplicated lives and to be friends with a lot of people is tiring. They prefer a small circle of dedicated friends; these are the people who are going to understand if the earth person didn't feel like calling or coming over today. A smaller, and therefore better, acquainted group of people means the earth person doesn't have to constantly worry about impressing them or going the extra mile in maintaining their relationship. Misunderstandings are less of an occurrence. Earth signs, where relationships are concerned, can be a bit lazy. They would prefer the other person come over their house because it's easier - that kind of thing. However, earth signs are also very loyal and stick with their friends, rushing to their rescue and supporting them in any way they can when they are needed.

3RD HOUSE

Air houses are also in charge of the native's mental functionality and, as in the 3rd house, their early experience with school. The mental levels of the 3rd include day-to-day thinking processes and learned, internal mental habits, as well as how and what the native communicates and to whom. This house asks the native with an earth sign to be fast and clever, and this is someone who naturally learns slowly and deliberately and learns best using a hands-on method, rather than a lecture. The house wants them to theorize about everything and talk a lot. Earth signs don't flash a lot of mental gymnastics; they just aren't interested in living in their heads. They want to feel something physical and see a tangible result of their work at the end of the day. Having a paper published is not exactly what they have in mind.

7TH HOUSE

Among other things, the 7th house is the area of communication with a spouse or significant other. This house is the shadow side of the native's communication, what they don't own about their own communication skills and what they must learn through a significant other. This house asks the native to search, find, and secure a permanent companion and share themselves with them. Earth signs can live alone very easily. They certainly aren't usually the aggressor in the pursuit of another. If they do find someone, the earth sign here attracts someone who reflects back to them, or embodies, earth in some way. They look for or attract safe people that have their feet on the ground, a little money in the bank, and a philosophy or goal that makes a lot of sense to the earth native. Earth signs are not into experimentation or deviation in this area of life and even if they happen to land in an avant-garde position due to their physical needs, they will still want partners who aren't going to rock their hard-won life-boat too hard. Their partner will teach them much about that side of themselves, yet communication won't be the number one pursuit in this relationship. Their method of connection will be on the physical, not the mental, level.

11TH HOUSE

The 11th house (among other things) is what the native aspires to on a mental level. Another word for this is vision: what is their vision? Also, how and what they communicate to acquaintances or groups of people. Earth signs aren't usually concerned with the future, except in the form of insurance against life's calamities. They feel that if you take proper care of the present, the future is assured. Once again, earth has a problem with theorizing or abstract thinking. Imagination is not their strong suit and they consider day-dreaming unproductive. What matters is here and now. They would look for a vision that has deep roots in reality. Any future goal would be headed for with a mind-set of easy does it, step-by-step, and patient plodding to reach a goal that is believable and workable with the talents they possess today.

As far as communication with whole groups of people, no one enjoys public speaking and it is safe to say, earth signs least of all. They usually don't crave the spotlight. They also dislike the distracting complexity of being in a crowd of people. It is too "out of their control" and they avoid them when possible. Yet here they are asked to take their place among a larger number of people and make the best of it. Working through earth, they would look to join a community that is doing earthly things; a community gardening project, for example. They would bring their earthly organizational and financial skills into an organization, sitting quietly in the back, collecting dues or making flow charts. In this way, they fulfill their need for reassurance and security within a neighborhood, organization, or community.

THE ELEMENT EARTH ON WATER HOUSE CUSPS

As previously mentioned, earth and water are the best of friends. This doesn't mean that they are exactly alike, however. Both elements work with sensations in the body to sense and analyze what is physically there, but earth's sensation is touch, concerned with that which is most tangible, while the water element processes the world with feelings and reads every emotion in the outside world for more information. They both prefer something that seems "real" and in the now, not theoretical (air) or ideal (fire). Earth on a water house would ask the native to be more emotionally consistent and use their emotional perception in logical or linear and practical ways to get ahead.

4TH HOUSE

This water house is the area of home and family. Earth here bestows a home life that is consistent and orderly, usually a family that is supportive, practical, and maybe a tad pragmatic. As we can see, this would give the native a good solid starting point with which to begin building a successful life. Other factors, like planetary placements and aspects to this house, may spin things another way, of course.

8TH HOUSE

The house of death doesn't seem like a great match for the earth element, but if we consider that mixing earth and death means chronic health issues, a steady, perhaps gentler decline, rather than high-speed collisions or unexpected brain aneurysms, we can see some advantage. This can make the whole transitional thing a bit more tolerable, but it depends on your point of view. Another very good relationship between this house and earth is the money aspect of the 8th. The 8th house is the opposite of Taurus's own 2nd. Here we find the money and resources of the partner and other people's money (taxes, wills, and estates) in general. Earth would be a great asset here, obviously. One other lesser known (or at least less talked about) quality of the 8th has to do with the spirit world. Some astrologers label this the house of the Occult. It is supposed to contain within it all that is secret and hidden on Earth. I look at this house as the area of life in which the spiritual essences *on the earth plane* (as opposed to not of this Earth) make themselves known. One example would be what we call ghosts: the essence of a spirit able to be seen or felt here on Earth. Another example of 8th house energies would be emotional essences contained, say, in a room. A person with a strong 8th house can sense the emotional temperature of an area, whether the people who made the impression or vibe are still present or not. All underlying emotional messages would be noticed by this person. The earth element, considered from these angles, would lend a practicality to dealing with the spirit world, like participating in ghost-hunting or bringing Occult knowledge down to application and usability. An interest in psychological counseling would be a great marriage of those enhanced emotional sensibilities, as this incorporates those practical intentions. Difficulties due to challenging aspects here would constitute a constant choosing between practical, hands-on applications of the physical realities placed in front of the native or going with their gut and living though their emotions. There is also another more sinister outcome of the more severe aspects, due to the raw or base-like qualities the earth element contains. This particular earth trait never mixes well with the 8th house energy Scorpio/Pluto. The 8th house et al. can sometimes take that idea to the depths, creating a scenario where the native is aware of the worst degradations possible in people. It can translate to a feeling at the native's core that they are not a nice human being. Most of the time, this is not true, it is only their acute awareness of the *possibilities* of negative human behavior that creates a blurred line between emotional understanding of the icky stuff at the underbelly of life and physical or true reality.

12TH HOUSE

The 12th is the third water house and the last one on the zodiacal wheel, so it is also the house that tries to encompass the symbology of all non-earth reality in a chart. Here, a sense of the "All" is found, a largess that goes beyond the bounds of Earth. Natives who have a 12th house emphasis (by planetary placement, etc.) in their charts are aware of realities other than the one they are in. The idea of God or a perpetuating, energetic, connective force is found here. It is also the place where a representation of the collective unconscious of humankind resides. Natives with strong 12th house emphases are a little unconscious in the real world because part of their attention is focused on the beyond. The difficulties of the 12th stem from: daydreaming, lack of attention to the here and now, and a constant need to incorporate spiritual influences into mundane living. This can be tricky, unless you're a priest. As one can see, an earth element here emphasizes this challenge of incorporation, as the native must live in both worlds and find a good balance between them. It also gives them gifts of awareness and perspective that may be lost on others.

Earth the Essential

Earth is always concerned with the physical and grounding things; that is, bringing things down to Earth. Water is emotionally grounding or taking an emotional temperature. Air and fire are not grounding energies; they are the elements that keep things moving.

After reading about the contrasts of fire and air with earth, someone could come away with the idea that earth can be a rather dull element in a natal chart. That could be true in certain situations, but consider this: without the earth element, we would not have the ability to solidify anything, to organize our ideas into solid, doable plans, or to execute them and continue to work at them until the job is well done. Without the earth element in our charts, we would have nothing in our lives of lasting quality.

Earth may not be a glamorous or exciting element in astrology. It doesn't explore or invent and it sure doesn't try and change the world, but take it from someone with only one earth sign in her chart: you really need it and can't get a thing done without it. There are many times when I am simply lost as to what step to take to get to my goal. I see other, more blessed souls with an innate knowledge of where to put their feet and where to invest their energy next. Everything runs in a straight line for them. If the element of earth is missing in our lives, we can't hold on to and harness the power of the human mind and spirit or find the determination to complete tasks. We will always need the strength and endurance it bestows in any major endeavor we take on. Earth stabilizes anything it touches, allowing the native or the event, to work well within the rules or boundaries of the earth plane we live in. It is essential for productive growth and success. So, well-placed earth elements in the natal chart are essential for the wellbeing of the body, the productivity of our life, and the balance of our soul. Without it, we just end up chasing our own tails.

Chapter 5
Saturn: The Surrogate

"Attachment is the great fabricator of illusions; reality can be attained only by someone who is detached." ~ Simone Weil
(1910-1943, French philosopher, Mystic)

"The human mind is not capable of grasping the Universe. We are like a little child entering a huge library. The walls are covered to the ceilings with books in many different tongues. The child knows that someone must have written these books. It does not know who or how. It does not understand the languages in which they are written. But the child notes a definite plan in the arrangement of the books--- a mysterious order which it does not comprehend, but only dimly suspects." ~Einstein

"Everyone takes the limits of his own vision for the limits of the world." ~Arthur Schopenhauer

Earth, Where Are You Now?

If planet Earth has been left out of Western astrology, then where have the traits or processes of this planet been hiding out over the years? Lacking a true home for earthly energies, astrologers did what they've always done: they observed a planet with the closest energetic signature to it and overlaid those attributes on that planet. In this case, it was Saturn. All this time, Saturn has worked as a surrogate for earth energy in Earth's absence, just as Venus has for Taurus. One reason for the selection of Saturn for rulership of earthly Taurian items might be due to the mythological link of agriculture to the Roman god Saturn.

The Astrological Process of Integrating Newly Discovered Planets

In astrology, when a new planet, planetoid, or point is noticed or discovered, interpretational information about that planet or point must be gathered, compiled, and studied. The first thing astrologers study for insight into its influence on us is the physical characteristics of the planet or point itself. When it comes to the properties of planets and stars in the solar system, astrologers are just as interested in this as astronomers are.

Through observations or explorations, data is gathered about a planet. Anything that pertains to an individual planet is added to a tally sheet of sorts. This serves as a reference guide to understand the planet and its characteristics: the way it moves, its orbit, the conditions of its atmosphere, its composition, orientation, action, and, lastly, any ongoing situation with it, i.e., what position (or constellation) it is in and what is happening to it (and us) right now. The study becomes a collection of traits about the planet on paper. Both astrologers and astronomers study the effects of a new planet on the solar system and our universe as a whole. Astrologers' part ways with astronomers when they ask: "How does this planet's orbit or characteristics affect the human population and, finally, what effect does it have on the individuals within that population?"

How the data is used further divides the astrologer from the astronomer. Astronomers always keep their studies to the physical data of a planet and astrologers go on to look at the gathered planetary information as it relates to us and our living conditions.

The list of physical planetary characteristics, together with how they have affected people and populations, place the planet in a symbolic category. The planet emerges as a ruler over, or a symbol for, certain types of things or ideas, energy, or actions on Earth that exhibit the new planet's characteristic quality.

Astrologers take information gathered about a planet and translate it to a symbolic level. For example: if Jupiter is the largest planet in our solar system, then it is taken symbolically in any astrological chart to mean any situation, characteristic, or problem made bigger, a larger-than-life-type energy. The planet Uranus has an orbit unlike any other in our local universe: it rotates on its side. That would be like having the north and south poles on our Earth at the equator. Hence, the planet Uranus, in astrology, has come to symbolize something out of the ordinary, an oddity.

This same type of physical symbolism should apply to Saturn. That is why I've chafed for years at many of Saturn's traditional correspondences that seem to include all Earthly characteristics; they just never seem right to me. Looking under "Earth" and "Saturn" in <u>The Rulership Book</u>, by Rex E. Bills, we see that as things now stand in the astrological community, Bills had little choice but to place the earth element under Saturn's jurisdiction in astrological rulerships. It is clear to me, however, that Earth must rule the earth element. With that idea of planetary symbolism firmly in place, let's take a good look at Saturn.

Saturn: An Illusion of Solidity

Astrology is the art of marrying mythology and symbolism with concrete, manifested reality, or, more succulently, spirit and science, into one workable system by which we can get a clear picture of our total reality for the purpose of understanding how to live better lives within it.

With that in mind, let's start with the notion that Saturn has been traditionally *the* grounding energy in natal charts for not only the human psyche, but the human body as well. If Earth is where we stand, live, and build our homes, then how can a planet that is 793 million miles from us be a better symbolic representation of our home and our stability than the one we are walking around on, our own terra firma?

The most important addition to this argument is the fact that the planet Saturn is barely even solid.

Saturn consists mainly of liquid and gas around a very small core. The gases are composed of hydrogen and helium. It might even turn out to be that the core is largely liquid. According to Space Today, "Saturn, which [was] formed more than four billion years ago, is mostly hydrogen and helium gases. There are lesser amounts of methane and ammonia. Saturn is a big ball of gas almost 75,000 miles in diameter held together by the pull of gravity. Hydrogen and helium also are the main gases in the Sun. While almost as big in size as Jupiter, Saturn's mass is only 30 percent of Jupiter's. And its density is lowest in the Solar System. It's so low, in fact that it would float in a bathtub"[1] if we had one big enough. Were we standing there, Saturn wouldn't "have a solid surface of hard enough ground we could walk on. What we see through telescopes is not a surface, but actually the top layer of a cloud of ammonia ice crystals."[1] It is not composed of rock and liquid rock, like Earth. You couldn't land there because there is nothing solid to land on. If there is something at the center, it might be a teeny core of rock surrounded by a liquid and then smothered in the very foggy atmosphere. "Saturn is a giant cloud of mostly hydrogen and helium gases. Gravity, the same force that brings things down to Earth, holds the gases of Saturn together."[1] Saturn is also a bit unstable, according to Alan Boyle, the msnbc.com science editor. A double aurora was spotted on Saturn by the Hubble Space Telescope. "The northern-southern light display is notable not only because of its rarity, but also because it shows that the giant planet's magnetic field is out of balance... But the peculiarities of Saturn's poles have intrigued astronomers for years. Some puzzle over a hexagonal cloud pattern circling the north pole. Others have found that Saturn's northern lights went all over the place, with dramatic ups and downs."[2]

By contrast, Earth (a medium size rocky body) is fairly stable, very dense, and has a solid shell. Earth is one of the terrestrial planets of which Mercury, Venus, and Mars are also a part. "Because of its high mass for its size, Earth actually has the highest density of all the planets in the Solar System. The density of Earth is 5.52 grams per cubic centimeter. The high density comes from the Earth's metallic core, which is surrounded by the rocky mantle."[3] Saturn's solidity is an illusion.

Just as Earth is for us the most tangible, most solid part of our reality, so our physical body is obviously the most solid thing about us, personally. So, the ruler and indicator of our physical body in the natal chart should be Earth, not Saturn. Any corporeal body on Earth is a solid outward manifestation of an inner life force. This description of a body can be likened to the structure of our Earth. The human body is a microcosm of our own planet's macrocosm of structure and composition. The body, like our Earth, is covered with a hard skin, a shell. Inside lies structure, bones, muscles, and a mass of liquids. At the core is heat, generated by electricity. We must have air, warmth, water, and a structure to contain it all in order to exist. In other words: air, fire, water, and earth, or the four classic elements. Our bodies are made up of the four elements, just as our Earth is. Animal, human, and even plant bodies are like fractals of Earth, the physical manifestation of the life on it. We are a product of the Earth and when we die our physical remains go back into the Earth, to replenish it, ashes to ashes, dust to dust, so we belong to the Earth, not Saturn.

Could it be that earthly traits have been pasted onto Saturn for so long that we've been missing something essential about Saturn and Capricorn as well? If we pulled the earthly mask away from Saturn, what would we find?

Saturn and Capricorn: The Highest Level of Earth Energy

Saturn relates to earth as the ruling planet of Capricorn, an earth sign.

Astrology uses an analogy of a human being's life to illustrate the stages of the zodiac. The zodiac is composed of the signs of astrology, starting with Aries. Aries is said to symbolize a baby just born. This energy is about beginnings, fresh starts, and breaking out. Aries and its ruling planet,

Mars, rule action. The downside of Aries, as you might expect, is their preoccupation with themselves and, like a baby, they can be selfish and think everything is all about them. Taurus is the next sign on the natural wheel of the zodiac. Taurus is said to be the toddler, beginning to explore the world around them and starting to assert their independence by entering the "no" phase that most toddlers get into. It progresses on up the line or around the zodiacal wheel until it ends with Pisces, the last sign that represents, among other things, an old man or woman of wisdom, approaching death, the end of life as we know it.

Capricorn is the last earth sign in the zodiac. Traditionally, the farther away the signs are from the beginning of the zodiac, the more sophisticated or abstract their energetic nature. In charge of the 10th house of public ambition and career, Capricorn is not a foundational sign by any means. There is nothing basic about Saturn; it is an outer planet. Capricorn, Saturn's sign, is still a perfect example of an earth sign, but it is the earth of outward ambition, goals, and the organization of what is already manifest, not the basic Earth/Taurus raw material, "build-it-from-the-ground-up" vibration. Capricorn is looking to convert earth energy into something beyond the basic bounds of earth.

Capricorn wants to carry earthly resources, the valuable raw materials of Taurus and the procedures, social connections, and perfectionism of Virgo to the height of possible achievement or the peak of operation. In this way, it takes full advantage of earth and, in the end, even tests the limitations of it. Capricorn asks: "How far can I go with this project or idea? I want to go further than anyone else has, and, in so doing, I may build the greatest empire of all and everyone will see that I am the best at working with earthly materials." They are the most ambitious of all signs; they want to see how much of earth they can build on, save, monitor, or control. Capricorn loves nothing better than to step in at the helm of a large factory or company that is floundering, pull the strings of the mechanism, and make-over its operation to the greatest efficiency. The highest manipulation of the most earth they can conquer is their ultimate satisfaction, keeping in mind that Cap also wants a material measurement of success for that endeavor, the rewards that earth has to offer: money, quality lifestyle, prestige, admiration, status, or power. The feeling of perfecting earthly processes to the height of their efficiency for monetary or self-gratification is indicative of Capricorn alone (The feeling of perfecting every-day life or the processes of life belongs to Virgo. Taurus isn't interested in taking the action or actions that make something perfect but they are very interested in having the perfect item or materials). Capricorn always understands how and where earth could be made better.

Saturn, as Capricorn's ruler, is also in charge of showing us how far we can go with the earth element and, not coincidentally, the limitations of earth as well. In the astrological chart, Saturn has always shown us where we lack proper earthly knowledge, resources, training, or procedure. Saturn's symbology may yet contain keys to a deeper understanding of our planet. Saturnian parental energy may extend to our Earth; Saturn may have something to tell us about E/earth and its properties. I say this based on the symbolic high level of E/earth - that is, Saturn.

Capricorn in the Natal Chart

With Saturn and Capricorn all about the application of Earth and its substances, the results give Capricornian people a rap for being cold and calculating. They appear unsympathetic because they are concerned with things other than people and the emotional attachments that can seriously hamper ambition. Capricorn's skill has to do with the organization of matter - that is, inanimate things. The organizing of people and their skills belongs to Virgo or even Aquarius.

Where we have Saturn or Capricorn in our chart, or when we experience a Saturn transit or have a Capricorn moment, we want to go forward with our knowledge of earth and test it by applying or using it. Our life in this area becomes about getting to the top of our knowledge or skill base. This translates to ambition, a keyword of Capricorn.

When the Capricornian person is in charge of a group of people (very commonly the head of a company), then the extreme practicality of the sign, added to the Capricorn/Saturn way of facing reality, produces a boss that appears to make harsh decisions easily.

A typical Capricorn CEO is usually foremost concerned with the health of the company, not its people. In a Capricornian way, a CEO of this sort has the idea that nothing is as important as the company because without it, everyone working there would lose their livelihood and starve. If an individual is causing a problem, they have to be let go for the good of the rest. This is logic and loyalty of another kind than, say, a Piscean brotherhood-(or sisterhood)-of-humankind-where-everyone-counts producing an altogether different mindset. That looks something like this: the company *is* its people and if one is unhappy, we must work with that person and when that person is happy again, then the company will heal as well and will all be strong once again. Here are two very different bosses with two very different attitudes and we can make the judgment that the Capricornian boss is harsher in terms of that one problem individual but does that make what the Capricorn boss did so negative? Both ways of operating will keep the company afloat for the good of the majority; both can work. Here is another part of that story to consider from the Capricornian viewpoint. That problem person, who is let go from this fictitious company by the practical, yet seemingly cold, boss may not have belonged in that line of work at all. Maybe he or she needed to find another type of job. While the firing of this individual may make for a difficult time for him/her, because the boss (with the hard, but ultimately practical, Saturn reality) stepped in to send this person on his/her way, the employee will, in all probability, end up in a better place. The old company is probably better off without the one who couldn't fit in and the new job acquired by the ex-employee not only makes him/her happier, but the new company gains a productive and satisfied worker. Everyone is better off. It also *may* be that the Piscean boss, although kinder in the short run, may have ultimately, and inadvertently, trapped, through ease and the following inaction, both the disgruntled employee and the company together in an unhealthy situation that will not end well for either. Sound judgments, especially when Capricorn/Saturn is involved, are always tricky because there is always more than one way to consider something practical. Perhaps our employee didn't want to enter into this difficult time period, didn't want to be challenged by the boss to find a job better suited to him/her, and would have complained to whoever would listen that being on the street, having to look for work, isn't easy. All that is true, and from an emotional standpoint, the firing may look *im*practical, yet

Saturn demands that the action be what is right in a permanent, usable, sensible way. It does not take into consideration feelings and emotions unless there are benefits in the long run. Although Saturn can be difficult in the area of emotion, it is always seeking for the highest and greatest good, willing to forgo short-term pleasure for long-term future success and happiness. Most of the time that means that "practical" isn't a kinder, gentler way to operate. It is the denominator of common sense, not Fun-o-Rama.

During visits from Saturn (transit) in our natal chart, it is natural that we end up testing our own limitations as well as Earth's. We see how far we've gone to push the walls of our own earthly reality and just how far we can go before we fall and fail. Through these lessons, we see where the bounds of E/earth are, what they look and feel like, and how they define our life. Much of the time, Saturn does this by reining us in or holding us down. The lesson, in this case, is not the punishment many feel it is, but to learn to think and work within this reality. The knowledge we receive as a result of dealing with those limitations actually assures us that we will do much better in whatever we undertake from here on. A better understanding of how the world works will always help us to succeed. Capricorn/Saturn holds the lesson, but also the diploma you get when you master the element of earth.

Capricorn/Saturn, with its higher earth function, bestows personal awareness that choices are available, but, at the same time, it makes sure that those choices are within the realm of possibility, given the space and time we are in. The layout or levels of earth action are cyclic in nature and may look something like this:

Concepts and principles of earth start with Capricorn. 1) Then basic *manifested* earth ingredients are presented in Taurus.

2) From the list of ingredients, Virgo selects the best pieces/people for the task.

3) Capricorn makes the final choice for its ultimate usability.

Saturn - Theoretical Earth and the Kabbalah

Capricorn (Saturn-ruled) as the cardinal sign of earth is the Alpha and the Omega of Earth; both the elemental etheric beginning of earth and the end result of it.

My statement "beyond the basic bounds of earth" in paragraph 20 refers to a paradox. Capricorn/Saturn does take earthly materials to their height on the earth plane, but, like a Mobius strip, Capricorn/Saturn energy also comes around to representing the beginning of E/earth, containing the basic principles of earth. Saturn is in charge of what I call theoretical E/earth. Theoretical earth is where the seeds and concepts of E/earth dwell in the energetic realm.

The energetic realm (as we understand it) is well illustrated in the Kabbalah and its Tree of Life. The Kabbalah is a branch of Jewish mysticism and another symbolic system or language that attempts to explain not only this world, but other planes of existence that produce or result in this world.

The Tree of Life is a way of showing how the energy might flow from other realms to this one and back. Its diagram of symbols allows us to organize and study all existence. It even covers the things that are difficult to conceptualize because they are so abstract. Kabbalah and the Tree give us a language to describe all the energy in the cosmos (and our reality included), just as astrology does. Astrology is also included/represented on the Tree of Life.

Throughout the Tree of Life are Sephiroths. They are repositories, vortexes, or concentrations of energy not unlike chakras. They mark significant points of reference in the matrix of the worlds of existence, and are a way of describing different types of energy.

The Tree also describes the path by which spirit descends, creating the material world. Physical existence starts above the Tree with nothing or a No-thing: that is, where God, or our concept of God, resides. Then it moves down into the first/top Sephiroth known as Kether, the idea of existence before the idea. Where is an idea before you get it? On some higher level, or other more ethereal realm, represented by Kether. The farther down you travel on the Tree, the more dense energy gets, until you have physical existence, Earth, reality as we know it. The energy of the Tree also shows the reverse. It is also the path a manifested being can take to ascend back into spirit or back to the ethereal planes that help comprise the physical world, but are not incarnated matter. For us, living on the earth plane, we are at the bottom of the Tree in the Sephiroth Malkuth. That is another name for the Earth plane.

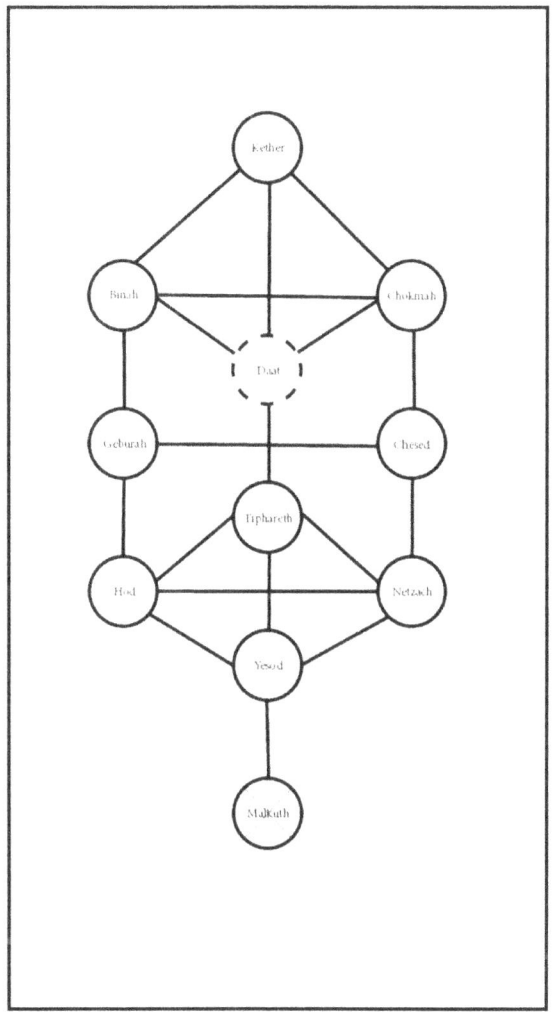

4

    In the Kabbalah, Saturn sits near the top of the Tree in the Sephiroth Binah.

    Situated as it is in one of the highest plane of existence, Binah is sometimes called the great Mother (of all), while Chokmah, on the opposite side of the Tree, is the great Father. Energies here are destined to fall to Earth and be manifest, but first they divide into a duality of the male/female or extrovert/introvert.

According to Gareth Knight, in his classic book: <u>A Practical Guide to Qabalistic Symbolism</u> (spelling varies on the word Kabbalah), "Binah is the first 'form' Sephirah. That is, although it is far above any kind of form as we know it, there is implicit in it the archetype or idea of form."[5] In a description that sounds very Saturnian, he goes on to say "Form can be defined as the interlocking of free moving force into patterns which then operate as a unity."[5] In other words, we cannot have form unless there is a restriction of free movement. Form limits movement and movement has to be curtailed at some level so that form can exist.

Since Binah is the first place that the idea of form exists or is formulated, one might say that Saturn, in astrology, could be the spiritual aspect of form or earthly manifestation. It is true that Saturn/Capricorn in the natal chart gives us quite a spiritual lesson in the essence of the material world and how to function within it. "In Capricorn the man reaches either the height of personal ambition or he becomes the initiate, attaining his spiritual objective."[6] Meaning, with Capricorn energy, one has a choice of attaining money and status, everything we might ever want in the physical level of existence *or* going much higher, becoming everything we have the potential to become, having the ultimate satisfaction of achieving all spiritual assignments here on Earth that we have been given in this lifetime. At the heart of that quote by the Mystic Alice Bailey is a very different side of the earth element. The idea she presented is that the best earthly attainments are not physical rewards, but ideally, perfected personality traits as part of an individual's psyche. They are, nonetheless, just as powerful, tangible, useable, and real. Here is a hint of the spirit or essence of earth that one rarely considers. This is what I believe Saturn and Capricorn truly mean to rule and represent. Currently, our Western culture isn't acknowledging internal achievements, or if they are, they are certainly not assigning any value to them. We tend to applaud fame, fortune, and gross materialism as the standards of success in our society. This is yet another sign that something is missing from our astrological interpretations of earth. All the nuances of earthly energy are not being understood or integrated into our lives. If we begin to consider Saturn, Capricorn, and the 10th house as symbols of the highest earth energy, what would that mean to us? How might that change us and our culture for the better?

Progression of the Earth Signs on the Tree of Life

The energy flow to manifestation within the framework of the Kabbalistic Tree of Life moves back and forth, starting from the right side (male and Chokmah) to the left (female and Binah) and proceeds all the way down the Sephiroths to Malkuth. The Binah energy trickles down to the next Sephirah, Chesed (Jupiter), and so on, crisscrossing and moving into the next lowest level (or dimension), and on, until the earth plane is reached and we have manifested reality as we know it.

What is interesting, at least for the earth signs, is that one can follow the Tree down from the idea of matter in Binah (Saturn), through Tiphareth (Sun), and then through Hod, Mercury's Sephirah (the original ruling planet for Virgo - Chiron has not been assigned to the Tree yet), then Yesod (Moon) and finally Malkuth, which is Earth. This lines up the earth signs perfectly:

From:
MATERIAL IDEA
Abstract spark or theory/spirit of earth
BINAH/SATURN/CAPRICORN
Saturn introduces the concept of restriction of form to a world that is energetically free and random.
To:
MATERIAL ESSENCE
The more limited freedom of thought/word/definition/choice/knowledge of earth
HOD/MERCURY/VIRGO
Virgo selects and refines what kind of form the energy may take.

To:

MANIFESTATION

The extreme limitation of physical existence on earth, solid matter

MALKUTH/EARTH/TAURUS

Taurus rules, understands, and works with the form. Emotion also helps to define and limit energy and, as we have seen, the Moon (Yesod) fits between Hod/Mercury and Malkuth/Earth but we aren't concerning ourselves with the water signs here. If we remember that there is a spirit, or, more precisely, a vibration in all forms, we get an idea as to the essence of Saturn and Binah. When we look around our world, we're really seeing two different levels of reality: the solid world of form and the vibrational essence that is behind it.

Shifting Saturn's Symbology: Illusions of Earthly Matter?

I read once that Saturn may actually symbolize the structural illusion of Earthly reality. This stuck in my mind because it made perfect sense to me. Taking Saturn the planet's dubious physical properties as a guide here, it is only logical that a possible future meaning of Saturn, for astrologers, would constitute some kind of deception or misimpression about our reality - something that appears solid, something that we rely on and take for granted, but may not be truly carved in the stone of E/earth. Saturn could become known as the way we fool ourselves about reality; how we think reality operates may not be entirely correct. With the advent of Quantum Physics, there are new ideas and exciting concepts of matter that the scientific community is discovering that lead me to wonder if Saturn's symbology (aside from being assigned a rulership of the essence of earth) should also preside over the *illusions* of Earth. I think this is an intriguing place of study as we move toward a greater understanding of what Saturn/Capricorn may really represent if rulership over form is shifted away from Saturn/Capricorn to Taurus and planet Earth.

The illusions that we humans historically cling to about our reality here on Earth would fill another book. This is not to say that we mean to delude ourselves, sometimes it's just simple ignorance that has kept us from the truth. We are a creative race and we don't like that feeling of "not knowing" something. What we can't understand right now we tell ourselves a story about and if that seems to fit, we'll stick to it until something better comes along. Even then, we don't seem to like to change very much and sometimes what we hold in our head long enough we make real by the energy we invest in it. Astrological symbolism, or any kind of symbolism, can also influence our attitude about what we believe to be right. When we change the way we think about things, we may even change our reality. In essence, it seems as if the Kabbalah may be correct in its explanation that everything begins as, or is in the end, energy.

Saturn's traditional interpretation of limiting our human exploits by reminding us of the framework we are working within, the limitations of earthly reality, always brings a question to my mind. If, as we say in the metaphysical community, "we make our own reality," then why can't we work outside of some of Earth's apparent boundaries of what we expect Earth to be? It may turn out to be precisely because of our, or others', expectations that there is a set reality at all. Perhaps Earth's rules haven't been as "set in stone" as we have all been led to believe. Physicists studying how the fundamental processes of earth operate have further discovered that our reality, especially at that subatomic level, doesn't seem to be any more stable or predictable. It stands to reason that since the subatomic or molecular level of reality is one that we cannot perceive with our senses (and for years on end never even knew existed), it would fall under this new idea of Saturn rulership.

Matter – All Illusion?

There is an illusionary aspect to matter and consequently some of our concepts of Earth; just as the physical planet Saturn is not solid. First, there was the shock in the 5th Century of finding out that matter was far from the solid thing it always appeared to be. Instead, it was composed of many atoms and molecules that not only move and vibrate, but are surrounded by a lot of, apparently empty, space. The empty space is now known as Dark Matter. Dark Matter seems to provide the structure or scaffolding that galaxies cling to. Although there are still many questions about it, from what we do know, it looks as though Saturn/Capricorn is a good candidate for rulership of Dark Matter as well.

Subatomic Particles and the Particle and Wave Theory

As we have seen, the principles and concepts of Earth, the precedents set for what E/earth is (not the physical world itself), fit well under a rulership of Saturn/Capricorn. Saturn/Capricorn, if now considered the highest level of E/earth, also seems to be a good match for rulership of the subatomic particle level of manifestation on Earth. This area of reality is the spiritual or vibrational level on Earth of a physical object.

Some studies of subatomic particles play an even bigger role in showing us our illusions around earthly reality. Called "the measurement problem" of Quantum Physics[7], atoms only appear in a particular place when they are measured. An atom doesn't seem to be in any location, or are in all locations, until a conscious observer decides to look at it. When a person looks at an atom, only then does an atom appear to stop and stay where the observer is looking. It may be that the act of observing the world creates the stable physical reality as we know it. In many of these experiments on the subatomic level, what we are testing for determines what our results will be. No one knows at this point what reality really is. It appears to be what our brains think it is: a holographic picture translated by the signals of light our brain receives from our eyes and the environment. It seems as if whatever we are looking for in our reality, we find. That may mean that if we change what we are looking for, the results may change, too. We don't yet understand the full ramifications of these discoveries.

Quantum Mechanics says the world around us seems to be in a specific state, yet describes it with possibilities and probabilities. All this leads me to wonder if Saturn should also be ruling over things like String Theory and the particle and wave phenomena.[8] It is all about "actual" versus "perception".

Another strange thing about the physical universe is that objects that have mass in the fabric of space warp the space, and to some extent, time also. Even very small objects, like people, do this. It is strange to imagine that if I take a walk down the street, the space-time around me is warping or curving, moving and vibrating, on such small levels that I don't notice it. I cannot see that I influence the space around me; that the reality I think is permanent and stable is actually a movable thing.[9]

Truth, Illusion, Form, and Fear

As matter, and some of our concepts of reality, turns out to be less than solid, Saturn steps in to rule the essence and illusions we have of our Earth.

On the other hand, the actual earthly forms we see that look and feel solid, those things we create from and build on, would then be, logically, ruled by Earth/Taurus. We proceed as if solidity is the reality and our assumptions seem to mostly work for us.

Taurus/Earth would rule what we think of as reality, in terms of structure, weight, and predictability. The information given to us by our senses, another thing ruled by Taurus, lead us to our perceptions of form in this reality. Taurus = our perceptions of form/reality.

Taurus/Earth rules what the physicists call "mass": the measure of how much matter an object contains or the amount of atoms in an object. Taurus would also rule weight. Weight is a measure of the force of gravity pulling a mass down. Taurus is also connected to the principle of inertia. Inertia tells us how hard it is to move something by applying a force.

Earth and Taurus rule reality as we see it, our perception of that predictable, manifested, or formed reality that we recognize all around us as immutably constant, i.e., things stay where we put them, plants grow upright, and walls meet floors. We count on these appearances and they give us our security, our peace of mind, so that we may get on with our lives. This is Earth and Taurus's jurisdiction. The apparent realities of stability, the forms that life takes, are Taurian in nature. Reality, as form and consistency, belong to Earth and Taurus.

Earth/Taurus works with what is in front of us and isn't interested in what it's made of or where it's coming from. Yet, it should be said that Taurus's fixed intensity goes down deep, to a visceral level, within the Earth Mother herself. Taurus has a deep connection to all the physical living things that have been produced and are a part of the Earth Mother. Taurus should rule the "Biophilia hypothesis."[10] The term "biophilia" means love of life or living systems and refers to how human beings seek connections with what is alive on Earth and tend to gravitate toward nature and natural spaces to rest and recharge their energy. In this way, there is a spiritual side to Taurus in its relation to Earth. In many ways, Taurus really is the essence of planet Earth.

Saturn/Capricorn concepts are what are truly behind all the forms on Earth. Saturn/Capricorn rule reality as it is on the quantum level, the structural illusion of reality, and the way time and space move and shift according to their own separate laws. Saturn also rules, for us, both the unseen truth and the illusion of our reality because Saturn is the molecular level of existence and also theories and ideas of E/earth. The truth is that everything on Earth is moveable and/or unstable on the molecular level and only by the movement/vibration (probably mutable Virgo-ruled on the earth level) of these particles do they create the solidity (Taurus) we are familiar with. Saturn also rules the human constructs and frameworks we invent and provide ourselves with to live by in a (so far) incomprehensible world. These constructs are somewhat illusionary but are also firmly attached to a whole human philosophy we've constructed about what it is we are dealing with here on Earth. Even though we can use the holograms of solidity as reference points by which to steer ourselves through our lives, they aren't the real reality. The real reality, and the illusion we perpetuate out of necessity, is ruled by Capricorn/Saturn.

    The schism between what we, as a species, have created with our human ideas about reality and the real reality is behind most of our fears. Fears are Saturn-ruled because our human fears are usually the result of not knowing something. We're always afraid of what we don't know or understand. What is out there: something that will confuse us? Change us? Harm us? What effect will it have? What will happen to our lives if life isn't what we thought it was? It is natural that illusion (what we know we don't know and what we don't know we don't know) and fear should go hand-in-hand, under Saturn.

The gap between what we want to believe and what *really* is keeps us from addressing, and ultimately solving, many of our problems, from our health issues to our ecological problems. We think of our Earth forms as unchanging and that everything will go on and be here, continuing tomorrow, just as it is today. This is not the truth.

Saturn, Ruler of the Earthly Illusion: Time

Time is another Saturnian reference point we use to function on our E/earth plane and another perfect example of the structural illusion of Earthly reality.

We believe that the concept of time, under the rulership of Saturn, is a basic part of life on Earth. We consider it part of our universe in general. This may not be the case at all. Physicists today are grappling with the idea that time does not exist on any level. This has come about because many of the equations they are currently using, including Einstein's General Theory of Relativity, to describe our reality have no place for the concept of time. These equations do allow for change, but time as we know it is simply not there. They can't find a way to show its existence and stay consistent with their theories. There may be no order of events in our universe or, if there is, we have not been able to find its true signature and integrate it to our satisfaction.

As Ernst Mach said: "It is utterly beyond our power to measure the changes of things by time…time is an abstraction at which we arrive by means of the changes of things; made because we are not restricted to any one definite measure, all being interconnected."[11] Lucretius's De Rerum Natura put it this way: "time by itself does not exist. Time gets its meaning from the objects; from the fact that events are in the past, or that they are here now, or they will follow in the future. It is not possible that anybody may measure time by itself: it may only be measured by looking at the motion of objects, or at their peaceful quiet."[12]

We started measuring time by counting the Earth's rotations and the movement of the Sun across a designated stationary graph, like a sundial. Now we find that even those movements aren't completely consistent. The Earth's rotation is actually slowing down about 2 seconds every century.[13] Earthquakes, and even weather, have an impact on the rotation as well.[14] Clock-time has always been nothing more than a human construct, definitely not an organic part of Earthly life. What does one or two o'clock mean to the other non-human, inhabitants of Earth? Nothing at all; we alone divide the day into smaller segments and label them so we can further manage our life, an organizational method for our convenience.

Time has other illusionary elements; it can be relative to our mood, our perception, or even our personality, as we experience it. We say that every minute lasts 60 seconds, and, in the same breath, we talk about how long some minutes are, as opposed to others. We all know people who have a different sense of time from us. They are always early or late for something. We have spouses who don't share our need to get something done now, before it's too late, or, conversely, try and rush us, when we think we have plenty of time left.

The concept of time is also different depending on where in the world you were born. Being part of a society (10th house and Saturn/Capricorn rulership) and learning its language also gives us our particular idea or understanding of time. Chronemics is the study of the use of time and the way we perceive it. This field studies ways in which cultures or societies differ in their perception of time. Two types of time measurement used in various societies are monochronic time and polychronic time.

MONOCHRONIC TIME

Monochronic is a time system where everything is done one task at a time. Time is divided into smaller, evenly divided units. Time is something to be managed and arranged and keeping to a schedule is important. The United States is a monochronic society. Our perception of time comes straight out of the Industrial Revolution. Factories were becoming a big part of our culture and wealth. A worker at a factory was required to arrive at a very precise time. Buyers wanted the items they ordered the day, or even the hour, that it was promised and no exceptions or they would spend their money elsewhere. Now, we use this carefully measured and predictable system in our day-to-day lives. We stick to schedules and, accordingly, expect everyone and everything - appointments, classes, repairs, even our entertainment - to be on time.

The communication scholar Edward T. Hall said that for monochronic cultures, such as the American culture, "time is tangible" and viewed as a commodity, where "time is money" or "time is wasted." Without the schedule, our business world would collapse.

Monochronic cultures include Germany, Canada, Switzerland, the United States, and Scandinavia.

POLYCHRONIC TIME

On the other hand, in a polychronic time system, time is sensed, rather than scheduled. Several things can be done at once as a part of the scheme of things, a large central whole. An even and precise accounting of every segment or moment is not that relevant. These cultures are more interested in traditions, not tasks.

Relationships count more than punctuality and they think nothing of arriving late for something if a friend or member of the family was visiting or needed them in some way. These cultures have very different priorities, so they are casual when it comes to calendars and schedules. The Native Americans see time in an even more fluid and intuitive way. They don't worry about what they consider arbitrary numbers or moments; when it is time for something to begin or "happen" they will know it and those that need to be there will show up. To them, a monochronic culture is too hung up on details that get them stressed out.

Polychronic cultures include Latin America, Saudi Arabia, Egypt, Mexico, the Philippines, India, and many countries in Africa.[15]

EASTERN AND WESTERN CONCEPTS OF TIME

Lera Boroditsky, an assistant professor of Psychology at Stanford University, has noted that if your first language is an Asian one, you might think of time as vertical and if your first language is Western, you might think of time as horizontal. Her theory is that English uses the horizontal spatial metaphors to express time (e.g., the good days ahead of us) and Chinese uses vertical metaphors (e.g., 'the month above' to mean last month).[16]

In Asian countries, especially China, language influences how people think of time, among other things. "In English for example, time is discussed in horizontal terms, for example, when one says "We are behind schedule" or "Let's move the meeting forward." In Mandarin, on the other hand time is talked about in vertical terms: Earlier events are said to be shang or "up", and later events are said to be xia or "down."[17]

Then, there was the discovery that the pace of life in each country can differ widely, leading us to feel that time is faster or slower, depending on where we live or visit.[18]

We do seem to be living in a place that has separated points of experience, whose sequence of events seem to move in a forward motion and, as far as we know, we cannot move backward in that sequence. Or, perhaps, it isn't time that moves forward at all but the creatures that live within a space, simply by moving forward, create time.

One definition of "time" could be a rhythm or pattern giving us a sense of movement that has duration and changes its speed and even its spatial shape depending on where you are born, your awareness, and what you are doing. Chronemics, culture, language, and self-awareness all influence and change our perception, our sense of time. Time seems variable, a Saturnian illusion, a human convenience, an integrated idea that is not real but we use it as if it is. If "time" was really based on reality, as far as we understand reality, it would be completely consistent and binding, but it isn't: nobody yet understands what "time" really is.

Saturn and Mythology

In Roman mythology, Saturn (known as Chronus to the Greeks, named after Chronos, meaning: time) was the king of the gods.[19] It is interesting to note that, although Saturn belongs to Binah, in the Kabbalah, the first and most high female energy, in our most common mythologies, Saturn is considered male. Of course, most mythologies known today come from patriarchal societies and so any god of great power must therefore, be male.

Astrology relied (and continues to rely) heavily on these patriarchal gods for much of its interpretations, so in the natal chart, Saturn rules the father. Throughout Western history, dad was considered the authority figure in the family, even when that wasn't true in individual situations. Throughout mythology, there have been cunning wives who manipulate, or even out-think, their royal spouses, but a goddess who rules straightforwardly over the other gods and goddesses as the ultimate authority is non-existent. In astrology, we have an equal number of female signs to male and yet most of the planets are named after mythological gods that are referred to as male. When it comes to its connection to astrology, the not-so-subtle perpetuation of male dominance in classic mythology has, in my opinion, also seen its day. Women are fast taking their rightful place of power, as equals to men, in most cultures. It is widely known and accepted now that both mom and dad are wage-earners, career people, home-providers, care-givers, and parental authorities. As an astrologer, this is one of the reasons I've never been comfortable using mythology as a subtext in astrology: it seems outdated and limiting.

Capricorn is a female sign, the ultimate authority over E/earth and anything relating to female. She is the queen of her half of the universe. The Tree of Life has one column or pillar that is male and one that is female. They are in equal partnership and their energies combine to create the middle pillar, the place where the world is whole and balanced.

By all symbolic rights, Saturn should be female, a goddess of great, and sometimes terrible, power. As we continue to develop a more balanced and equal attitude to the questions of male/female power in our society, how we will correct or reconcile this gender discrepancy in astrology is a question and one that I do not know the answer to yet.

Speaking of Rome, an interesting parallel to the illusionary side of Saturn is played out in the festival of Saturnalia. In ancient Rome, this pre-Christian "Christmas" party began on the date the Sun entered Capricorn. In the time of the Julian calendar, that date was around December 17th. However, our current calendar puts the date on the Winter Solstice, around December 21st. The festival of Saturnalia lasted about a week and many of our Christmas traditions have been carried over from this celebration. Gifts were exchanged and the night was lit with colored lanterns and candles. It was also a time when everyday masks were temporarily dropped and roles in society were exchanged. Everyone's status changed and everyone swapped their responsibilities for a little carefree frolicking. For those seven days, if you were a slave, you became the master. If you were a master, you waited on your slaves. All social and sexual mores were relaxed. Reality was turned upside down for a short, happy time. This is almost counterintuitive to Saturn's current temperate reputation.

A Small List of Comparisons

Based on the mythology, the physical characteristics of the two planets, the metaphysical properties, and the symbolism derived from these sources, here is a partial list of possible splits between the astrological energies of Saturn and Earth:

SATURN/CAPRICORN--EARTH/TAURUS

Earthly Concepts--Earthly Form

Earthly Essence--Earthly Weight

Earth Theory--Mass

Earthly Illusion(human constructs)--Solid Perception

Time--Consistency

Subatomic particles--Solid objects

String Theory--Structure

Abstractions (of Earthly things)--Solidity

Fear--Stability/Security

Unknowns of Reality--Known reality

Metaphysics--Measurements/Physics

Limitations of perception--
Limitations of structure/form

Refinement--Coarse/Raw/Crude

What we don't know yet about earth and Earth--
What we substitute in its place

On a more personal level:
SATURN/CAPRICORN
How do I create form?
How does my perception of reality influence
 or interfere with, my creating form?

EARTH/TAURUS
How do I work with form/raw materials?
With the results, what form does it take?

A Note on Illusion and Earth

I do not mean to imply here that Saturnian (and its sign Capricorn) illusion is in any way related to the illusion of Neptune. Neptune's illusions have nothing to do with Earth. Neptune is about that which is not part of Earth and separates us from our E/earthly reality and incarnation.

New Possibilities of the Higher Octave Planets in Astrology

Neptune, as we all know, is the higher octave of Venus, Uranus is the higher octave of Mercury, and Pluto the higher octave of Mars. It seems as if we could now position Saturn as the higher octave of Earth, lending a wonderful symmetry to our inner planets. Each inner planet would have a higher octave, 4 inner planets to 4 outer planets. Jupiter is the only singleton in this situation, along with our other "planet" Chiron, Virgo's possible new ruler. There is a lot of debate in the astrological community over whether Chiron belongs to the sign of Sagittarius or Virgo. Personally, I feel Chiron rules Virgo. The "wounded healer" descriptions of that planet, along with my own personal research, studying of transits, etc., has convinced me that Virgo is a good match. It makes sense in so many ways. However, I agree that Sagittarius is an attractive assignment when it comes to the mythology of the centaur, Sagittarius's symbol. I think the confusion comes from the fact that Sagittarius's ruling planet, Jupiter, may be the higher octave of Chiron, or even vice versa. These two planets do seem connected somehow.

Spiritual Earth

As astrologers or metaphysicians, we don't really consider the earth element very spiritual or define our planet Earth in terms of spirituality, leaving those labels to water signs or planets, yet its forms and functions still come from the source, the spiritual ethers of other dimensions, emanating down to a solid, object level. When we consider this aspect of E/earth, it becomes important, maybe even imperative, to embrace the idea that apparently solid objects around us can indeed be maneuvered within the spiritual dimension of Earth into some new reality, as long as we understand that earth is the element that works the slowest and most deliberate of all. There is no magic wand in earth and things don't appear or disappear spontaneously as a result of magician-like incantations. Still, changing your mind or your attitude has concrete results. The results are earthly in orientation, meaning that when our attitude changes, the earthly things or forms around us begin to change in an earthly way: our jobs are changed, our friends shift, we move our homes, we lose or gain money. These are the simple changes of every-day life and we are used to experiencing them. What we may not understand is the connection between who we are at that moment, what we are thinking and doing, the type of energy we are holding in our bodies, and those changes. The shifts are so gradual that we may not see how we have, personally, caused those changes.

    I believe that readjusting our perception of Saturn and, more appropriately, letting it occupy a loftier position in astrology, a higher-earth-energy function, can help us understand that connection and cause an awakening of sorts in our lives.

Changes in the Natal chart

After placing Earth in the birth-chart, Saturn started embodying the questions I have about reality. What are the limits of our reality? Does it even have limits? Where can we go from here? Do things really have to be the way they are? How much do I really know about the fundamentals of earthly processes? Am I using the earth element correctly in my life? How can I use my fear as a gateway to deepen my understanding or knowledge of life? How do my fears reflect what I won't see or am unwilling to acknowledge about life? How do my thoughts and ideas about what is real make my reality, and are they correct for what I want out of life? Do my actions make sense in the context of where I want to go and what I want to get out of life? What if there was no time as we understand it? How do I live more fully in the present?

In a more negative sense, how do I limit myself and my reality within my own mind and, in turn, my life? How do I delude myself about my reality? What more do I need to know about earthly life or acknowledge that I am ignorant of? What do I fear and why?

When we're having a reality check in our life, we're taught to look at Saturn transits, but when we are forced to deal with limitations, in my mind, there is always a question: Are these limitations really earthly, physical barriers, or are my own narrow concepts about the situation holding me back?

What would all this mean then, when we read or approach Saturn in an astrological chart or transit? It might mean that we should look there for where our perception of reality has been working or functioning, but is not, at its base, completely grounded in fact. This is the place where there are deeper truths about our reality and we are not seeing them yet.

Saturn's energy in the natal chart would show us where and how we have a flaw in our perception and are forced to face it and then discard it, in favor of real reality. No wonder Saturn transits can be so hard!

More Radical Shifts Involving Saturn Likely

It will be a long, and perhaps sticky, process to add a new planet to our astrological system, even if it *is* our own. More traditional Saturn rulerships may shift if/when planet Earth takes a more prominent place in astrology.

If we decide, as an astrological community, that the element earth rightfully belongs to Earth and transfer the more mundane earthly things away from Saturn to Earth (and perhaps Taurus), then Saturn, and Capricorn, can shed its Earthly mask and show us the illusions we have acquired over the centuries around both earth the element and Earth our planet.

There is nothing basic about Saturn; it is an outer planet. It doesn't belong in a basic earth function area, while

Taurus's simplicity and sensuality always bring us back to basics.

In lieu of Saturn's proposed ethereal nature, crystallization, a process that has always been under Saturn's jurisdiction, may more likely fall under Earth's rulership. Crystallization is the process of making something solid by knitting together what was once loose or flowing. One of the methods of rock formation, crystallization seems to scream simple Earth (Taurus) not a more advanced planetary energy like Saturn (Capricorn).

We can now see that Saturn is a loftier earth energy. Its position on the Tree of Life, in metaphysics, and even on the molecular level says to me that it couldn't be concerned with something as tangible and physical as the human body and some of the other things placed in its care over the eons. Taurus/Earth, and not Saturn, may be the ruler of the entire physical human body, more on this in the next chapter "Earth and the Body."

[1] Curtis Ed., Anthony . "Exploring Saturn." *Space Today*. Space Today Online, 2005. Web. 17 May 2011. <http://www.spacetoday.org/SolSys/Saturn/SaturnHistory.html>

[2]. Boyle, Alan.,"See Saturn's twin light shows." Cosmic Log on NBC News. NBC News, Feb 10 2010. Web. 6 Aug 2012.

<http://cosmiclog.nbcnews.com/_news/2010/02/11/4350413-see-saturns-twin-light-shows?lite>.

[3] Cain, Fraser. "Earth's Mass." *Universe Today*. N.p., 09Dec2009. Web. 17 May 2011. <http://www.universetoday.com/47217/earths-mass/>.

[4] Smith, Puck. Tree of life bahir hebre. 2006. Drawing. WikipediaWeb. 1 Sep 2013. <http://en.wikipedia.org/wiki/File:Ktreewnames.png>.

[5] Knight, Gareth. *A Practical Guide to Qabalistic Symbolism*. 2nd ed. 1. New York, N.Y.: Samuel Weiser, 1980. 87. Print.

[6] Bailey, Alice. *Esoteric Astrology*. 15th ed. Vol 3. New York, N.Y.: Lucis Publishing, 1997. 93. Print.

[7] Krips, Henry. "Measurement in Quantum Theory." *Standard Enclyclopedia of Philsophy*. N.p., 22Aug 2007. Web. 19 May 2011. <http://plato.stanford.edu/entries/qt-measurement/>.

[8] Anastopoulos, Charis. *Particle and Wave: The Evolution of the Concept of Matter in Modern Physics*. Princeton, N.J: Princeton University Press, 2008. 7, Introduction. Print.

In the book: "Particle and wave: The evolution of the concept of Matter in modern physics" About the images of matter in modern physical theories, author Charis Anastopoulos states: "The key principle of modern quantum theory is the remarkable assertion that the elemental and the atomic aspects of matter coexist. In technical language, this principle is referred to as the *field-particle* (or wave-particle) duality. I argue that the field description of matter is obtained from the development and refinement of basic insights of the theory of the elements, and in a similar way the atomic theory carries the conceptual germs of the particle description.

However, such identifications are neither simple nor straightforward. Even though a central thesis of this book is that the complex concepts of modern physics can trace their origins to simple and intuitive ideas, we cannot ignore the fact that modern physical theories weave these ideas in a distinctive and complex pattern that cannot be perceived unless one follows the twists of every single thread. If the atomic perspective of particles moving in the Void remains fundamental to modern physics, the three words "particle," "moving," and "Void" involve so many more associations and properties than their traditional counterparts that they appear substantially different. And whereas some scientists have seen in modern physics the rebirth of ideas about intrinsic powers of matter, the carrier of this idea is a mathematical object, the *quantum field*, which is so abstract in its character that its true essence, if such exists, remains hidden from our eyes.

[9] "Monster of the Milky Way." *Nova*. Public Broadcasting Service: KSPS, Spokane, Television. 19 May 2011. <http://www.pbs.org/wgbh/nova/blackhole/program.html>.

According to Einstein space is curved and made even more so by the objects of matter that pass through it. Matter warps space time. When I walk through space time it warps ever so slightly around me, but because I am not very massive it is so infinitesimal I can't notice it.

Time and Space curve and warp relative to such factors as <u>movement</u> or <u>gravitation</u>, but are also used in reference to more fantastic notions of discontinuities or other irregularities in spacetime.

Theory of Relativity. Nova: Monster of the Milky Way (Black Holes)

[10] Killert, Stephen and Wilson, Edward O. . *The Biophilia Hypothesis*. Washington, D.C. : Island Press, 1993. Print.

"Biophilia hypothesis." *Wikipedia*. Wikipedia, 11 Mar 2011. Web. 19 May 2011. <http://en.wikipedia.org/wiki/Biophilia_hypothesis>.

"Welcome to The Biophilia Foundation ." *The Biophilia Foundation*. N.p., 2010. Web. 19 May 2011. <http://www.biophiliafoundation.org/>.

[11] Barbour, Julian . "Scribd." *The Nature of Time*. Scribd.com, 25Apr2011. Web. 19 May 2011. <http://www.scribd.com/doc/53886013/J-Barbour-Nature-of-Time>.

[12] Healey, Richard Edited by Craig Callender, *Time, Reality and Experience*. Cambridge, UK: Cabridge University Press, 293. Print.

De Rerum Natura by Lucretius

[13] Suggested Reading:

- Ropeik, David. "Strange twists on our spinning planet ." *Mysteries of the Universe*. MSNBC, 19 Mar 2001. Web. 20 May 2011. <http://www.msnbc.msn.com/id/3077334/ns/technology_and_science-science/t/strange-twists-our-spinning-planet/>.
- Hamilton, Donald . ""The Geophysical Effects of the Earth's Slowing Rotation". *Novan.com*. N.p., 2006. Web. 20 May 2011. <http://novan.com/earth.htm>.
- Chang, Kenneth. "Quake Moves Japan Closer to U.S. and Alters Earth's Spin." *The New York Times*. NYTimes, 13Mar2011. Web. 20 May 2011.

<http://www.nytimes.com/2011/03/14/world/asia/14seismic.html>.

- Schechner, Sam. "Earthquakes vs. the Earth's Rotation." *Slate*. N.p., 27Dec2004. Web. 20 May 2011. <http://www.slate.com/id/2111443/>

[14] Suggested Reading:
- Cook-Anderson, Gretchen. "NASA Details Earthquake Effects on the Earth ." *Nasa News*. Nasa, 10Jan2005. Web. 20 May 2011. <http://www.nasa.gov/home/hqnews/2005/jan/HQ_05011_earthquake.html>.
- Weather Schirber, Michael. "A New Spin on Earth's Rotation." *LiveScience*. N.p., 25Feb2005. Web. 20 May 2011. <http://www.livescience.com/178-spin-earth-rotation.html>.

[15] "Chronemics." *Wikipedia*. Wikipedia, 09May2011. Web. 23 May 2011. http://en.wikipedia.org/wiki/Chronemics

[16] Boroditsky, Lera. "Does Language Shape Thought?: Mandarin and English Speakers' Conceptions of Time ." *Cognitive Psychology 43 Stamford University* 43. (2001): 1-22. Web. 23 May 2011. <citeseerx.ist.psu.edu/viewdoc/download?doi=10.1.1.11>.

(www.idealibrary.com) PDF file

[17] Kitayama, Shinobu. *Handbook of Cultural Psychology*. !st Ed. . New York, N.Y.: The Guilford Press, 2007. 573-574. Print.

Google Books: http://books.google.com/books?id=i-ZEIgFfXGgC&pg=PA574&lpg=PA574&dq=Asian+culture,+vertical+time+perception&source=bl&ots=oIZTyegDqv&sig=maPKNC42NRTDwpAZLM-Ste3Xwew&hl=en&ei=Lu6cTOb8OobSsAPWnu3VAQ&sa=X&oi=book_result&ct=result&resnum=7&ved=0CD4Q6AEwBg#v=onepage&q=Asian%20culture%2C%20vertical%20time%20perception&f=false

[18] Levine, Robert. *A Geography Of Time: On Tempo, Culture, And The Pace Of Life*. Basic Books, 1998. Print.

[19] The Greeks called Saturn Κρόνος (Kronos) who was the God of time

Chapter 6

Earth and the Body

"What we call reality is an agreement that people have arrived at to make life more livable." ~Louise Nevelson

"If there is no reason why something shouldn't exist, then it must exist." ~Murray Gell-Martin

On Earth and Rabbit Holes

When I began this book as a result of a short article I wrote for The Mountain Astrologer magazine, I was a little naïve. I was excited about the idea of including planet Earth in the astrological chart; something I felt was right, logical, and long overdue. Then, in typical Mercury-in-Gemini fashion, I didn't think too far ahead about the long-term ramifications or where my train of thought might take me. As I began to tease out the more mundane and solid earthly traits Saturn has always ruled, in order to give them over to the "new" planet Earth using astrological values, I suddenly found myself questioning some very basic principles of astrological thought. I didn't want to end up writing this chapter, I really didn't. As Lewis Carroll tried to warn us in Alice in Wonderland, once you go down the rabbit hole, there is no telling where you will end up.

As I have stated in Chapter Five, "Saturn the Surrogate," Taurus/Earth, and not Saturn, seems the logical choice for the ruler of the entire physical human body. The reason for this conclusion was obvious once I got past my traditional prejudice. The corporeal nature of our bodies demands kinship with our home world, Earth. The Oxford Illustrated Dictionary defines corporeal as "tangible, material, hereditament of material objects." In other words, corporeal means substantial and related to the material world. As we have seen, the characteristics of Saturn the planet are much more ethereal than our Earth. Since planet Earth is *the* place of material reality for us, and, similarly, our bodies are the most tangible and material part of us, they go hand-in-hand. It may be argued that no matter what the animal or plant on Earth, the body is always the crudest, the most solid, part of what are, in essence, fairly energetically, or spiritually, driven beings.

  I realize the idea of shifting the rulership of the body from Saturn to Earth is disconcerting to say the least for most of the astrological community and I include myself here as well. I do understand that this throws some of our most basic concepts right out the window. If Saturn doesn't really rule the body, then what does all this mean? It threatens some of our old reliable doctrines. Yet these kinds of shifts have always occurred when a new planet is introduced. Life is something that is never still. The sky and our reality, is always changing, and astrologers know this better than anyone.

I think that Saturn will still preside over some parts of its traditional areas of the human body, such as the skin. The skin is tangible, yet there is an illusionary aspect to it; it has a surface substance, making us appear solid, yet it is quite permeable. It also "contains" all our parts. The symbology there seems sound. The body part that stopped me dead was the skeletal structure. The Saturn rulership of the skeleton has always been undisputed, even sacrosanct. Structure in general, along with the crystallization of anything, was always definitively Saturn. However, when I began to look at charts of people that had broken their bones in an attempt to better understand rulerships, I began to see that planet Earth could also figure prominently in these charts as well as Saturn. Although this data is difficult to come by and not completely trustworthy because no one looks at a clock when their leg or arm is in tatters, this still makes sense from another perspective. The fact that Earth is permanently linked by opposition to the Sun in any chart and breaking a bone is a fairly traumatic happening to the self, it would stand to reason that the Sun, and consequently the Earth, would be involved in a "bone-breaking incident" transit to the natal chart. Anything that happens to a person that is life-altering in some way must involve the Sun by transit and anything that involves the Sun, with very few exceptions, would include the Earth.

Proceeding along purely symbolic lines, the Earth could eventually take center stage as the ruler of bones and the structure of the physical body. Many more chart studies will have to bear this out. As one friend pointed out, when we die, we are buried in the Earth and all that finally remains of us are our bones and our bones rest in the Earth.

While air is the mind, water the emotion and fire the electrical system that keeps the heart beating and everything moving, earth must be about the physical presence, the formed structure of the energetic creatures that are, in this case, known as human beings. Crystallization will also, in all probability, fall under an Earth planet rulership. It is the Earth, after all, that runs this process, deep underground taking minerals and compressing them into rock like structures or gems of great beauty.

As far as the physical body though, where does that leave Capricorn (and Saturn) and the other earth sign, Virgo? I specify the earth signs because the physical body is all about substance and form and therefore: earth. If the body in general (as illustrated in metaphysical and biblical writings) is the resulting manifestation of ethereal energy, a "Kabbalistic" last step destination of some spiritual essence, then there are more layers to our bodies, existing in energetic form on other levels or dimensions.

Levels of Physical Form

According to physicists, the physical universe of form is created by the movement or vibration of subatomic particles. The type and rate of this movement creates the variety of forms we encounter. Within this realm, scientists keep discovering smaller and smaller particles responsible for creating our recognizable reality. Will there come a time when we learn what is beyond the smallest particle and what will that be? At this point, it is believed that subatomic particles may give way to "strings" of energy. Metaphysical or philosophical disciplines have always taken up the reins where physics has dropped them, when it comes to discussions of energy beyond physical particles.

If it were possible to trace a physical object to its energetic roots, how many energetic levels of existence might there be and what characteristics would these levels reflect or explain?

It is reasonable to assume that where physical matter gives way to energy it would still be somehow bound or related to the physical object, perhaps by sympathetic vibrational levels. If the object is alive (like an animal), the energy might be one of the factors that drives that object and if the object is inert (like a table), the energy level might be the deciding factor on what that object would look or feel like. If we could stand within the realm of these energies and see them, would we be able to identify the characteristic energies or match the traits of that energy with its physical counterpart?

If the object is a human body, we can speculate that there may be matching layers of energetic material that are in partner with the physical form. These energetic layers may explain the physical form but also influence the way that form functions or doesn't function. Some of these energetic layers we know well: mundane levels of energies like feelings and emotions, mental attitudes, stress levels, etc. The astrological chart can give a read-out of these energetic signatures. For me, that is a big part of the information the natal chart imparts.

Genetics may explain why we are tall or short or have blue eyes instead of green, but the kind of energy we pull in, resonate to, hold within us, and consequently exude or express into the air around us has a great effect on the way our life operates and that ultimately determines the final appearance of our physical body. Whether we feel calm and happy or haggard and angry most of the time is etched into not only our faces, but remembered by every cell in our bodies. This is our energetic signature and it contributes to the health and efficiency of the physical body and even defines what diseases the body is prone to.

Multidimensional Bodies

Now we pass from the more accessible and tangible levels of energy we experience in conjunction with our bodies to a more spiritual or theoretical level of existence. These are the energy levels or signatures known in metaphysics as multidimensional bodies.

There seem to be dozens of names, descriptions, and levels for these various energy bodies with a lot of confusing and overlapping information on the many multidimensional bodies we are supposed to have and how they interact with the physical body. Beginning with Eastern esoteric teachings and moving right on through to some of the more well-known Western occultists like Madam Blavatsky, Alice Bailey, and C.W. Leadbeater. The latter two equated the astral body with our emotional "body," asserting that emotions had their own life apart from the physical.

These bodies relate to our manifested corporeal being but are the energetic components or more abstract portions of it. Some proof of the existence of an astral body is offered by those that have had out-of-body experiences or astral projection. The astral projection process is the act of separating from the physical body and traveling around using the astral body. Instances of interacting with other energetic bodies than the physical one may be: seeing or perceiving the aura, dealing with chakras and acupressure points, and even possibly feeling another's "personal space" or energy field when we are close enough to them.

There is conflicting information as to which energy body is the lowest or closest to the physical body. Some say it is the astral while some say etheric and some say they are one and the same![1] What *is* agreed upon is that there are levels of incarnation before the physical form on other, more spiritual or ethereal dimensions that are attached to the physical body and accompany it throughout its life. For purposes of this book, I am going to streamline, simplify, and label them thus:

1) Astral (highest = spiritual, where the body begins to form)
2) Etheric (midway = energy body)
3) Physical (lowest = on the earth plane)

Keep in mind that there may be many other bodies or levels that can fit into and around this list, depending on the discipline.

A Sampling: Three Earthly Levels of Incarnation to the Physical Body

If there are truly energetic levels that are "above" form, mirroring the physical in the etheric plane, then this is the category in which I would put the Saturnian rulership of the body. Symbolically, it fits better than the rulership of the physical form. Earth is earth, form or physicality, and Saturn/Capricorn vibrates to a higher earth level energy, so it would most likely rule the astral body or perhaps the causal body which is considered the highest body and the seat of the soul.

In astrology, the planets closer to the sun in our solar system rule the more basic signs. The "inner" planets, as they are called, when applied to human beings, are all about simple, straightforward internal processes of the life-form.

SUN: Consciousness and life force
MOON: Feelings and emotional nature
MERCURY: The mind: thought and communication
VENUS: The heart: love, social connection, expression of feelings
(EARTH)
MARS: Movement: desire, action, anger, drive, sex

The planets that are farther out from the sun embody more abstract and symbolic, less easy to define, concepts:
JUPITER: Belief systems, philosophy, rules to live by, exploration, growth
SATURN: (Traditionally) reality, discipline, restriction, responsibility
CHIRON: Wholeness, balance, health, sickness, connectedness and symmetry
URANUS: Universal Truth, independent desire, higher will, community, equality

NEPTUNE: Spirit and spiritual side of life, diffusion, relating, imagination

PLUTO: Death, decay, intensity, transformation

In our solar system, Earth sits between Venus and Mars. It follows that Earth should also rule something simple and straightforward, some kind of basic concept. Could that concept be the physical body of earthlings? Symbolically, Saturn should be in charge of something more abstract than a physical body or structure, those two items fit more readily into Earth (and Taurus).

Here are some proposed levels of incarnation of the human body and their rulers:

1) Astral Body

Saturn/Capricorn: Rules the body from on high, in charge of the body's energy level and its characteristic markers, the beginning of containment that will become our body and where the physical form emanates from. Changes to the body may first occur here and trickle down through the various dimensional bodies, or like the Kabbalah, may move back and forth both ways. This level is the highest energetic form of our physical incarnation; it would be our essence as seen or experienced from the most abstract or spiritual realm.

2) Etheric Body

Chiron/Virgo: The energetic body is the closest to the physical level of incarnation; also called the vital body by some, it is in charge of organizing and maintaining the vitality and health of the physical body.² This energetic body attunes and connects our consciousness to the physical body and to the other energies on other planes of existence that are attached to us, weaving them all together. It is the last stop of the energies from the higher bodies down into our physical consciousness and form. The chakras are found here, as is the aura. This works because of Chiron's symbology of wholeness and health. At this point, there is still a lot of speculation over Chiron's rulerships and alignments, but the majority of the astrological community is beginning to agree that Chiron has to do with (among other things) acknowledging and correcting errors in body/mind/spirit. There are many reasons I attach the sign Virgo to Chiron, but this propensity for showing us where our wounds (errors) are and how to heal (correct) them is chief among them. This is very Virgonian. In addition, the flip side of constantly cultivating wholeness, symbolized by Chiron, can be translated to perfectionism, which is a great desire to have everything just right, and another major Virgo marker. Virgo is the sign that best understands "what's wrong with this picture?" Virgo is the sign of the healer. The best healers are those that can look beyond the illnesses or maladies of the physical body to the causes or "dis-eases" of them. What gives a healer that picture of health or what tells them what is out of alignment and why? They see or sense on some extra level what has gone wrong with an unhealthy soul. They possess the ability to feel and work with that creature's energy levels. They manipulate that energy, finding the right "place" of ease where that being can thrive once more. This would mean tapping into and using the etheric level of a physically incarnate body.

3) Physical Body

Earth/Taurus: Here we have the solid form of our being. This is the vehicle we walk around in, the end result of the energies that have come from more ethereal levels, all contained and concentrated in one area (the body) with (in theory) the appearance, health, and attitude emanating from those other various dimensional levels. Once incarnated in a body, these levels of energy continue to flow through the body and into the atmosphere that surrounds the body as well as being contained within it. This sets up a sort of magnetic field, as well as an aura, attracting the same kinds of energy back to the body and person. The astrological chart also maps and explains this energy. Our bodies are made of earth and clay, as in the familiar funeral phrase: "ashes to ashes, dust to dust," meaning after death, our bodies return to the earth of their origin.

Earth/Body Consciousness and Our Western Health Crisis

In astrology, the Sun is the symbol of, and the repository for, the life-force and is carried by and animates the body. The Earth and Sun are opposite in the chart because one is life-form and the other life-force. (This is a tidy match-up to the Kabbalah's pillars of Form and Force.) They work in tandem as two partners in a dance of life. What happens to one immediately affects the other until death, when the life-force separates from the body, or life-form. While alive, the body is just as important as the life within it. There is a balance to be achieved here and that balance is called wellness or health. Here in the West, we are having a very difficult time maintaining the health of our bodies. Even if you haven't had the lecture (or worse, the diagnosis) from your doctor, you can't miss the constant rhetoric about the sorry state of health our bodies are in. It's on the news, in the bookstores, and on everyone's mind just about everywhere you go. We have issues with nutrition, obesity, and disease like never before.

Here is another indicator of a lack of Earth in our astrological charts and consequently a lack of Earth-consciousness in our lives. The astrological chart is the sum-total of everything that is possible to understand about the human condition, and Earth (our body) is not represented.

With the exception of the medical astrology branch of our discipline, when we conduct readings for clients, we generally do not enter into lengthy discussions about the needs and challenges of their bodies. At least I haven't noticed it. Unless a client already has a health problem or a loaded 6th house, it isn't something we spend a lot of time on. We don't place great emphasis on how the client's particular body is built, what state it is in and how they can work to improve this important component of their life.

In Chapter 2, "The Sun-Earth Opposition," I talked about the universal theme, the macrocosm, of the Sun-Earth opposition and how studying the opposition gives us another philosophical perspective about the duality of the world we live in. For various reasons, over the centuries we've lost our immediate connection and a more intimate relationship with our planet. In the process of losing touch with the Earth, we also lost touch with an awareness of our bodies, the earthly part of us!

Here is where we encounter the microcosm of that Sun-Earth opposition and have a very personal experience with that duo. The Sun, as representative of our spirit, and the Earth, a representative of our flesh, held for a lifetime in this natural opposition, give us immediate insight into how hard it is to be a creature of both. We are sick because we don't know how to maintain a balance between our spirit (Sun) and our body (Earth).

This has to do with personal attitudes that don't include any emphasis on the importance of the body and all it does and is doing for us every moment of our lives. We don't really connect to our bodies anymore. We have "out-of-kilter" ideas about what we want our bodies to do and we run the gamut of its physical abuse, from ignoring its needs to pushing it beyond its level of endurance, with very little in between. Most of the time, though, we just live our lives without thinking of it at all, and when it breaks down or gets sick, we are caught by surprise. The body is half of a dual system that includes our spirit/mind and, as such, must always be considered carefully.

Most of the health problems we now face have a lot to do with maintenance. Taurus (and Virgo) probably rules maintenance, ongoing daily work, an investment of time, nourishment, conservation of energy and resources that keep a machine, a planet, or a body going. Although the signs of Taurus and Leo are typically a square by aspect, when we look at these two signs as underlings to their oppositional planets (Earth and Sun) for interpretive purposes, we have a nice portrait of our dilemma.

At their most basic level, Leos and Tauruses both want what they want when they want it. For the most part, the human mind and spirit want comfort and pleasure. This is what we call "being happy." The body wants comfort and pleasure too, but the way these two get that comfort and pleasure differs greatly. The body wants whole, natural food in its most raw state and lots of physical activity. Our species evolved that way because that was what the environment offered, even demanded. Then we got a little too creative and invented the lifestyle we have now, a brand new environment of our own creation. We live and work in structures that separate us from the natural environment. Closed off from interaction with the land or sky, we can forget our true habitat for days, weeks, and even months at a time if we want to. Other than a bird or an occasional squirrel, most of us never see, or even hear rumors of, the other animals we share this planet with. At present, their images are only used to sell cars or breakfast cereal: something abstract, compartmentalized, and easily forgettable. Then came a little creative license with our food. We loved the sweetness in our fruits and vegetables, so we went on to extract it in order to eat it in greater quantities, invent sugar, and get diabetes. Then we extracted fat and oil, and discovered salt, high blood pressure, and heart disease. Over time, we started to think that if a little tastes good, more will be even better, and so here we are in the obesity era of our evolution. Our current health struggles are the result of forgetfulness and the ability to detach from our natural roots.

We don't consciously think about how our bodies evolved or what they need anymore. We don't ask ourselves what our constitutions would thrive on, what would give them energy and drive. The body is our earthly component, the thing that is still very much attached to the natural, earthly environment. It may be a drag, but we cannot dictate to our body what it should need: it needs what it needs. Our spirit/mind has needs too, and it's a balancing act of opposing forces between mind/spirit (Sun) and physical body (Earth): both needs must be met or the individual suffers and dies.

Our mind/spirit frequently overrides the body's needs on a daily basis and forces it to make do with what our mind/spirit craves. Our bodies are truly amazing because they work so hard to adapt and use whatever we give them to live on. We really don't want to eat vegetables; next to our invented and contrived taste sensations they seem pretty dull. The body can live on Doritos and Dr. Pepper for quite a while. Ultimately though, this takes its toll. Then we run to the doctor and ask for pills or a stomach stapling, or some other such thing, to give us our lives back.

Similar to Taurian energy, the body is fairly passive. Although set in its ways, it is tolerant, low key, and easy-going *for a while*. After years of being taken for granted though, it *will* dig in its heels and get most painfully willful and stubborn. It will have its day, eventually.

We may say that the mind/spirit is the steward of our body, a somewhat selfish, Leonian leader of our consistently earthy, practical, and stubborn Taurian needs. Yet, the best leaders make sure everyone has what they need to be the most efficient for the good of all concerned. We can no longer afford to be detached and forgetful of the earthy, physical side of our life. We must embrace the see-saw duality of human existence, the life of the spirit/mind *with* the attached and ever-present body. It isn't easy to have two opposing wants and needs yammering at us every day.

Therefore, the combination of Sun and Earth signs should probably be read and interpreted together at all times. I envision a future where the importance placed on the Sun Sign will always include the Earth sign as well. They will always be talked about as a duo: the duality of the earth plane and the duality within us create a mirror of each other. A living creature on this Earth is both a Sun and an Earth-ruled entity. This, among other things, is what the symbolic opposition of the Sun and Earth in the astrological natal chart says to me.

In the future, the question won't be "What is your Sun Sign?" It will be "What is your Sun/Earth sign?" or "What is your Spirit/Body opposition?" because (along with the Moon and Ascendant) this is the combination that will give a true (albeit abbreviated) snapshot of our being. This is our spirit/body combination, the dynamic that becomes one of the most important personal challenges we face throughout our lifetime. Understanding the give and take of what both planets and the signs they are in have to offer will help us in our quest to answer the questions of what we need for both optimum vitality of the body and a happy, or at least satisfied, spirit/mind.

For further information and descriptions of the human body with regard to planet Earth in astrological signs, see Chapter 10, "Delineating Earth."

[1]The Experience Festival (Global Oneness)

Global Oneness. N.p., n.d. Web. 24 May 2011. <http://www.experiencefestival.com/a/Astral_body_-_The_astral_body_in_Theosophy/id/611907>.

Astral body - The astral body in Theosophy

"Blavatsky used the term "astral" to refer to the double (*linga sharira*), which was the lowest but one of the seven principles (immediately above the physical).

Later however, C.W. Leadbeater and Annie Besant (Adyar School of Theosophy), and following them, Alice Bailey, equated the astral with Blavatsky's *Kama* (desire) principle (the fourth of the seven principles of man, and called it the *Emotional body* (a concept not found in earlier Theosophy).

In this way, astral body, desire body, and emotional body became synonymous, and this identification is found in much of New Age and theosophically-inspired thought since.

The astral or emotional body here is understood as a sort of psychic body or aura that is made up of emotions, just as the physical body consists of matter. In occult thought, emotions are not just subjective qualia, but have an existence apart from the individual consciousness, and exist on a cosmic plane of existence, in this case, the astral plane."

(2) "Etheric_body." *Wikipedia*. N.p., 14Apr2011. Web. 24 May 2011.
<http://en.wikipedia.org/wiki/Etheric_body>.

"The Etheric body" - energy ruled by electrical Uranus - "a name given by neo-Theosophy to a vital body or subtle body propounded in esoteric philosophies as the first or lowest layer in the "human energy field" or aura. It is said to be in immediate contact with the physical body, to sustain it and connect it with "higher" bodies."

Chapter 7
The Essential Taurus

"The Earth has music for those who listen."
~William Shakespeare

"It'll be no use putting their heads down and saying, 'Come up again dear!'... If I like being that person, I'll come up: if not, I'll stay down here...."
~Lewis Carroll

Taurus the Homeless

Out there in the Milky Way is the constellation Taurus, a sign bereft of a ruling planet, astrologically homeless for millennia. For many astrologers, Taurus is a bit of a lurker; just in the background with easy labels like stubborn, slow, or quiet assigned to it. I don't see anyone going to the depths with this sign. Most of the time, we give it all the regard of a comfortable, old chair. Taurus may hold its own in a natal chart, but many of the old interpretations make it sound more like a period at the end of a sentence than a dynamic energy to be reckoned with. While it's true that Taurus *is* the sign that can be tranquil to the point of inertia, it's all in the angle of observation.

Foundational Energies

The fixed signs Taurus, Scorpio, Leo, and Aquarius are the astrological foundational energies of their own elements: earth, water, fire, and air, respectively. Foundation signs are the backbone of any element and the fixed signs, by their very nature, are the most stable. The movement of fixed signs is similar to that of a spinning chakra, the energy moving around and around but staying in one place. This creates an intense concentration of any element the sign represents. Taurus is *the* foundational *earth* energy and really the base of our sense of reality here on Earth. Our most immediate impression of what is real is through solid objects or the way things apparently stay in one place for lengths of time. Our sense of touch, which allows us to feel solid objects, is how we know where we are, that we are here and not some other place. Having contact with something solid, like the ground, is literally our touchstone for reality. Taurus rules the senses in general, but most especially touch. With touch, we feel and know a solid framework describing this reality, laying out a basic idea (the feeling of solidity) of what is real. This allows us to operate from an idea of stability. We couldn't even begin to live our lives or plan our moves until we felt that everything was going to stay where it was yesterday.

In this way, Taurus is dynamic. Just holding something still that has a propensity to be in motion, like life, long enough to work with it could be considered a Herculean task. Creation may be a force, but we have to have form and consistency for progress or growth. Planet Earth is obviously our number one foundational reference point for existence through consistency and stability, and Taurus's energy is its equal match.

My fellow astrologers would be quick to point out here that Taurus already has a planet, the planet Venus, and to that I say: "bunk." Most of my astrological career, I've balked at the idea that Venus was in charge of my Sun Sign. The 150 degree gulf between Libra and Taurus isn't an easy distance to negotiate and it's a nasty, hard angle, as an aspect at that. My Mercury in Gemini is always asking: where is the logic in that?

Co-rulerships in Astrology

When a planet has been linked with a sign, weak or strong, the human belief in it over thousands of years creates an enormous amount of energy linking the two. So, any planetary connection with such a sign will only die hard. Tremendous Venusian energy has been invested in Taurus for eons, so Venusian patterns and influences continue in this sign, partly because Taurus does share some commonality with Venus. The reason why Venus was such a good match for Taurus in the first place asks the question:

In the beginning were the traits of Taurus that close to Venus, or did certain Taurian traits get emphasized because Venus became its ruler? It doesn't erase the fact that other planets may be closer to the true Taurian energy level, but it is natural that a spark of Venus will forever flicker within the sign of Taurus, even if we someday decide to assign Earth (or some other planet) to Taurus. The same has held true for all of the signs that once shared rulership planets with other signs and later found their home world within our solar system:

- JUPITER: once ruled both Sagittarius *and* Pisces, then upon planet Neptune's discovery, Pisces was reassigned to it. Pisces still carries some Jupiterian overtones.
- SATURN: once ruled both Capricorn *and* Aquarius, but Aquarius was later given to Uranus. Aquarius still has connections to Saturn.
- MARS: once ruled both Aries *and* Scorpio, but Scorpio is now ruled by Pluto. Mars still sits in as background of Scorpio.
- MERCURY: for many astrologers, Mercury still rules Gemini and Virgo, but the discovery, study, and integration of the planetoid Chiron into Astrology has shown that Virgo may be a perfect match for this planetoid. The dialogue over whether Chiron is to be the ruler of Virgo continues to this day.
- VENUS: in my opinion, the last of the planets with dual rulership (I have assigned Chiron to Virgo) Ruling Libra and Taurus and now, perhaps only

Libra. Taurus will historically, continue to have associations with Venus.

- EARTH: last I checked, Earth is in our solar system, but it has never been considered for rulership of any astrological signs (until now)

Of course, it is the very nature of an ongoing, dual-sign rulership that tends to, over time, meld together and blur boundaries between separate signs and their character traits. As a result, astrologers have gotten in the habit of ignoring or passing over the many differences between the two signs (Libra and Taurus) remaining under Venus's rather decorative roof. The planet Venus, historical co-ruler of Taurus, is the lazy man's match for it. Though certainly some similarities exist between Libra and Taurus, a closer inspection shows more holes in that pairing than the county roads in Northern Idaho.

The Quincunx or Inconjunct

Taurus is not Libra. That may seem perfunctory, but I think we all need reminding. I almost feel like a parent heading for a lecture as I say that: "Astrology is too old to be fooling around with dual rulerships." We have added Chiron, Ceres, Eris, and Sedna to our repertoire and still Taurus and Libra are uncomfortably joined at the hip. It's time to take a hard look at what these two signs have (or don't have) in common.

If you look at the two signs in orb as an aspect, you get a quincunx or inconjunct. What kind of companions can they be, when mathematically their natures are 150 degrees apart from one another? In my opinion, the inconjunct or quincunx is a major aspect that creates tension and discomfort. In <u>The Yod Book</u> by Karen Hamaker-Zondag Johannes Kepler is quoted as describing this aspect as "cutting sharply"[1]

Here is a quick glance at some great sample interpretations of quincunxes in Horary Astrology. Although horary charts differ from natal charts in terms of what the chart is describing, much of the interpretive information is the same. The negative power potential of the quincunx is really striking here. We get a host of actions that all predict difficult outcomes in a horary chart.

Meanings of Quincunx/Inconjunct in Horary Charts:
- A need for radical change and adjustment
- A definite "no" to the question
- An impossibility under the current circumstances
- Obstacles and/or obligations
- Discord

- Dramatic changes in life
- Dislocation, long distance travel, change of residence
- A health issue (in relevant charts)

"Inconjuncts were derived by signs once upon a time, the sign next or before to the one we care for, has no elemental affiliations and therefore no likeness or alikeness or even enmity. It wasn't a match, it wasn't an opponent, it wasn't a friend; it was a strange foreigner, a misfit, an inconjunct. The sixth sign and eighth sign from the one we care for, are similarly inconjunct as they share no connection (either good or bad) through triplicities.

This strange lack of connection between the inconjuncts made astrologers intuitively reach the idea that their influence is disruptive. Further studies proved – to some degree – that quincunx seems to bring an upsetting incident or situation and therefore is considered a negative aspect. It is an aspect that demands changes and adjustments." [2]

Here are signs that, when connected by the right degree, form a quincunx or inconjunct in the chart:

- Cancer / Aquarius
- Gemini / Scorpio
- Leo / Capricorn

- Libra / Pisces
- Virgo / Aquarius
- Aries / Scorpio
- Sagittarius / Taurus
- Capricorn / Gemini
- Leo / Pisces
- Aries / Virgo
- Taurus / Libra

As you can see, the action and attitude in each of these pairs is alien to the other. They have no sympathy by polarity, element, or mode. When you ask these pairs of signs to take action together for a common goal, they are at a loss. Consider a negative (receptive), cardinal, water sign like (private) Cancer forever tied to the positive (driven or public), fixed, air sign like Aquarius:

- Cancer likes to stay near home base or at least within the walled-off parameters of their latest project and tend their ongoing crop, be it a business or a family.
- Aquarius's arena is the public eye. They prefer interaction outside of home base, meeting many kinds of people. They want to study humanity and see what makes us tick.
- Cancer people process the world around them through their emotions, using their feelings as a filter to tell them what's what. How everyone else is feeling is

usually just as important as Cancer's own feelings because the temperature of people around them directly affects the quality of Cancer's attitude and surroundings as well. They use the past for perspective in understanding where they are going.

- Aquarius lives in the head. Open, intellectual thought and discourse are important, as it leads to important truths that may allow great changes in the way we conduct ourselves. For Aquarius, emotions are an inconvenience; they keep us stuck in the past, clinging to old ideas that have outlived their time. They want to stay pure and detached because you can't please everyone and they want the truth of any matter and change, even if it may prove devastating.

Of all the aspects, signs in a quincunx are the least likely to have any ease working together. Looking at Taurus and Libra this way, it's a wonder that they were ever paired up under one planet in the first place. With a quincunx standing between them, what makes these two signs so different? What makes a Taurus a Taurus? Let's start at the beginning of a Taurian life.

A Taurian Childhood

When I was young, I always wanted to be outside. Outside was more intriguing than inside, or as Anne in <u>Anne of Green Gables</u> liked to say: "There is more scope for the imagination" there [3]. Even though I lived in pretty typical middle-class neighborhoods, I always managed to find wild places in which to play. It almost seemed as if they were "made available" to me or maybe my searching made my finding them inevitable. Since I spent so much time outside, whenever I had all manner of troubles, it was there I found my answers. A sort of trust was established between the Earth and I. It was a familiar place with stable, repetitive cycles that I could count on. I craved a sense of oneness with the apparent peace in the plants and rocks about me. Yet the organic variety of Earth was always endless and entertaining too. In the fresh air, various scents slid down the wind, colors of every shade or tone were a treat to the eye, and bird song: cheerful notes for jangled nerves. My senses were engaged at every level, and it was an inspiration. The ground beneath my feet always comforted me, because it was solid. Trees don't talk back and it didn't matter what people said or did, or how confusing life was, the Earth's plants and animals were there just as they were the day before and the day before that.

When I got older, I began to realize that I could change my earthly surroundings. I could move rocks to more pleasing patterns or plant favorite flowers where I could see them more often. I could sketch and paint pictures that captured that beauty and reminded me of my forages. Shaping my world, to help create something from nature's raw materials, was an intriguing idea. I found I also had a bit of control over Earth's basic elements and, in the process of rearranging them; I could creatively make something that more closely matched what I felt at that moment in time. With this co-creating, I could make for myself a place with even more reliable beauty…and more peace.

Now, when I am out in my garden, or have finished a painting, I can see the tangible results of long hours of work. I have invested energy there and there is great satisfaction in seeing the work bear the fruit of flowers, vegetables, or mementos. It all belongs to me and me to it. With gardening and painting, I have, at last, achieved a kind of mind-meld with the Earth.

This is not a description of a Libra childhood. The expected hint of Venus in this scenario is the pleasure and creativity present in painting and making a garden beautiful. But even there lies a difference between creating something beautiful to share with others (Libra) and creating something for reconnection, reassurance, or sensual pleasure (Taurus). It is the intent that separates Taurus from Libra. Even if a Taurus grew up in New York City, individual relating would be with something more inanimate than fellow New Yorkers. Museums (a little of that Venus creeping in), parks, or just a favorite spot in the park would be sought out in times of stress. Of course, Taurus enjoys other people, but more one at a time than a group. Under some pressure, Taurus doesn't immediately run off to chat about it, they pull in. Pure Taurus is a true introvert in that they absorb energy when alone and give it off when with other people.

Libra is the opposite: an extrovert absorbing energy with people and shedding energy and feeling depleted mentally and emotionally when alone. If this were a description of a Libra childhood in times of trouble, this child would not go out alone into the woods for solace, but rather seek out friends to confide in or engage in some other busy social activity that would take her mind off her unease. Libra needs people, not plants. For them, the comfort is in interacting with other people who might share their dilemmas; a kind of "we're all in this together" scenario.

General Taurian Truths in the Human Personality or Natal Chart

The energy of Taurus can be described as *the* energy of the earth plane. The way Taurus works is really synonymous with the way things work on the earth plane. Their sense of what is, what is necessary, and what needs to be done (without sentimentality) is similar to the way nature operates. While it's true that Taurus adores comfort, they will not ignore practical reality to have it.

At the core of Taurus energy is one keyword: authenticity; to be real in every sense of the word. For Taurians (and wherever Taurus is in the natal chart), that would mean wanting to be real in what they do, how they think, and what they feel. This is the main contrast to Venus and Libra.

A short list of where Taurus is contrary or opposite to Venus and Libra:

Taurus:
- Doesn't mince words
- Doesn't go in for pleasantries, superficiality, or exaggeration
- Embrace "what is" and leave "what might have been" alone as much as possible
- Don't let feelings or desires interfere with practicality
- Dislike or distrust things that are charming, glossy, showy, or "prettied up"
- Have little patience for weakness or the inability of others to embrace reality
- Cannot comprehend short-term success at the expense of the future success
- Have an aversion to anything appearing abbreviated or seemingly rushed
- Tend to dislike crowds and/or parties

- Enjoy time alone or doesn't see a great need for socializing
- Has no desire to smooth over things that are less than perfect or have rough edges if that is their nature.
- Shy away from or are bored by intellectual discussion and deliberation
- Have definite or "fixed" ideas about everything
- Decisions are easily reached based on their facts with no waffling or insecurity
- Does not procrastinate or hesitate when the way is clear and there is something to be done even if the task is unpleasant.
- Are generally not pliable, cannot be sweet-talked into things
- Need the security of the well-defined or tried and true
- Doesn't need to get involved in a contest or argument
- Avoids controversy
- Relies on instinctual, gut feeling, not intellectual thought for their sense of truth or knowing
- Enjoys or finds comfort in a regular routine
- Attracts people or situations to them rather than leading or initiating action themselves
- Doesn't "push the river;" comfortable with the timing of things
- Interested in inward sensual rather than social outward pleasures

- Attends to unpleasant tasks first to get them out of the way

Where Taurus appears in the chart, there is always a pressure to be authentic; that is, to see what is real or true and walk that path even if friends, family, culture, or society says otherwise.

A complete comparison with Libra will be discussed in the Taurus, Libra and Venus chapter.

The Real "Typical" Taurian

To truly understand Taurus, one must move away from accepted astrological stereotypes or at least go deeper into them. Obviously, there are good reasons that stereotyping occurs and, in astrology, where would we be without our typical cook-bookish characteristic traits? Yet, if we get too comfortable, lazy, or dismissive, we'll never get to the heart of a sign's energy.

For one thing, some astrologers assume that the energy of a sign is only emanating *from* the individual with their Sun in a particular sign. In reality, I believe that the sign the person is born into also speaks volumes about the *situation* they find themselves in. It is the energy that surrounds the native as well as what is inside that person that makes them a Taurus, a Leo, or a Scorpio. The sign describes what is reinforced time after time in their experience of life, setting up the things that happen to them that then dictate what they are set up to learn and experience from life. That is what their Sun Sign is all about.

I also have an idea that a Sun or other planet's sign operates like a filter or a barrier, keeping those bits of reality that pertain to that sign forever in the native's magnetic field or surroundings and allowing other sections of life to be let go and forgotten. The sign is what gets caught in the native's (or planet's) sieve, what is always noticed, used, and digested.

Either way, what a Taurian experiences is that life is precious, yet uncertain and precarious. Remember that Taurus's opposite sign is Scorpio and (due to the dual nature of our level of existence) any Sun Sign is born with an awareness of its opposite embedded in their consciousness. The opposite sign of anyone's Sun sign acts like a bumper, guiding and giving the native something intangible yet instinctual to bounce their natural energy pulses off of, helping to keep the native down a certain path. So, Taurus natives want to start right off with creating something that stands up against Scorpio's world of disintegration and decay. As a child, they gravitate to things like building blocks and very quickly realize that if you aren't careful and take things in the right order, everything falls and you have to start over. Rather than quit, the fixed, determined energy of that sign will not let them give up until they have completed what they started. They instantly hate the feeling of wasting any time or energy which would mean a lot less acquisition in the form of physical skill, mental knowledge, emotional satisfaction, or material gain for them. They always want to feel some progress has been made and make the most of what they have. For Taurus, the inevitability of death is rallied against by collecting, building, or even hoarding that which whispers life, while Scorpio is born with a subconscious (Taurian) awareness of overwhelming excess in all departments, precipitating the immediate need to shed stuff and get down to what is essential.

Over time, the Taurian attempts to build invariably lead to moments of collapse, an action that always leaves those born in late April and May shaken. So begins a lifetime of worry that life means change and that things don't always happen the way you expect them to; this idea that, whatever your intentions, there are unknown and unforeseen factors that are always waiting to undermine your success. Taurians are left fearing any change they know full well could occur and made so much worse if they don't foresee it or plan on it. They learn at the beginning, on a basic level, that if they want something solid they must find a way of building things that stand up to these forces, things that stand the test of time. They must anticipate any kind of disaster that could lead to the destruction of their project and construct some kind of shield or back-up plan for it. They spend their life on a quest, looking for that which is permanent and unbreakable. If they can find it, they will feel safe at last from the uncertainty that seems to permeate the world around them.

Taurus becomes a bit like a chemist of the physical world, learning what ingredients are right for lasting quality and how to make any surroundings stable and consistent as a platform for the building of the object, relationship, lifestyle, or idea. Sizes have to match up, the work surface has to be conducive, and action must be taken in a certain order. Starting with blocks and slowly graduating to building the life they envision, make no mistake, unless terribly wounded, the Taurus has a vision of what their life should look like. They are planners. Planning a life makes the world seem manageable. Manageability means control, and control means safety and security. Of course, this is somewhat of a happy delusion, but as the expression goes: "If it ain't broke, don't fix it," an expression against wasting time that must have originated with a Taurus.

To obtain the life they want, Taurians follow a blueprint crafted in their psyches, ever-searching their world for items that must be located and secured: people, places, and things. Effort is made and energy applied when the time is right and for the length of time that makes sense for the results desired. Cost effectiveness is king. In other words, if the energy put in to a project is not going to produce the same amount of satisfaction when completed, the Taurian will see no reason to start it. The energy put forth must be proportionate to the end result. There is no action or adventure for its own sake: why take more chances when life is risky enough? They do not invest time or energy in things with little or no payoff and, if possible, they prefer insurance and guarantees. Like other earth signs, Tauruses look for dependability, quality, and longevity in every aspect of life. At their heart, Taurus always looks for consistency; something or someone they can count on no matter what.

Digging Deeper

There are generalities that can apply to any aspect of a Taurian life. It is always good to keep in mind that individuals are far more complicated than simple Sun Signs suggest and, as always, check natal charts for what kind of actions (planets) are tempered by Taurus, where (houses) these traits manifest, and how (aspects) well they work, since everyone has Taurus somewhere in their chart.

Of course, there are always enough people exhibiting astrological cookbook-type characteristics to display those recognizable patterns, but be that as it may, it is a little too easy to label Taurus as the sign that is "plodding, dogmatic, stuffy, or conservative." The truth is always more intricate. There are layers to these traits that have not been mined lately, if at all. It isn't just Taurus that has been short-changed by our sound-bite society; it is EVERY sign and planet, and house, too, for that matter. When we continually sum up astrological traits for brevity and convenience, over time we fall into comfortable, easy-pat answers, and our depth of knowledge is lost, leaving astrology open to criticism and more credibility problems.

If you are looking for a "look" that says Taurus, you may miss the less obvious. Of course, there are plenty of Taurian stereotypes around, otherwise there wouldn't be stereotyping. Keep in mind, though, that much of an astrological chart consists of the interior, not exterior, experiences of an individual and their reactions to them. In other words, what someone's interior language told them about the world because of the template (astrology chart) they were given. Many times it is an *intent* that precedes an experience of a Sun Sign that makes someone embrace the traits of that sign. Therefore, the *reason* the action was taken must be looked at. The Sun Sign is who people feel they are at the core, the place where they feel normal and truly themselves.

At the core of every Taurian is practicality, something that is normal and natural. There is an Al Stewart song called "If It Doesn't Come Naturally Leave It," a good title to illustrate Taurian philosophy. Tauruses have a need for things to make sense, and to see that things are in their natural state, so doing what comes naturally is what makes the most sense. Let things live as they need to live and operate the way they need to operate (This is what allows Taurians to accept the outrageous if crazy is, in that case, natural). When things are in their natural state, everything flows with ease. When that happens, there is consistency and then security. Taurus's way of wanting ease, of wanting relaxation, is right here. Luxury is simply an overabundance of flow, an overabundance of things making sense, of god-is-in-his-heaven-and-all's-right-with-the-world. Having things be natural is very practical. It is practical for things to be in their natural state; there is consistency and security. Monetary abundance is another way of saying all is flowing, everything is consistent, in balance, and nothing can happen that will be jarring, unpredictable, or ugly. All is possible, easy, and beautiful.

If we miss the small subtleties in signs, it can make big differences in understanding what is really going on with our twelve astrological energies. Skimming over something and giving it only a first layer value can leave us scratching our heads when we run into what looks like an exception, because contrary to the Taurian trait of "conservative," some of the world's most radical and cutting edge people were Sun-Sign Taurians.

The Taurian Salvador Dali

An example of such a "radical" Taurus is Salvador Dali, who was not only a Taurus Sun Sign, but had a stellium in Taurus! Who would match keywords like plodding and predictable to someone as avant garde as Dali? Yet he was quoted saying that he had a "love of everything that is gilded and (Taurus) excessive, [and a] passion for (Taurus) luxury[4]. Dalí was highly imaginative, and also had an affinity for partaking in unusual and grandiose behavior. His eccentric manner and attention-grabbing public actions sometimes drew more attention than his artwork to the dismay of those who held his work in high esteem and to the irritation of his critics."[5] If it became practical for Dali to be a little crazy in order to get himself noticed and his paintings sold, so be it. His unusual pictures set him apart and made him feel secure in himself. However, we know Salvador's father (as indicated by his Sun-Sign Taurus) had to be more conservative (he was a lawyer) and the strict disciplinarian that he was.

Dali's Childhood

Dali's childhood home was the inland town of Figueres, Spain where his father, a very practical man, worked as a notary. His family also had a second home on the coast at Cadaques, Spain. The family spent a lot of time outdoors, recreating in the Spanish sun. For all his Taurus energy, Dali had something of an identity crisis most of his life. Living an isolated and sheltered life in the beginning (Taurus), he was born into a family that coddled him and treated him as someone special because they believed he was his own recently deceased brother reincarnated.

This gave Dali an odd mix of arrogance and insecurity. He was always interested in who he really was and, needing self-examination, he embraced anything that could give him more insight into himself so he could feel alright about himself. He spent a lot of time looking within, one would assume in order to capture and secure the elusive, unshakable center of his persona, one that should have, by rights, belonged exclusively to him alone. By becoming obsessive about himself, he ended up a narcissist. Narcissism always lurks in the dark side of Taurus. Dali then used his paintings as a way to self-medicate and for self-exploration and, for the most part, his paintings were all about him.

Dali and Nature

Dali had his share of fears and they were a psychological force in his life. He had a few nasty surprises when it came to nature, as might be expected with his Sun/Mars/Mercury in a Taurus conjunction and of course, on the opposite side, Earth, in an exact square to Saturn in Aquarius in the 8th. Taurus would demand that a relationship with nature be strong, but aspects are the things that describe whether that relationship will be negative or positive. In this case, Taurus (and Earth) gave him a connection to nature that was very important, but difficult aspects to the Taurus sign and Earth set up a negative reaction to nature, which was still prominent in his life, just not very comfortable. So, being a Taurus, Dali often noticed and interacted with the natural world and his aspects foretold of great difficulty with it.

As a child, he picked up a dead bat to bury it and found it crawling with ants.[6] This unexpected and ugly occurrence frightened him and he forever associated ants with death. Grasshoppers were another creature he had issues with, their voraciousness reminded him of the way he felt around his father, like he was being eaten alive. He even attributed sex (another fear) to them. You see these symbols in his paintings again and again, standing in for fear and death. He didn't know how to relax and accept the unpredictability of life on this Earth, and the things he couldn't control frightened him. He was uncomfortable with himself and wanted to jar or shock others as he'd been shocked. Becoming a surrealist was the perfect vehicle for sharing his thoughts and feelings. His paintings were a cathartic release for him, showing people, in his mind anyway, the scary side of nature and of life itself.

Dali's Quest for Self-Understanding and Self-Expression

Salvador Dali was also very eccentric, of course, but eccentricity was his consistency, what he found comfort and security in. In Dali's chart, Uranus in Sagittarius (aspecting his Moon, Venus, and Mars, and then, consequently, Mars pulling in Mercury and the Sun) yields free and boundless (Sag) experimentation with truth. This, tied up with the urge to express himself in so many ways (emotionally, physically, and mentally) would yield a pattern of expression that told him: "when following a course for the permanence of solid success (Taurus), saying whatever crazy thing comes into your head no matter the consequences (Uranus in Sag) will work in your life and in the world of art," and it did. He liked to make up and embellish stories about himself (Sun/Mercury/Mars) and never worried that they were not physically true: to him, it was about the emotional truth (Uranus/Moon/Mars), not the actual truth. It gave him his problems, too, when he wanted to change any of these ideas, he had a hard time with it (due to the Taurian fixed nature). He always needed to relate to, but also stand out from, the crowd (Sun, Mercury, Mars conjunction in the 11th house), there was familiarity and security in groups of friends and acquaintances, which was another ground wire for him. It is hard to sum up the many complexities of a human being, but with all the squares to his stellium by Saturn, I am sure that in his mind there was a fear that if he did not keep up his rebellious behavior, he would lose the reputation that had brought him his status, and Taurus would cling hard to the success he enjoyed and the personality he had now discovered, developed, and was deeply invested in. The inability to face up to the realities of his eccentricities (Saturn in Aquarius) caused him grief and estrangement with his family, his father (Sun in Taurus) in particular. Still, it was *practical* for Dali to remain eccentric throughout his life. It was who he was at his core: a fixed Taurian who needed attention and to belong (so much so that he ditched his religion in order to join the surrealists, later re-embracing it), all the while using his work as assurance, insurance, and an opportunity to express, exorcise, and heal his fears of his father and the natural world.

Earth in Dali's chart is loaded with difficult aspects reinforcing in a big way that love/hate relationship he had with nature. The basic premise and bottom line of all Dali's Taurus and Earth connections was whether it was a good thing (easy aspects) or a bad thing (negative aspects), he was inescapably drawn to nature and nature to him. He couldn't ignore it even if he wanted to and his life and paintings certainly reflect that.

Looking at the lone sextile to his descendant says to me that his wife Gala did a lot to allay and sooth his fears. Still Dali also had a great fear of women and sex (typical of Saturn in the 8th, squared his sun).[7] He wasn't comfortable with physical touching at all, yet he loved his wife and was always loyal, in his fashion, to her.

Dali's intentions were to have a safe place in the world that gave him means, self-support, self-confirmation, and self-satisfaction. Notoriety or fame is always self-affirming if you put stock in what others think and with the 11th house planets and Moon on the M.C. (Medium Coeli), Dali did. These attributes, all attached to difficult aspects, mean that what he did to be safe and feel secure he did without thinking too deeply about the way the rest of the world would react, even if it worked against his own and his family's expectations. He didn't dwell on the ramifications of what he said or did; it was simply what he needed to do to survive. Having almost all of his planets above the horizon meant the public was always going to notice and respond to him. His life was lived in the public eye. Based on all the Taurian energy, he probably had a love/hate relationship with that as well.

It looks like a difficult task to reconcile all the Taurian energy around Dali with the odd outer circumstances of his lifestyle. In this case though, his chart tells a better story of his inside life. The Sun and the personal planets of this man don't lie. They describe Taurian intentions and how he achieved them and, in this case, they were definitely atypical. We can't know what it felt like for Dali to live the life he chose. It is easy enough to note aspects and the other factors in his chart that indicate diversion from normal society, but knowing what really drives a Taurus gives us an insight into Dali's very soul. Understanding the inner motivations of a person makes the difference between superficial skimming and a deep understanding of an individual, not to mention ending confusion over how someone like Dali could be a Taurus in the first place.

The City Taurus

A lasting stereotype for Taurus is the frequently used statement that due to their love of nature, Tauruses live in the country.

Obviously there are lots of Taurus people living in cities all across the globe. Again, for any sign's description, it is the approach to life and not the lifestyle that makes a Sun Sign anything. Again, one must look at the intent, the internal perception, through the Taurian lens. Although it can be typical to find a Taurus personality keeping to the country, there are many reasons a Taurus would prefer life in the city, convenience being number one. In the city, everything is laid out and there for you. You don't have to drive long distances or lose time and energy to find the things you need to get your projects done. The safety in this case is not physical, it's material and mental. Although peace and quiet is something that is fully appreciated by a Taurus, they don't have to have it. They are able to tune out the incessant noise that would distract or upset a more delicate nervous system like Libra or Gemini or even Virgo. Taurus is tough, at times even non-reactive. They take things as they come and don't think too much about a couple sirens blaring in the distance. Easy access to museums, art shows, and concerts would be thrilling to them. Still, the citified Taurian will always have plants on the window sill, or bowls of rocks or shells from the world outside their door. They may consider the noise and crowds a necessary evil. When a craving for the country life inevitably comes up, they satisfy it with walks in the park or vacations to national parks and quiet out of the way "bed and breakfast" surrounded by natural landscapes. Knowing that everything they will ever need materially is around the corner makes the city an attractive locale to a person who longs for that kind of practicality, and that in itself can produce the peace of mind Taurus is looking for.

Taurus and Nature

In the Northern Hemisphere, the sign of Taurus is in the month that pushes the Earth from slumber each spring, deepening a new cycle and helping it to take root in the land. Pure earth energy is elemental. For us, planet Earth is the place of birth for all things and is far more appropriate in the 2nd house with Taurus, the very first earth sign we encounter in the zodiac

For Taurus, nature has a seductive siren's song that not only lures them from their homes, but gives them the secret of their tranquility. This is another area where Venus has made some sense in the Taurian rulership because we are talking about a sign that prefers a realm of peace and beauty. Still, it may be argued that:

A) nature belongs to Earth

B) nature is most often beautiful

C) tranquility can be attributed to earth energy

D) earth signs are always looking for the stability that brings peace of mind

For Taurus, nature is always the inspiration for artistic pursuits (where they paint landscapes, photograph animals, or make pottery from the very clay of the Earth). In scientific studies, they will take on issues like geology, ecology, or wildlife management. Their musical aspirations might be geared toward capturing a sunrise with symphonic harmony or musically reminding them of a walk in the woods. The businesses Taurus would run, besides providing something very necessary to the customer, tend to be "green."

Nature, by its very nature, is calming to Taurus. As in my childhood story above, it is the pinnacle of stability, or at least it is perceived that way. It seems at rest, in a permanent and sleepy, slow cycle to us humans. One may count on its grounding abilities. More than that though, it is beautiful, giving Venusian pleasure in an *earthy* way. Taurus loves pleasure; pleasure is the best part of having sensory input. Nature engages and stimulates all the senses and Taurus is most decidedly in charge of the senses.

Taurus the Sensual

Mimicking nature and mirroring earth, Taurus presides over the senses, *exclusively*. Senses are the most basic, earthly thing installed in living things that allows that them to operate in this world. Senses bestow on every life some form of perception and this perception tells any creature where they are and what situation they find themselves in. Senses give us information about our immediate environment and help us in every way to negotiate our way through the day and through our life. Senses connect us to our surroundings, telling us what is real and what is not. They explain to us how things work in the natural order of the world. We understand basic and important information about everything around us. With that understanding, our senses then tell us how we should proceed. With our sense of touch, we can feel where our bodies are now and know where we want to move next. We can feel what is against our bodies and protect ourselves from the harm of heat, injury, or cold. We can take pleasure in seeing color change and move around the shapes of things to watch out for danger. We can hear the glorious song of birds or the wind telling us that we should pack it in when a storm is due. We taste our food and know what is wholesome and good to eat and what may be spoiled and make us sick. Smell also allows us to avoid contamination by warning us to stay away from what is disease-ridden in addition to delighting us with the sweet scents of mouth-watering goodness. They are our protectors as well as our entertainers. They are the basic operating system for ease of travel and health of any organism throughout its life.

The sign that is ruled by Earth should be in charge of this and all sensory input. The sign that rules these senses is the sign that understands reality at its most basic level because Earthly reality is brought to us by the senses. That sign is Taurus.

This also makes Taurus rather sensual. Having a more heightened awareness of sensory input makes one attuned to that sensuality. They want to experience it on every level and as a result they embody it. It's natural when a Taurus moves with grace because they can feel that an awkward, lop-sided gait feels wrong. They crave things that are smooth, soft, comfortable, and beautiful in every realm, physical, mental, or emotional. As an outcome of their rulership, they also want the things around them to be as natural as possible. On their table, they want real flowers, not silk. On their bodies, they want one hundred percent cotton, not polyester or man-made materials. They prefer houses made of wood and stone, not synthetic textures. This keeps not only their senses occupied and happy but their connection to the natural world maintained at all times, with earthly vibrations emanating in what they own, wear, or live in. Nature feeds Taurus's senses, bestows peace and tranquility, and grounds them into reality. Nature *is* life to them and if they were to get locked up in a plastic room for a year, I suspect they would shrivel up and die.

Fertility

Taurus has been associated with fertility and when attached to a ruling planet Earth, the reasons become pretty obvious. Fertility can be nothing more than a fixed lack of motion that allows something to *stabilize* and grow, or it can be a *wealth* of ingredients *collected* into a primordial soup of possibilities. Taurus stabilizes and collects and values what it has to the point of hoarding which can all contribute to fertility. Fertility also has to do with being in touch with earth, the basic ingredients needed, and understanding the conditions of any "soil" used so you know when to make your move for the best result. Taurus has these qualities in spades.

The Stubborn Taurus?

Stubborn is another word that comes up around Taurus but I think it is less "stubborn" than resistant. When making decisions, Taurus energy moves slowly, either physically or mentally, and this has been incorrectly distilled down to indicate stubborn and dull-witted. Taurus only resists change because they want time to assess what any change will mean in the long run. They are not against change; they just want good solid reasons for it. They want the reassurance that they are not going to go from the frying pan into the fire.

Resistance is that thing that says: "Before I discard something old and true in favor of something new, I need to explore any lasting worth or value that the old may still have before I turn it out into the street." As long as something has some value, it is still worth using, worth keeping. Taurians are the keepers, the holders of what is good right now, where Cancer is the keeper of what we used and loved in the past.

Resistance also translates into a faithful and loyal person that will uphold whatever has had value to them, be it a person, a pledge, a cause, or a thing.

However, there is some justification in assigning the stubborn gene to Taurus. Taurus is the sign that says: "Until I think it is the right time to move, I will not move," and no amount of prodding from anyone or anything is going to change that. It is also where determination comes from. Determination is what helps one stay on course until a task is done. The attitude is, until a course of action is proven unwise (to them, mind you), why should movement away from it occur?

This is another earthly trait, for nature does not discard a species that, due to changing conditions, begins to struggle for survival. First, it works on ways to overcome. Nature keeps and uses all that it is in a predictable, careful, and steady way, with the effort of evolution moving a species along, bestowing a new beak or a habitat adjustment without a true end to the species until there is nothing more that can be done.

Basic, not Blasé`

Ruling essentials, like the senses, Taurus is concerned with the basics of the life force. Taurus is the second sign of the zodiac, so one would naturally suspect the sign would be about beginnings in some form.

Aries begins the zodiac with pure life energy, wild and untamed. Taurus takes that energy and gives it a holding pattern, a starting place. Taurus is concerned with the foundations of life. In the context of the life force, Taurus catches the Arian incessant movement and holds it in place. This allows energy to solidify into some-THING. Solidity is Taurus's middle name, a most important quality for all life-*forms* because nothing could exist as we know it without it. When energy is held still, it turns the energy in on itself and develops repetition, like the beating of a heart, breathing in and out, conscious thought, reproductive cycles, seasons, orbits, and all manner of predictability and consistence. This gives life the ability to exist.

Foundations are, quite simply, the base of anything. This is no small thing. In building a house, it would be the conditions of the ground that the house will sit upon, and then the footings of the structure itself. Here is just one example of a place where you find Taurian essence manifested into something you can see and study as a parallel to more abstract foundational ideas.

The foundation, whether it has been laid down with thoughtful care or distracted haste, always sets the stage for the future success or failure of anything, be it a philosophy, a relationship, or a structure. As you might expect, with anyone who has prominent Taurian energy in their chart, there comes the ability and the interest to lay foundations of any kind. Taking anything on an energetic or idea level and manifesting it into the material realm is Taurian. This parallels, for us, the essence of our planet Earth. This planet is where everything is caught, manifested, made solid, and exists.

While also preserving that which has value, the development and stability of tried and tested ideas, projects or people are the Taurus's life task.

Value

Although Taurus is always associated with money, I think about that aspect of the sign more in terms of value. Nature is concerned with value. It has a web of life, in it each life-form, no matter how small, has a place. Each life-form has worth: even the rocks themselves are necessary. Everything contributes to the whole. Nothing is overlooked.

The eco-system of the Earth was designed just like a set of blocks, each one stacked on top of another from this age to that, from millennium to millennium, each block holding and contributing something essential to the whole. Our Earth planet also holds anything of value until that value is at an end and so does Taurus. Value is an important keyword that belongs exclusively to Taurus and it isn't used enough in conjunction with the sign. Taurus is all about value: what is valuable, why is it valuable, how valuable is it and how can I hold and preserve its value? Taurus instinctively knows the answers to all these questions. Value is worth. It's not just what people are willing to pay for something, it's what that something can contribute to a situation. Taurus assigns value to everything:

- By productivity and endurance: how many and how much will I get out of this?
- By stability and longevity: Is it strong and durable? How long will it last?
- By usefulness: How many ways can I use it? Does one thing have other uses?
- By beauty and luxury: how good does it make me feel? How much joy do I get from it? How attractive is it so that others may want (and buy) it?
- By effectiveness and satisfaction: Is it accurate? Does it do a good job? Does this do the job and even more than originally thought?

Taurus is the sign or the essence that ascertains whether something or someone is worth its own advertisement.

Self-Concern

Self-concern is often mistaken for selfishness. Self-concern and selfishness (or even the extreme Narcissism) are two sides of the same coin, but one side is positive and one lives on the dark side. Taurus is a self-concerned sign, but that isn't necessarily a bad thing. All of the personal signs (Aries through Virgo) tend to be focused on the self or individual, just as the public signs (Libra through Pisces) focus on others and the outside world. Self-concerned simply describes the motion of the sign's energy; where it is supposed to go and what it is supposed to do. Being self-concerned means that the nature of this sign is to first study, understand, and improve the self, with outward expression or exploration coming later after the self is developed. The public signs seek expression immediately with other people and other people's needs, leaving holes in the individual's awareness to be filled in later. Self-concern is not inherently selfishness. Selfishness is an obsession, a sickness, or a laziness that keeps an individual focused on the self out of some fear or some feeling of lack that instills in that individual the idea that they will never have enough so they must grab all that they can. Selfishness is never thinking of others. On the other side, philanthropy is a wonderful thing, but not in the extreme and at the expense of individual growth. How much can one person give when they haven't taken the time to hone their skills, sharpen their intellect, or deepen their hearts? This is what the personal signs concern themselves with.

Proper use of self-concerned energy has to do with balance. It is proper and healthy to attend to one's own needs. If someone is always giving their energy out to others and never recharges, they will soon be burned out and have nothing left to give. Joy and vitality are gone. If one is always giving to oneself with no thought of others, they have no outside stimulus to open them up and inspire them and they become lonely, miserly, and miserable. The trick is to give to both one's self and one's community in whatever proportion feels right, never completely taking sides with one or the other. When self-concern is balanced with generosity, everyone wins.

Conservation

A typical cookbook description of Taurus always alludes to how slow or lazy Taurus is. Again, sound-byte thinking has allowed us to skim over and superficially label something without considering the true functionality of the energy. Taurian energy is not, by rule, lazy. This label comes from the fact that they like ease. There is no doubt that a trademark of the planet Venus is ease. Venus picks the way that has the least resistance, the best flow, because that is the smoothest, "nicest" way to go. Venus (and Libra) detests blocks or barriers and that feeling of having to push oneself against something or someone (just the opposite of Mars of course). Venus looks for and craves harmony. Taurus has embraced a good portion of that need for harmony.

I suspect, though, that the Taurian side of Venus's sympathetic love of ease may stem from a need other than the Libran "go with the flow" kind of harmony. Taurus is not the most energetic of signs. In fact, I wonder if they aren't the sign with the lowest energy in the zodiac.

Remember, Taurus is fixed earth and has all the energy of a rock. Despite my sarcasm here, I really don't mean it in a negative way. A rock's energy is simply contained. A rock's energy isn't in what it does, it is in what it maintains. Its strength comes from sustaining a tremendously dense and seemingly impenetrable form. The strength is passive, not active, until you try to hit it and break it.

Tauruses hold their energy and their strength in reserve and it is considerable, but it follows that they only have so much effort that they can apply to daily life. This is not weakness, it is only that their energy is like a deep pool and Taurian people aren't always able to tap into it for immediate use: it sits there in reserve, not easily accessible. When times get rough, when there is a need, Tauruses can hold their own: they are survivors. Yet because of the energy that is set aside, almost dormant, the rest of the time, they are at a disadvantage.

Having limited energy then, Taurus quickly learns to collect or conserve. Conservation is a Taurian word and idea. The concept of spending what you have in a step by step, slow and practical way, to hold some back in reserve and never over-extend and end up with nothing, or find yourself in the way of "too little too late". Taurus has an instinctive, abject fear of "not enough" and "too late."

So, as Tauruses go along their merry way, they avoid distractions. They simply cannot afford to be pulled away from their business, their thoughts, or their goals. There is a need to be a bit insular to get where they are going. To get too involved in something that doesn't directly concern them, to go fight another's battle, or join some cause, that's just too much busy work, too much trouble, energy that can't be spared. Their actions become deliberate: one step at a time, while they weigh what reserves are in the balance. They need time alone to recharge and to think and process and take inventory on what they will need and what they have left. They are cautious. Their movements are usually slow and steady, but this isn't because they are lazy or even dull; it's to ensure that they have enough energy left to finish whatever they start. Sometimes slow and steady action has another perk: it lends itself to absorbing and understanding things in more depth than others who move faster. There isn't much they are unprepared for, and there isn't much they overlook or miss when it comes to their own business. However, they can be very ignorant of what others are thinking and feeling.

Taurus oversees all types of conservation: the inner conservation of their own energy, but also the outer form, a kind of conservation one would expect from a sign that is ruled by Earth. Conservation of the Earth and its resources is on the mind of every environmentalist these days. Earth-ruled Taurus is in charge of this. They are in touch with Earth processes and understand why resources cannot be squandered and wasted. They understand that there are finite amounts of useable material and are at a loss as to why others don't see the danger in overextending the use or even ignoring the reality of our world of limited resources.

Taurus is always practical. Taurus asks: "If we are to survive, what is practical about using up everything that is sustaining life for the glory of a moment?" All earth signs are interested in investing in long-term vitality, just like Earth the planet. What is the point of all the energy invested if it is all gone to nothing in a year or two? Our planet invests its energy to insure that all will continue. It protects, *conserves*, and doles out what it is able to or what is needed for future life. This is what we must learn to do, too. Taurus works to avoid the pain and discomfort that comes from poor planning and they never ignore facts because they know that won't change them. The way Taurus (and the Earth) functions can show us the way to a brighter, comfortable, and continuing future for our environment and all life.

Willpower and Determination

Taurian people are blessed with a great and natural willpower if they choose to use it. Between the resistance factor and the holding in or containment of their "earth rock" energy, the result is a force of nature they can tap into that becomes a block wall of impenetrable strength. As far as contained energy and the silent stillness available to them, they are probably the strongest sign in the zodiac in this respect. They are survivors because they can "wait it out" until the end of time, if necessary.

Common Sense

Common sense is literally "common" or collected knowledge that has been held onto for so long as to become instinct or a sense. Having been tested over time, this knowledge is accepted as useful or correct and is consequently utilized by people all the time. Taurus is tapped into this reservoir as a direct result of their desire to follow what is tried and true. What has always worked in the past is good enough for them.

This contributes to the Taurian hold on what is practical at all times. They will always see what is logical in any situation and head in that direction. They can easily spot something flimsy because it deviates from the formula. This applies to phony people too. They aren't usually taken in by charm or manipulation. They don't get bewitched but they can be too trusting once a relationship has been established. Since they aren't devious, they don't immediately suspect another might be.

Comfort, Luxury and Pleasure

Taurus is *the* sign that craves comfort. This trait has become mixed up in Libra/Venus's love of ease. There are slight motivational differences between ease and comfort. Ease implies no resistance, a lack of opposition or tension. Libra does not handle conflict well, so the driving need for a lack of tension in and around Libra means that resolving differences between opposing forces becomes an essential Libran skill; hence their flair for diplomacy.

Pleasure, for Taurus, is knowing what they want, why they want it, and how to get it and if when they find that something, if it is decorated in a beautiful way, pleasing the senses, even better.

Comfort, on the other hand, is a lack of need or necessities; having all that one requires in order to live a good life; a desire for protection against any afflictions (cold, hunger, poverty, or filth/disease) that keep one from a state of contentment. A result of security is comfort and extreme comfort is luxury.

Security

Taurus's need for security is legendary. Some explanation was offered at the beginning of this chapter, where I mentioned that Taurus carries around (sometimes unconsciously) the knowledge that life is precarious. They want to fortify their existence and anything they create against this fear of what they deem is abstract chaos or a slide into nothingness. Using the idea of investment, we can see that Taurus would ask: "What is the point of all my efforts if I can't see that there is enough stability here to sustain it? I will not waste my energy if it is all for nothing." They want guarantees. This is the basic, central, underlying force that drives the Taurus. They attempt to create guarantees through ownership and possession. They own material things because they are solid and therefore must be real and will last. They are a talisman against nothingness. If I have possessions, I can count on them to be there day after day; I have proof that life is indeed stable.

If you possess something, you also control it. Here is where the line between Taurus and its opposite, Scorpio, gets a little blurry. Both signs have tendencies to micro-manage things in their life because if they are in control, then they can directly influence the action and, especially in Taurus's case, anticipate any problems and keep things easier to deal with; that is, safe.

Scorpio tends to control people or situations, while Taurus tends to control property. Taurus controls through ownership: "Hey! That is MINE and I'll do what I want with it, so hands OFF!"

Scorpio controls through manipulation: "If I say this particular thing or take action this way, then people will react the way I want them to and the situation is in my favor."

A Taurus that has absolutely no control over the wild winds of fortune in his life is a very unhappy being. On the other hand, they don't have a problem bowing to authority, but only if they can trust them to be sensible. They would rather "experts" be in charge anyway, as this relieves any burden of blame from their shoulders should something go wrong. More importantly, if they are working for someone who knows what they are doing, Taurus can just mind the business at hand, do the one thing assigned to them, and let the others worry about the big picture. They really don't like to lead; it's too much bother keeping tabs on all those details and "what ifs." They don't want people looking up to them, either. They are uncomfortable with flattery, as they know nobody is perfect and it's just a matter of time before any "building blocks" they put up will fall down and then there is sure to be trouble. If the person in charge proves hapless, though, Taurus's practicality won't have a problem stepping in and, through necessity, grabbing control and running the place.

They will adopt accepted philosophies or religions that have been established long before they came around, since, having been tried and tested, they must be right. They rely on family that has been there for them their whole life and friends who are loyal no matter what. These are the things that Taurus pursues: consistency and order. Here is safety. Here is predictability. With a hold on reality that is based on volatile things like the rules of society, relationships, and transitory matter means that, for Taurus, when things change (as they are wont to do), Taurus will be threatened. They will cling to what they have known; a life preserver against the chaos they can see before them. It is very hard for them to give up the safety of the known for the unexplored and therefore unsafe, *un*known, even when what they have isn't working so well anymore. Still, at least they understand the old ways. For Taurus, tried and true means security, safety, and sometimes a pretty mundane existence, which leads us right into the negative side of Taurus.

Taurus: The dark side

No section on interpretation would be complete without looking at the dark side of the sign in question.

Negative traits of any sign come into play with an incorrect use of their energy.

This occurs when:

1) The energy or sign is not understood well enough and then misapplied.

2) It is taken to the extreme and, as a result, thrown out of balance.

Any sign, planet, or house energy is vulnerable to being misunderstood and misapplied in someone's chart. Any energy taken to the extreme is out of balance:

- Capricornian restrictions can be seen as a wall to progress instead of a structure that one must learn to work within for the best result.
- The Piscean need for fantasy is best used to imagine a new reality, not escape from it.
- Gemini's craving for new facts or ideas should be utilized only when the need arrives for them, not run on a loop so that the native is caught up in one long distraction.
- Scorpio's penchant for getting down to essentials can lead to the extreme of getting rid of anything and everything, following the "throwing the baby out with the bathwater" scenario.
- The Aquarian idea of breaking down old, outdated rules can lead to breaking down everything for its own sake and ends with total anarchy or chaos.

- Arian action can become purposeless, non-stop activity ending in complete exhaustion.
- Constant Cancerian care-giving leads to personal burn out.
- The Sagittarius exploration of the "hill beyond yon hill" disallows any attention to important or imperative details here and now, that need tending.
- Virgo, on the other hand, can get so lost in the perfecting of daily minutia they lose all perspective.
- Leo's passions can easily mushroom into fanaticism.
- Libra's desire for living a gentle life can create one of complete passivity and superficiality.

Sign and planet characteristics bestowed on any individual are talents to be recognized and utilized, tempered with the knowledge of how and when to use them, not hyper-extended or sucked dry.

Security Issues or the Paralysis of Fear - Immovable and Resistant

When Taurian energy is misunderstood, it carries a signature of fear.

The very basic Taurian need for security, stemming from that original subconscious feeling that life is fleeting and tends toward chaos, can constitute a climate of fear and the worst of Taurian motivations are a result of that fear.

Holding onto that which has worked before can be a very good idea when appropriate, e.g., building a skyscraper, meeting new people, places where the tried and true are not only comforting but even expected. Yet, life is change. To stay vital, vibrant, and alive, life moves forward, growing and changing all the time. This includes human life and throughout a lifetime it is helpful, nay crucial, that a person change first physically and then mentally. Change requires a leap of faith; a crossing from what has been known to that which is unknown.

When fear enters into any situation, you have a person (especially a Taurus person) who will instinctually cling to the past and its apparent predictability because going forward into the unknown is just too scary for someone who wants guarantees.

Sometimes this fear is a result of simply coming to the end of known ideas or paths for a Taurian person. Within its normal range, Taurus enjoys (metaphorically) building with materials readily available, in an accepted way, with what is in the present surroundings already. They don't go in search of new material or ideas; they are not explorers like Aries or Sagittarius. So what do they do when they have nothing left to construct? It may not be natural for them to forage for new items to add to their arsenal and even less natural to adopt a new stance on some point, but they can do it, as the song says, when they "do it their way."

The Importance of Understanding and Working with Unique Astrological Signatures

The trick for any Sun Sign (or charted) persona is knowing when a particular type of action is appropriate. Sign or planetary energy is a tendency; it is not locked into someone's action without any chance of manipulation on their part.

People with fixed water or earth signs can always begin new sequences even if they are not natural initiators, just as signs who are initiators - (generally speaking) fire, air, or cardinal signs - can stop exploring and build on something as long as they are using their own unique methods of astrological operation.

Natural tendencies can be worked around by including steps that make that sign feel comfortable through a compromise. For example: in order to stay focused and stick with a long assignment, cardinal, mutable, fire, and air signs have to find ways to avert boredom. This may entail breaks in any routine that is conspiring to bog them down and make them restless. Another ploy might be doing things out of an established order to keep them challenged, etc., or whatever works for them.

Fixed, water, and earth signs, when called upon, can explore new horizons; they can change and adapt in their own fixed, earth, and water way. For Taurus (or any earth and sometimes water signs), exploring would be slow and steady, one step at a time. They would employ calculated risks to keep to their comfort zone and make sure certain safety measures are in place. Mutable, and to some extent water, signs would do well to find other people to support and work with them.

When Taurus, or any sign, doesn't understand their unique way of doing things, such as having a choice in the way they change, a choice in the process, and instead feel that they must adhere to more standard methods of operation, they will clench up in fear, thinking they must either run headlong into it or stay where they are at until atrophy sets in. The other Taurian tendency to fall back into a basic pattern seduces them into not wanting to know too many new facts that might complicate their simplistic, and therefore comforting, stance. If they choose this path, they may become unable to ever learn or act on anything new, ultraconservative, dull-witted and stagnant, backing away from life.

Ownership and Hoarding

For Taurus, ownership is another way of securing something, to have it consistently there for them. Taurus sometimes goes way beyond material items and wants to own inappropriate things, like people. Once again, it is fear that is the motivating factor, an idea that if they don't own this person, controlling everything they do or say, they might challenge Taurus too much or even leave the relationship. Of course this is irrational and usually guarantees the very result they feared, but whoever said emotions were rational? In this case, the Taurus must find their own trust in whatever happens; that it will be in their best interest. Real love can only exist when there is freedom and trust.

Another pitfall of obsessive ownership is hoarding. Over-collecting and storage of things one doesn't really have a need for: hoarding is an emotional compulsion stemming from a feeling that one never will have enough. Again, hoarding can involve anything from material items to people.

It is overcompensation for inadequacies, real or imagined, in one's self or one's life. When Taurus people cannot give themselves enough credit, comfort, love, or support, they will overcompensate with collecting. The results can leave them feeling stifled and trapped under a mound of stuff or a crowd of people that don't contribute in any healthy way to their life.

Ownership and security can also become all about money and then it's anything for a buck. The more money they have, the stronger they feel they are. They suffer from the illusion that enough money can solve any problem.

Selfishness and Sensual Pleasure

The negative side of Taurus definitely includes selfishness. As afore mentioned, being a personal sign automatically insures that their first priority or their first concern is with the self. This can be self (small s), as in self-obsessed with their own small concerns, or Self, (large s) meaning an awareness of their path and their charge to grow into a mature, well-rounded human being. Like any personal sign, how that concern of self materializes, is up to them. When they choose the small self, Taurus can be petty, power grabbing, money-making, and all for themselves. This spills over into the sensual area, and then we have a person who is all about their own pleasure and how they want everything to feel good to them with no thought about another's discomfort or needs. Hedonism is a Taurian word. They will crave foods or drinks that make them feel good, like chocolate or alcohol, and not care what it does to their health. They will become didactic in their opinions or habits because their own ideas are what makes them comfortable and they see no reason to change or even compromise. The love of ease they acquired from Venus can trigger a craving for convenience that stands in the way of living life to the fullest. Convenience is not the essence of a life well lived.

Taurian Creativity: The Banker and the Artist

Lastly, there is a certain dichotomy in the sign of Taurus, an apparent surface inconsistency that I wish to analyze here because it has been a source of some confusion. Taurus energy, as we've discussed, is about the simplicity of getting back to basics, yet in conjunction with those basics there is a sensual, rich, and lush creativity. Like Earth and nature, animals and plants have a basic job to do: live, reproduce, die, and contribute to the Earth's fertility. Yet nature accomplishes this with infinite creativity and much beauty.

Within typical Taurian occupations there is a list that includes both the banker and artist. How do you reconcile these two seemingly divergent outcomes of human experience? By looking inward again, at intention, and also going deeper into what these occupations have in common.

The first intersection between bankers and artist is in the realm of that Taurian exclusive: value. Both artists and bankers must understand what makes something valuable. The artist captures and expresses value (sometimes with beauty or wonder) and then perhaps can sell his/her work for money. The banker must invest wisely in what he/she is anticipating will ultimately have value with the resources he/she has at his/her disposal. The artist uses his/her resources by rearranging them to produce something of value either to himself/herself or to others so that they will be inspired and have the reaction that the artist has anticipated or envisioned. Taurus's understanding of value also makes them a natural in the banking business or any business. They can't abide nonsense; that is, things that don't make sense but they also want to make *cents* too.

Taurus is one sign that is very concerned with basics, the foundation of anything. Gathering resources or raw materials is always the most practical way to begin and they make sure those materials possess a lot of potential.

Whether banker or artist, you still have two people who create something from basic materials or, put another way, create something from nothing. The act of creating is manifestation, and in astrology that is an earth word.

The banker and the artist both work to manifest, that is, to build something tangible for the purpose of seeing or experiencing a desired result. They want to feel not only a sense of accomplishment (as with any earth sign), but a feeling of outward flow of their ability, the action of creating: construction. Leo, another very creative sign, wants to feel self-expression as a duplication of or an outward flow of their own personality, but Taurus wants to feel that their talent or ability is being utilized to bring about the best possible result imagined. Creating is the need to see something envisioned come to fruition.

The creativity comes in the form of making the most of the resources or tools at hand to create something there that wasn't there before. It is the act of creating that is the most important to the Taurus, not usually the end result, as in Leo's case.

For the banker and the artist, the act of creating is the same, and the reason may even be the same, but the end product is quite different.

Of course, art or creativity may also be used as a message or to share a thought or feeling about something. The reason may be intangible, but the result is not. If human perception is shifted or changed as a result of someone's creativity, it has a lasting impact. Taurus is always interested in things that last, things that make a difference. This is not the same as wanting or eliciting change, however (art as a medium for change would fall under another sign's jurisdiction, such as Aquarius).

Taurus would certainly like its art to have an impact on others, though their goal in creating is not usually to change their audience's thinking. It is more to impress upon them a feeling of pleasure, relation, or connection with the subject. With Taurian rulership of the throat, singing, of all the artistic pursuits, is the pinnacle of Taurian art. A singer, with their own rendition of a song, builds an emotional connection with the audience and then it is reciprocated with applause. The applause tells the singer their interpretation of this song, their creative flow, has been successful. If the audience leaves happier, humming the tune, the performance has had all the impact a Taurian needs.

Taurus asks: "How can I make something that has lasting impact out of the raw materials at hand? How can I make it attractive, enhancing the value of it, and how can my own senses be engaged or get involved so that I may become enmeshed in this process?" The answer is through the act of building, applying strength and tools in proper places to make something useable; through singing, the sensual pleasure of vibration that inspires; and through painting, seeing and melding brilliant color or feeling the molding of clay (which must be the ultimate in physical, earthly sensuality) into something beautiful to look at that no one has ever seen before. The act of creating is a form of pleasure for the Taurian, which is their first goal, not giving pleasure to the public, even though that may be the final result. In a perfect world, Taurus would also prefer that the results of their labor be functional if possible, which would give them the ultimate satisfaction.

  The Taurian connection to the natural world always attracts their attention and their human nature entices them to tinker around with it. They want to know how one color would look with another or how that stanza of notes will sound. This is their area of play and experimentation. Art and nature are familiar places, a home, and they trust their instincts there, so they lose their innate caution when it comes to art forms. Their love of the sensuous keeps them coming back again and again to satisfy their craving for deep rich colors or smooth satin finishes. These are just a few of the things that make them fine artists.

Money can take the form of artistic self-expression too, a banker deals with the concepts of worth and wealth, worth being how much value is placed on something or how much something can do or contribute to a situation. Money is a uniquely human representation of an earthly raw material in its potential form. It is energy waiting to be used. Money can also take the form of self-expression and there is a great deal of creativity in it. It is the ultimate basic tool for the building of anything. A banker's reasons for controlling money is to manifest an idea or a vision, and they do this by creating wealth (Taurus) which bestows value (Taurus) on whatever the wealth touches or, conversely, they bestow value on something and it makes money. The banker decides what will be valuable and the creativity comes in when they give the money to businesses or contractors to make things happen. What buildings or businesses are to be built? How will the town look and who will use the building/business and what will this building/business say about our town? The banker builds and creates through the wealth he or she has at their disposal. If he/she is good at using their creativity, more wealth comes in and more creation can happen. The business community is the banker's brush and the town or community is his canvas.

The artist is trying to materialize an idea or vision too, or start a debate, give inspiration, create emotion, or give an experience through emotion. By putting an idea on paper or in a sculpture, they have made a physical representation of it. They have done what nature does and with some of the same materials (color, form, etc.) nature uses. Music, in many ways, duplicates the sounds nature uses (bird song, wind whistles) and it also creates emotion for the purpose of sharing that emotion and something more; something that is not readily understood or communicated on a mental level: an emotional connection with the world. Musicians bring in and create a feeling or mood that wasn't there before. They are manifesting and sustaining an emotional experience while the music plays and sometimes long after that. An artist wants to make a picture or sculpture of something to look at because it makes them feel a certain way and they want to experience that feeling over and over. Sometimes this pertains to something beautiful and sometimes it does not. The banker wants to see the results of his/her work in the form of a community that he or she has helped to build or create.

Creativity is the Earth asking that something be manifested and it would be better if the result was not the same thing as the last time because monocultures are not only dull and boring, but unhealthy. To have everything the same, made of the same materials, have the same function, look the same, and feel the same is not a good thing. It is not sustainable. The Earth needs diversity so that its creatures can survive. If all the animals of the Earth ate the same thing, they would soon run out of food, and if all plants needed the same soil and rainfall, the places they could grow would be very limited. It is diversity and variety that distributes life all over the globe, each eating and growing and living where their particular form dictates they live. People are the only creatures that alter their environment, when they move to make it the same as where they left, upsetting the balance and ruining the more efficient system that came before them.

    Another reason for Taurus's penchant for creativity (when linked to the Earth planet) comes in an even more profuse or lavish way with the concept of co-creating. If God is the creator and we are god-like, then we have some of his/her abilities and can, with his/her help, create like he/she does. For example, take the typical Taurian activity of planting a garden: you pick a spot where the garden will be, you select the kinds of flowers or vegetables you want to grow there, you plant the seeds, you water and feed it, then the garden grows and the rest is out of your hands. You may weed out or cut back, but ultimately the rest is up to the life force or God, if you like. Still, you have changed the way the Earth looks and functions in that particular place. A bad example of co-creating is the damage we have done to the environment. We've all been co-creative there, boy howdy, but in this case it wasn't a good thing.

    Co-creating can be the ultimate power trip; to feel in charge of what you are doing and, for the most part, responsible for the end result of a creation or a living thing is a heady feeling. Taurus would do this to align with or mimic the power they feel emanating from nature. For Taurus, nature is an outward, tangible manifestation of some inner force or energy that is called God by some. Taurus enjoys power; it helps them feel strong, solid, and alive. However, they wield power to align with something larger than themselves, to feel the connection with the natural world, not to dominate or control (as Scorpio might), and to experience strength, something they admire. When co-creating, there is a synergy, a give and take of the universe, that they can feel they are part of and it becomes another big, sensual experience, perhaps the ultimate sensual experience for Taurus. Bankers and artists are both co-creators that use basic elements to manifest something in the material world, to make something of value that involves the senses, has an impact, and ultimately stands the test of time.

Now let's explore Libra energy and see how it contrasts with Taurus.

[1] Hamaker-Zondag, Karen. *The Yod Book*. York Beach, Me: Samuel Weiser, 2000. 9. Print.

[2] Wroskopos, . "Quincunx aspect in Horary." *Wroskopos's Blog*. Wordpress.com, 14Feb2010. Web. 24 May 2011.

<http://wroskopos.wordpress.com/2010/02/14/quincunx-aspect-in-horary/>.

[3] "Episode 1." Writ. Kevin Sullivan and Joe Wiesenfeld. *Anne of Green Gables*. Public Broadcasting - Wonderworks: KSPS, Spokane, . Television.

[4] Gibson, Ian. *The Shameful Life of Salvador Dali*. New York City: W. W. Norton & Company, 1997. 1. Print.

[5] Saladyga, Stephen Francis. *The Mindset of Salvador Dalí*. Vol. 1 No. 3. Niagara University, N.Y.: lamplighter (Niagara University), 2006. Print.

[6] Dali, Salvador. *The Secret Life of Salvador Dali*. New York, N.Y.: Dover Publications Inc., 1993. 14. Print.

[7] Martínez-Herrera, M.D, Jose. "Dalí (1904–1989): Psychoanalysis and Pictorial Surrealism ." *Images in Psychiatry*. The American Journal of Psychiatry , May 2003. Web. 24 May 2011.
<http://ajp.psychiatryonline.org/cgi/content/full/160/5/855>.

Chapter 8
Taurus, Libra, and Venus

"Appearances often are deceiving." ~Aesop
"Adversity Makes Strange Bedfellows" ~1837 Charles Dickens: The Pickwick Papers

Venus is to Libra…not Taurus

For millennia, Taurus and Libra have shared Venus as their joint ruling planet and planet Earth's place in the astrological natal chart has been limited to an observation point providing the zodialogical houses or wheel base for the planetary position in our charts. This is not an insignificant thing, but I believe Earth has a much bigger job to do for us (and we for it) and that includes more symbolic contributions to our psyches for astrologers, their clients, and possibly even the world at large. With Taurus and Libra still crowded together in an unsatisfying and even stressful room, a line has been drawn across the floor there. The sign of Taurus, in relation to Libra, forms a 150 degree angle, a quincunx aspect, and a quincunx does not peaceful pair make. The old reasoning for this Taurus/Libra dual-rulership-arrangement is becoming insupportable. It is time for some fresh ideas. Venus is a different planet from Earth and Libra is quite different from Taurus.

In her book <u>Esoteric Astrology</u>, Alice Bailey flags Venus as "Earth's complementary planet" its "polar opposite esoterically considered."[1] Of course we can't know what she would say to the material presented in this book, but when considering the separation of Taurus from Venus, and the long term changes to Taurus if/when this connection takes place, it may be that these two signs and their respective planets are destined to be tied together always…on an esoteric level at least.

Astronomically or physically, in the solar system, Venus and Earth sit side by side, Venus being Earth's closest neighbor, at times a possible 38 million kilometers or 23.7 million miles[2] as opposed to Mars at 54.6 million kilometers.[3] Venus also shares a similar size (diameter) to Earth,[4] 7000 miles as compared to Earth's 8000, and, like Earth, Venus has a rocky crust and an iron-nickel core. We all know the similarities end there, especially when it comes to atmosphere and temperature.

In astrology, Venus and Earth reflect those differences.

Exploring Differences (and *Some* Similarities) of Venus/Libra and Earth/Taurus by Keywords

ATTRACTION AND VENUS

Symbolically, the planet Venus has always been about the concept of attraction. This can be akin to magnetism. In physics, magnetism (a sub-force or division of electromagnetism) depends on specific properties of objects.

Magnetism can either pull the two objects together or push them apart (this aspect of magnetism in astrology could fall under Uranus/Aquarius), depending on which way the magnets point. This has to do with the way the electrons are situated in the material. Most materials are almost insensitive to magnetism because the magnetic properties (electrons) are pointing every which way, with almost equal numbers pulling or pushing. However, once in a while, these can all be lined up so you get really big magnetic forces. This description of the way magnetism works in physics could also be a symbolic description of the human reaction we know as attraction and love. Throughout our lives, most of the people we meet have little effect on us. They are pleasant and we like them fine, but we have no desire to hang out with them for long periods of time. A small percentage of people we meet rub us the wrong way and we avoid them. Then, once in a great while, we run into someone whose "electrons" are lined up with ours in such a way that we can't stay away from them! They fascinate us and we want to be with them all the time. We fall in love and want to live with them.

EARTH

Planet Earth's symbolism hasn't really been officially recognized, which is what this book is all about. When we refer to Earth in astrology, we usually mean earth without the capital letter that is, the element earth. Still, we can gain a lot of insight using the element as a descriptor. In the physical world, Earth would probably rule gravitation and gravity, which is, respectively, the force of attraction between you and other objects of mass and the force of attraction between you and the Earth. Although they sound like similar concepts, magnetism and gravitation are very different forces. However, both magnetism and gravity are relatively weak forces and can't affect objects at great distances. Both get weaker as objects they hold get farther apart in distance.

Sign Dynamics of Libra and Taurus

Libra is a cardinal sign. Fixed signs like Taurus are foundational and grounding-type energies, the building and holding of a specific (in this case earth) element. Cardinal signs are initiating; cardinal signs are essences. In Chapter 5, cardinal earth was discussed in the form of Capricorn. Libra is cardinal air. Cardinal air would be initiating, activating, theoretical air, which is almost a redundancy. This is the idea of thought; all that thinking about something can make it be. Because the emotional level is not triggered when Libra is involved, it lays out an impartiality in that section of the natal chart or the Libran person.

LIBRA AND TAURUS

Attraction is a word associated with both signs and my guess is it will continue to be. They both appreciate beauty and enjoy making things attractive, up to and including themselves. Libra's sense of attraction is more proactive and outgoing. It isn't as if they are beyond making themselves attractive for the purposes of catching someone's eye, but it is also about their attraction *to* people, places, and things. It becomes a mutual thing.

Taurus is much more passive. Attraction, for them, is so someone else will do the work and make the effort. They feel infinitely safer seeing who will approach them, rather than risk rejection by making the first move themselves. Attraction and making themselves attractive assures the Taurian that someone will show up.

Love is in the Air

Here is a strange little omission for a Planet Venus rulership of Taurus: Taurus has never been associated with one of Venus's primary functions: love and marriage. Taurus has nothing much to do with relationships or socializing. Another little oddity is that many descriptions of Venusian operations in astrology seem to suggest it operates on an emotional level (water element) of the human psyche, but it's matching sign, Libra, is an air sign. At first glance, this is an incongruous element for love. Why should it be so? It must mean that Venus (and to some degree love) expresses itself through air qualities.

Marriage

Of course, Leo (fire element) and the 5th house of the zodiac, whose natural ruler is the Sun, is where we find romantic love affairs and Mars (Aries) rules passion, desire, and sex. Marriage may be the end result of a passionate love affair, but it is also a powerful beginning and we better have more than love or passion in common with our new spouse if we expect to have a good one. Venus, in the context of Libra, tells us that in order to be fully and deeply in love, we need more than desire and affection. We must have mental fellowship and camaraderie. We must understand each other and be able to communicate on an intimate level with our loved one. This breeds companionship and, ultimately, lasting friendship. Lastly, Libra tells us that we need to think of the other before ourselves, at least fifty percent of the time. These marriages are the most fulfilling; these are the marriages that last.

Partnership

Romantic love *is* associated with Libra as well as Leo because romance is an idea as well as a noun or verb. The reason Librans are romantic is they've been paying attention. They know what will make their partner happy, what turns them on. They have an inborn sensitivity to how their loved one (or anyone) will react to whatever circumstances the Libra chooses to put into motion. There is a great advantage to winning the object of your affection's heart when you put that person's needs before your own. It's also very addictive to the one being pursued and it certainly deepens any attachment they may have.

There is also a selfish side to Venus/Libra's flattery and adoration. They know they can "catch" whoever they want to with their considerable people skills and then thoroughly enjoy having that personality living within their sphere. Ultimately, there are cases when it is for the Libra that the Libra makes sacrifices or does favors for a loved one. Yet, unlike Taurus, they don't want to own their partner, they really just want to share their life with someone interesting who stimulates and inspires them. They ask: "How can anyone play the game of life on all the levels it's meant to be played with no fellow players?" For Libra, to be alone cheats them out of an essential life experience; life is in danger of becoming flat and boring.

Self-Adornment and Self Worth
VENUS/LIBRA

The planet Venus contributes to self-worth as well. Just to know that we are loveable, that someone feels about us the way we might feel about ourselves gives us a confirmation that we are on the right track. We must also be beautiful or at least attractive in some way for others to want us. These are affirmations that we simply can't get by being alone. To keep drawing in the people we have chosen and ever enhance those compliments we receive from them, we decorate ourselves. This is Venus: she knows how to look good and she uses whatever she can for an improvement in that area. It is a perpetuating circle: we wear something beautiful, we attract people who compliment us, we feel good, we gain more self-esteem, and we look for more ways to be beautiful.

EARTH/TAURUS

Earth/Taurus doesn't look to human outsiders to confirm or deny what they know about themselves. They usually keep their own counsel, sometimes to a fault. To them, people are nice and their company is enjoyable, but they aren't their main concern. The Earth/Taurus energy is not even about people, except as part of a whole. Earth is about sustaining life and ways of living, growing, prospering, constructing, fertilizing for consistency and stability. Earth/Taurus is interested in enhancement and decoration, but it isn't for compliments and human attraction. It is to increase value. Aside from monetary value, this is also about how much something is enjoyed, treasured, or revered as much as how much it is worth.

Money

VENUS/LIBRA

Venus has always ruled money in astrology. Money does make things attractive and it is also a way of placing value on things. The more we love something, the more money we will pay for it. It's an easy fit for Venus.

EARTH/TAURUS

Of course, money belongs more to the sign of Taurus and the 2nd house than to Libra (7th house), so if Earth becomes Taurus's ruling planet, money will be under Earth rulership. This does track, as money is the concrete and tangible (or knowable through the senses) representation of the value of something. We exert our energy for someone in the way of providing a service and we are paid, a concrete manifestation of effort made that (hopefully) matches in value what it was worth to the client or customer. Although money and the making of it can be mystifying at times, it is certainly an Earthly contrivance. It usually follows that what we put out, we expect to get back in a reliable, linear way. Money is the earthly representation of something's or someone's worth, and Taurus is all about the concept of value tangible or intangible.

Harmony, Gaiety and Happiness
VENUS/LIBRA

Venus is in charge of the lighter side of life. It is essential to our well-being to be able to look on the bright side, to feel that everything is going to be alright, and that life isn't always hard. Buoyancy is a word for Venus. Without it, we would all commit hari-kari. In order to have the time and be in the mood for gaiety, one must feel that their life has some harmony, or a balance. This helps with satisfaction and its end result: happiness. Many of us actively seek gaiety. We drive for miles to go on rides in theme parks, call in sick to work and hit the beach or buy tickets to dances or concerts just to have some fun. We yearn to feel better about things; we want ease, and it feels good to laugh. It gives us strength and inspiration to go on living. The idea that life can be fun is all here under Venus.

Some people (usually with an afflicted Venus or heavy earth influence in their chart) can feel that this kind of frivolity is a waste of precious time. For those people, their lives are about productivity and that does not cover such nonsense. They do not inherently understand the value of nonsense to our nerves and our equilibrium. They don't 'get' the need to let all the seriousness go and just goof off, but as long as we are balanced about it, goofing off is very good for our health.

EARTH/TAURUS

Earth is not concerned with making something lighter or brighter, only the concrete facts of the matter, and Taurus at its core isn't comfortable with silliness and doesn't really approve of goofing off. Part of this judgment comes from a sense of dignity that they guard and prize too heavily. It is part of their security issue. We have to be very confident people to give ourselves permission to be playful or silly around others, as this requires letting down our guard. Taurus doesn't do that easily.

Women
VENUS/LIBRA

In the astrological chart, Venus (along with the Moon) describes women in our life. For the female's natal chart, Venus gives insight into their femininity and describes their outlook on being female and the female friends they have. For the male half of the population, Venus (along with the Moon) in the chart explains the male's attitudes toward women and the experiences he has with them.

EARTH/TAURUS

There are a few female connections with this combination. Taurus is a female sign and we refer to Earth as Mother Earth, but that alone doesn't say very much about any "women" connotations. However, when we look at it from the Sun/Earth opposition angle, we see what could be the Yin (Earth) female to the Yang (Sun) male and we might be talking about more universal female energy symbology when we refer to Earth/Taurus.

Art and Creativity
LIBRA/VENUS

Venus is all about attraction and allure and this includes beauty and the arts.

Since Venus uses beauty as part of their attraction principle, at its core, Venus understands what makes people sit up and take notice. Much of art has to do not only with making things more beautiful but also getting some attention. Venus is also considered the most creatively artistic planet. When I think of Venus in terms of Libra, I see the oil paintings of Renoir and Monet, jewelers polishing stones to a translucent sparkle, or an orchestra playing a pleasing Brahms symphony - something taken from this Earth to the airy height of human creativity.

Art with a message, e.g., protest art or art that is meant to shock or shake people up, would not be ruled by Venus. That would probably fall under Uranus. The result of Venusian art makes people feel inspired, nice, calm, or happy.

EARTH/TAURUS

Earth and Taurus are a creative duo as well, but they haven't the refinement of Venus/Libra. The creativity of Earth /Taurus is a bit more basic, but it doesn't lack for beauty. Once again, we see the Earth influence predominant in Taurus, the sign of the gardener or the architect. Earth/Taurus's creative flow tends more toward crafts, construction, and working with the Earth's resources (including, of course, currency) on all levels. Marrying art with both Earth and the element earth is a Taurian aspiration, and if the results are ultimately usable, even better.

Love and Companionship

LIBRA/VENUS

Venus/Libra is the planet/sign ruling love and companionship. There are many different kinds of love and as many ways of expressing it. While the Moon sorts through our feelings and emotions internally, in the human domain, Venus/Libra describes our personal outward experience of love and companionship from the time we are born. What we attract or draw into our lives is a result of the expectations we acquired during our time here that finally become our whole approach and attitude to the idea of companionship, ending with the outward visible expression of our way of showing affection, loving, and marriage.

The Venus/Libra duo, in this respect, is essentially about the intimate social structures and the more lighthearted aspects that go along with being human. We are a very pleasure-loving, social species and where Uranus/Aquarius governs our desire for community, Saturn/Capricorn rules our desire for public recognition, and Neptune/Pisces our place as brothers and sisters in the global scheme of things, Venus/Libra holds our needs for a connection to carefully selected individuals.

EARTH/TAURUS

There are no particular astrological references for this area in regards to Earth and Taurus.

Sociality

An outcome of companionship is sociality, the need to connect with others of our kind.

VENUS/LIBRA

Like its ruling planet Venus, Libra is an *outgoing and extroverted sign* and does quite well as a party girl. It is the one sign of the zodiac that really needs both revelry and company. Libra is the perfect people person, understanding and allowing everyone to have their say. They are very concerned with social mores and manners, the refinements of the species that makes the race more human: cultured and gentile, not to mention pleasant.

People with heavy Libra or Venus energy in their chart are essentially nourished by the presence of other people. As a species, we all crave feedback on some level to check or register our intellectual and emotional temperature. We like to feel a thread of commonality with our own species. When we are alone too much, we may feel there is nothing to validate what is happening to us and how we feel about it.

Venus/Libra says: "We are a species that looks beyond our singular reality, seeking to compare it with someone else's in order to know ourselves better." Other people have the power to help us to better understand ourselves. Sometimes this can border on a feeling of being unsure of ourselves, like we need backup from others to know that we fit, how we belong, and where we are attached to our surroundings. I've even heard people say that the things that happen in their lives are not even real until they share them with someone. For them, it's in the sharing of the happening that somehow moves it from the realm of theory to reality. Here is a subtle bleed-over from Taurus and its long stay with Venus, the fact that Venus can help ground us and fix our reality (still in a Libra way) by our *social interactions or within a social sphere.*

EARTH/TAURUS

Taurus is a *quiet and introverted* sign. Earth/Taurus is quite happy, or at least comfortable, with being alone. Taurus does enjoy a few close friends, but, in general, does not require constant companionship. Taurus may even be the sign of the loner. They prefer the simplicity and ease of working alone. They find that others distract and interrupt them in their work and they are not crazy about the interference they cause. They feel the more people on the project, the less say they have about the process and end result.

Social etiquette and human diplomacy have never been Taurus's forte. To Taurus, etiquette is an unnecessary construct, a burden to learn and negotiate, a phony way of acting, and sometimes even nonsense that is a hindrance to all that is natural or true about us.

They are not talkers and especially detest small talk, something that Libra excels at. Libra does not see small talk as the waste of time that Taurus does. To Libra, small talk helps people get comfortable with each other so that we can all get to the deeper kind of talk. On the other hand, if Taurus has something to say, they will say it. Why pussyfoot around wasting time on idle chatter? They dislike the feeling of social pressure, the idea that they must hold up their end of the conversation, which is probably boring them to death anyway. They are more into doing it than talking about it. Venus would balk at Taurus's reserve around public gatherings and their dislike of excessive conversation.

The Light and the Dark side of Libran Shared Experiences

Venus/Libra wants to experience and understand cooperation. The dynamics of people working together fascinate them. The darker side of that goal is designed for Libra's own comfort level. They cannot abide conflict. Yet there are many times when disputes or arguments are beneficial, even absolutely necessary. People must have the freedom to declare opinions and discuss (or yell about) their side, but for Venus/Libra, any anger or frustration in the air threatens to overwhelm them, disengaging their sensitive nervous system and shutting them down out of a sort of self-preservation. Therefore, they have an expectation that others will be cooperative and they might even demand it. Making sure everyone is getting along is as much for them as it is for the others, maybe more so.

Venus/Libra also feels that when two or more people have the same experience at once, the shared experience becomes richer. The happening has more layers for everyone because they each have their own unique impressions and reactions to it.

If we see someone smiling or having fun, we smile, too. We remember what it is like. We are influenced by those around us. We want to try out what others are doing, from drinking a glass of wine to riding on a roller coaster. If they are enjoying it, we think we will, too. We love to enjoy ourselves.

EARTH/TAURUS

Earth/Taurus gets pleasure and enjoyment internally through the process of stimulating their senses while creating, acquiring, and stabilizing, like the Earth Goddess Gaia herself busily pushing up mountains, receding lakes, and blooming flowers. It doesn't require any company, though. They aren't afraid or threatened by a good argument, either. Although they can have an artist's sensitivity, it is almost always overridden by the practical necessity of the situation. If the air needs to be cleared, then clear the air, and if it comes at a price, so be it. Earth/Taurus is likely to have a "what will be will be" and "things happen for reason" attitude.

To stay within the social sphere, Venus/Libra must have talents that lead to popularity with a certain amount of social stability and status. The first is charm (which Earth/Taurus may see as being phony) and the second is niceness.

Nice-ness

VENUS/LIBRA

Enjoyment and pleasure is also part of being nice. Venus/Libra has within its realm and rulership the idea of nice. Nice is not only a human attitude or action for the Libran, it's a way of life. Nice is smooth and gentle. It has no sharp edges to hurt or bruise. It is sweet and easy and avoids the rough and harsh. They feel that there is no reason to get angry or nasty in difficult situations, since it only makes everything harder to deal with. Revenge or making enemies (even if it might be justified) means that some unpleasantness will remain indefinitely with the Libra. No thanks, they would rather not. That kind of ongoing tension is never worth it to the Libra.

Nice is also about not too much or too little. It is the absence of intensity, being overwhelmed or, the discomfort of some kind of lack or poverty. Even if that intensity is joyous, if it is out of control or over the top, they will gladly avoid it. They are the extreme opposite of an adrenaline junkie. A lack of extremes helps the Libra to remain famously impartial in almost everything they think and do. As we know, they also have a terrible time with decisions because of their constant "middle ground" philosophy.

Nice-ness helps our species cope with some of the less pleasant aspects of life. How can we make it through hard times, not to mention the downright horrible times that some of us encounter in living our lives, unless we can focus on what could make it gentler or at least easier? This is not the denial or pink foggy thinking of say, Neptune/Pisces. This is acknowledgement that "bad" or "icky" is out there and we must avoid it or talk through it quickly and gently (maybe just changing the subject) as a way to bring otherwise difficult times back into a perspective, to get beyond them, and make things beautiful and peaceful again. The essence of equilibrium, Venus/Libra doesn't concern itself with the harsher truths or raw reality; it craves ease, a gentle lightness of mind and spirit.

EARTH/TAURUS

Earth/Taurus, in contrast, has to do with the physicality of what IS. With Earth there is a heaviness, a bulky reality. Taurus isn't about ease. They may enjoy abundance, and while it could be argued that, symbolically, there is a quick jump from luxury to the concept of ease, at its core, Earth/Taurus feels there is no sense in avoiding unpleasantness, they would just as soon face up to it so that it can be worked out and fixed once and for all. Taurus (along with any other sign) would like everything to go well, of course, but it's really more about facing reality, because in the Taurus's mind, facing reality ultimately makes things easier.

As an outcome of nice, Venus/Libra gets caught up in justice and fairness. When something is wrong, it is unpleasant. It is out of balance, and equilibrium should be sought out. Earth/Taurus understands that life is not fair and never expects it to be.

Beauty, Art, and Creativity
VENUS/LIBRA

There are many reasons Libra is concerned with beauty. Libra uses beauty and art to feel better about the world and to make the world a better place. Art is an enhancement or a beautification of an object or place. Art is a refinement of life to Libra and it is a pleasant joyful thing to participate in it.

EARTH/TAURUS

Earth/Taurus is interested in enhancement or beautification for the purpose of increasing something's value. Another reason art is in Taurus's court is because it is sensory enhancement. Taurus loves color, sound, and pleasing tactile experiences. The field of art offers intensity in those sensual areas. Taurus also likes to tinker, to craft and lose themselves in the focus required to create. The act of creation is usually a solo affair that takes the crafter's mind away on a pleasant trip, relieves stress, and makes the world seem safe for the time being.

A Few Words about Libran and Taurian Houses
LIBRA AND THE 7TH HOUSE

Venus, the current ruler of Taurus, is of course in charge of Libra's 7th house. The 7th house is all the way over on the western edge, the descendant of the wheel, diametrically opposed to the 1st house. Called the house of "the other," it does not have an immediate affinity to the native. It is as far from the native as it can get and still be part of him/her. We cannot even access our seventh houses without aid from other people, at least not until we've had some major life experience in that area and maybe not even then. We don't recognize that part of ourselves, because it is so far away from our concepts of ourselves and what our environment holds. This house asks us to attract another into our life that will teach and show us that side of ourselves. Libra's bottom line is the quest for a partner or the "other." Libra's biggest challenge is to mesh the dual and complex personalities of two separate individuals (and thereby unite their own split psyches as well) into a thriving and happy whole.

TAURUS AND THE 2ND HOUSE

The 2nd house sits next to the first. In the natal chart,

the 1st house is all about the owner of that chart. It explains what the native looks like, what their approach to life is, their attitude and what their resulting surroundings look like. The 2nd house evolves out of the 1st. It is a house of resources, worth, and value. Some astrologers call this the "money house" and certainly money fits here, for it is valuable. However, I see money as a symbolic physical representation of energy expended or knowledge acquired; just one of the possible valuables we have to spend throughout our lives. Personal resources are of great value to the owner of the chart. Resources can be talents and abilities the native is born with, but also any skills that they have learned or acquired throughout their life. Personal resources are just like our Earth's resources: to be dipped into with reverence, used appropriately, and made even stronger with proper use or exhausted and/or squandered, and then suffer from neglect. Our human resources are our own building blocks to a life well-lived. We make money from them and they are what give us our sense of worth.

This house is also about what we value in our lives. What do we hold in highest esteem: people, art, cars, morality, stuff, fame, technology, justice, home, family, wealth, ideas, work, or accomplishment? Developing and then having a set of values is a deceptive endowment because it is so passive a powerhouse in our human lives. A set of values have the power to create purpose, expand personal potential, and make us even more of what we are. Put another way, by going backward on the house wheel from the 2nd to the 1st house we get: *what we value leads to what we become.* When it comes to the 2nd house, each of us must learn to understand value and to use our resources to the best of our ability.

This area of life is appropriated by the 2nd house of the natal chart: the nature of natural intrinsic talents, the development and use of basic (human or otherwise) resources, and the journey to understand value, making this is a very appropriate house for planet Earth to rule.

Summary

Although they will always be tied together historically and esoterically, sharing some characteristics, Libra and Taurus have many differences, as well they should, sitting at a 150 degree angle from each other. They have more than enough separate characteristics to go their merry and separate ways. Taurus deserves its own planet and the characteristics of this sign lend themselves quite well to planet Earth.

[1] Bailey, Alice. *Esoteric Astrology*. 15th. Vol 3. New York, N.Y. : Lucis Publishing Company, 1997. 24. Print. ISBN 0-85330-120-4

[2] Coffey, Jerry. "Venus Distance From Earth." *Universe Today*. N.p., 08May2008. Web. 26 May 2011. <http://www.universetoday.com/14152/venus-distance-from-earth/>.

[3] Cain, Fraser. "Distance from Earth to Mars." *Universe Today*. N.p., 04 Jun2008. Web. 26 May 2011. <http://www.universetoday.com/14824/distance-from-earth-to-mars/>.

[4] Cain, Fraser. "Interesting Facts About Venus." *Universe Today*. N.p., 05May2008. Web. 26 May 2011. <http://www.universetoday.com/14070/interesting-facts-about-venus/>.

Chapter 9
Planet Earth in the Astrological Chart

"When we look at a rock what we are seeing is not the rock, but the effect of the rock upon us." ~Bertrand Russell

Placing Earth in the Natal Chart

If we are now to consider placing the actual planet Earth in an astrological chart, how would we go on to interpret its meaning? Logically, we could begin with the element earth and then, presumably, add Taurian energy to that. With that formula in mind, how is Earth recognizable in the birthchart?

Note: When a question starts with WHERE I am always referring to the house in the astrological chart and when the question begins with HOW (and sometimes WHAT) it is always what sign the planet, in this case, Earth, is in.

The position of the planet Earth in any chart (problems or skills depending on aspects) would seek to provide:

- focus
- realism
- predictability
- security
- support

- basic fundamentals (of anything)
- permanence
- linear or smooth flowing ideas
- clear paths for growth
- creativity
- safety
- assurance
- value
- wealth
- plenty or luxury
- determination
- productivity
- limitations
- resources
- framework or systems
- organization
- experience
- understanding of limitations: realism
- the seeking or understanding of value
- ownership
- stability
- grounding
- foundational layers of work
- sensuality or connection with senses
- ability to build

- dependability
- insurance
- material things
- physical proof of existence, including the physical body
- money
- possession
- a connection to the natural world
- common sense
- connections
- stamina
- tangible proof

In the astrological chart, houses always reflect areas of our lives, such as home, spouse, career, etc. Depending on which house the planet Earth falls in at our birth (this can also apply to any planet we may have in the sign of Taurus, by the way) in that part of our life, we would:

- desire support
- need safety
- look for tools to help us build or better something
- want to be steady
- be basic
- be creative within a framework
- crave beauty
- be fertile

- be fearful of unknowns or unpredictability
- be systematic
- be firm
- crave abundance
- have plenty
- be reliable
- be dependable
- go slower
- understand rhythms and patterns
- worry we don't have enough
- be simple
- be straightforward
- want the uncomplicated
- crave an easy flow
- be logical
- be self-concerned
- be sensible
- be possessive
- be sensual
- collect experience
- hoard
- be realistic
- use common sense

- be traditional
- be subjective
- take things personally
- stock up
- be stubborn
- be persistent
- be productive
- want possession
- want usability
- be no-nonsense
- wish for fullness
- want saturation
- be satisfied
- crave symmetry
- be attractive
- want attraction
- work on the physical
- look for satisfaction
- need richness
- be rational
- understand values and worth
- make necessary sacrifices
- be hard-working
- do what is necessary
- be practical

- be grounded
- have or crave luxury
- be a bit too easy-going
- be naive
- be narrow or limited in thoughts or actions
- be self-indulgent and/or selfish
- buy or collect material proof or things in that area
- collect or develop resources
- use resources
- invest
- make plans
- have physical body awareness
- earn money
- love/hate nature
- look for peace of mind
- want to build something
- make connections
- want reliability

This is what we *want* or are *asked to experience* in that *area* of life; because that astrological house has the planet Earth (or Taurus) in it. The aspects would tell us whether we get these things easily or have struggles and, consequently, issues with them.

Earth is the thing that holds us together in that area of our lives when we are scattered and distracted by showing us where we can have consistency. It reminds us that stability is possible in our lives because no matter what is going on at the core of our planet or our own core, the planet Earth for us looks and feels solid and permanent and the ground we stand on is firm. Wherever Earth is placed becomes the physical center of the chart, the place where reality is sensed, touched, smelled, and tasted.

Earth's position in a chart shows us where (house) and how (sign) we are being asked to tread a concrete, workable path with great regard to how things work here on whatever level (house/sign) we are talking about within set laws or rules, which may include the rules of our human family, the laws of our community, the expectations of our culture, or the physical laws (physics) of the earth plane itself. When we have the right formula, we become powerful, wealthy, and influential in whatever part of life is affected, creating ever more opportunities for building and growth.

Integrating Earth in the Natal Chart

To begin the translation of our own individual planet Earth within our natal charts, we can start by asking ourselves some questions around Earthly traits.

Safety and Stability

When thrown off your game, how (planet Earth's sign) do you find your footing again? How do you feel tethered? How do you ground yourself? How do you look for stability and feel safe and secure? Where (earth house or planet Earth in a house) do you look for security? What must you have to feel secure? What tethers you to reality, how do you assess what reality is? What is real to you and how is it real? And on a very individual level: how does your particular earth energy (Earth in what sign and house) serve to ground you and give you perspective?

Astrologers cannot assume that an individual's need for grounding will follow traditional method of activities such as sitting home with a cup of hot tea. If someone had Earth in Aries, they might be out rock-climbing to get their bearings and feel normal again. People with strong or well-aspected Earth signs in their natal chart feel safe and secure most of the time. When they do hit a wall, they can easily find their feet again, confident that who they are and how they think will lead them out of any difficulties, just as it has before. Although they feel most comfortable when things today go on as they did the day before, if change makes sense and seems logical they will embrace it or at least be willing to give it a try. Having a sense of stability that comes from within and having been born with support systems in place gives them the ability to allow change and even to see it as a potentially good thing while retaining any remnants of the original idea that still have merit.

Safety and Stability Affected by Lack of Earth

When someone is lacking an element (or energy) in their chart, they will naturally draw a blank when it comes to its stronger suits or talents. It isn't in their DNA. In this case, they could be missing the point of Earth and all it represents. They lack knowledge of it and it just doesn't have a place in their life This could occur on the inside of a person – in other words, as awareness of a weakness or barrier they have – or it could be physically missing, such as living without basic creature comforts, tools, or opportunities. This can also lead to that peculiar opposition effect: overcompensation of Earth. This occurs because the native is so acutely aware of an emptiness that they grab any trait of earth they can find and take it to the limit. With a little earth savvy finally in hand, they have to make it bigger, to have it stick out from everything else so they can see it and know that it is there. It becomes like a child of theirs, a child that was in danger, so they now smother it and won't let it go out to play with the other kids. They may even become paranoid, thinking (unreasonably) that people are trying to take away what little stability they have worked for and now, at last, possess. The results are the earth extremes of paralyzing rigidity and ultraconservatism. In this case, earth issues are out of balance for the native, another issue in the way of understanding how to work with it.

Safety and Stability Affected by Hard Aspects to Earth in the Natal Chart

If a native has difficult or challenging aspects involving Earth in their natal charts, they rarely feel safe. They have probably been witness to a world that has at times been a scary place, one with few absolutes. They tend to cling to whatever they've known as their only sure route to safety. They clench up when change appears and it doesn't matter if that change could be an improvement, because they would have to shift what they have been doing or thinking which would leave them feeling like they have lost their tether.

Since they can't find or feel stability inside of themselves they must have routine to serve as a substitute for stability all around them. Having hard aspects to Earth creates a basic distrust of progress and forward motion. They are also confused because they feel they have tried earthly ways of doing things and, for them, they didn't work very well. Earthly ways don't feel right; earth is at odds with the other elements in their chart and the other personality traits in their make-up. As with all hard angles in a chart, the native has to find a way to incorporate the earth element with all the other elements of their chart (and their personality) and make them work together.

When people have little success trying to understand or follow earthly laws or society's structure, there are certain paths they will take to fix the problem. Most of the time they will look outside of themselves for something structured, like a system to study. They place themselves into a system in order to understand how the rules, the scaffolding, the routine, or the laws of this system, work to contain and regulate the whole and keep it functioning. They may do this by going back to school, joining the military, finding a job in corporate America, being an integral part of an organized religion, or becoming a mathematician/accountant. There, they find the challenges they need to face in order to settle their own internal disputes and acquaint themselves with an earthly organization. It's a very uncomfortable process and there are many days of painful reality checks.

Another course of action open to people who don't understand or want to work with the earth rules given to them is to invent their own rules and attempt to live by them. Sometimes this works, but most often it doesn't. Many rule-breakers end up on the dark side and, while there, they never seem to think that, in the end, they will fail. They are unrealistic (this is how an embezzler or Ponzi schemer is born).

Lastly, they may just give up altogether and drink themselves to death or something similar. It depends on their personality, of course, but I sometimes wonder if a lack of earth or having all the worst aspects to Earth in a chart isn't the hardest of the elements to deal with because it is so essential to basic survival skills.

Building and Productivity

What (planet Earth's sign) is your method for working to bring things about? How do you manifest things in your life? How do you produce? What is your method of production? What and where do you want to build from the ground up? Where (earth house or Planet Earth in a house) do you enjoy the process of putting things together step by step? Where do you look for the satisfaction of a job well done? What kind of finished product gives you a thrill? It could be a building built, a book published, a loving relationship, a theory accepted, a child grown, a room clean, etc. People with strong and well-aspected earth in their natal chart understand how the world works. That is, which tool to use, where and when to invest their energy, how to organize the job, and proper methods of process or construction. When they get in the groove, they work long and hard for the sense of completion they seek. As a result, this slice of the population is the most productive of all the other elemental personality configurations.

Building and Productivity Affected by Hard Aspects to Earth or Lack of Earth Element

These are the people who can't help but fritter away valuable time trying to find the right time, place, or way to start a project. Lacking an understanding of method or of what works, together with being unorganized, they make many false starts or mistakes and get exhausted way before the project is completed. They may struggle with the most basic concepts, like beginning, middle, and end.

The result is a lack of confidence in their ability to figure things out correctly, put things together in a way that will produce the result they want, or hold up under pressure or scrutiny, all ending up in unsatisfying outcomes. You can bet they won't be anxious to take on anything new without great guidance. Unless they can find where their other talents lie, they may go through life feeling like a failure.

Creativity

How (Earth sign) are you creatively productive? What kind of an artist are you? What are you likely to get creative with? Where (An earth house or planet Earth in a house) do you long to see earthly beauty? What do you consider beautiful? How is beauty practical and applicable to you? Where do you work to achieve flow and symmetry? Where do you crave beauty or at least, luxury in your life? How do you judge beauty? What is your basic criteria for beauty? In what way do you need beauty? People with strong and well-aspected earth in their chart are physically creative. They yearn to see ideas or inspiration brought down to Earth and manifested into something one can see, taste, hear, touch, or smell. They love the control of having a hand in this process; holding the brush or the reins of a production and weaving the spell that will create the reality of what they have envisioned. Monitoring and testing the layers of development as they work to fit one piece onto another: this is one area that they can trust or even enjoy some experimentation. Making it real can mean many different options with regard to color or design and they love the fact that beauty can actually be honed or created by them here on Earth.

Creativity Affected by Hard Aspects to Earth or Lack of Earth Element

There will not be a problem in this category unless what they create has to be useful (like furniture) or want to make what they create into a business. Creativity does not have to be either physical or permanent. Hard aspects may create someone who believes they have no talent in the creative arena or it may be that they are artistic with no technical knowledge of the media that they work in, even though it has a tendency to work out just fine.

Nature

How (Earth in a sign) do you connect with nature? What does the natural world mean to you? Where do you see nature's role in your life? Earth people usually relate to nature as a source of beauty and/or inspiration. They use nature as reliable and tangible proof that life is stable and continues on no matter what happens to them personally. In times of stress, going out into nature, taking a walk in the wind, or sitting in a meadow gives them a sense of peace and helps them recharge their batteries. They have a desire to be close to the natural world, by gardening in it, recreating in it, or living by it. They lean toward natural elements in their home decorating and are constantly collecting pieces of nature and displaying them in their home. They understand the need for the preservation of nature, instinctually knowing that we, as a species, still rely on the marriage that is humanity and nature.

Attitudes of Nature Affected by Hard Aspects to Earth or a Lack of Earth Element

In the chart, this creates a situation where the natives either don't consider the natural world at all (lack of Earth) or think about it with fear and/or loathing (hard aspects). There are many people who have lost their connection with nature, seeing it as a decoration or not at all. Our culture has made that fairly easy to do. We don't see where our food or water comes from anymore. We go to the grocery store and everything is prepackaged; we turn on the faucet and we have water. The availability of these essentials removes any reason for thought about the sources and sustainability of our most basic needs and, with it, any idea that they could run out or become contaminated. It's a dangerous convenience. The other extreme are those natives who think about the natural world a lot because they are uncomfortable with it and worry that they might be exposed to it. For them, nature is harsh, too raw, or even gross. Animals are predators looking to attack or kill, insects are bizarre, unpredictable, and alien. Even plants are capable of sticking or stinging. Forests or deserts are scary havens of the wild, the exotic, and the dangerous; places shrouded in mystery where you may go in but you might not come out. They are all to be avoided if it is possible.

Quality

What (Earth in a sign) items do you spare no expense to have the best of? What things in your life must last? What in your world must be built strong, tough, or particularly beautiful? What items must be "top of the line" for you? What is your idea of luxury? What are you looking for durability in? This could be people, relationships, places, things, or even ideas. Although frugal, earth people are also willing to pay more for anything of quality. This seems contradictory but their philosophy in this area is simple: when you pay more for something of quality it lasts longer (and gives more pleasure), keeping you from having to spend for it again for a long time, in the long run this saves you money, and gives you an experience of happiness every time you use it. Aesthetic sense is strong in earth people. They want clean, lovely conditions where they live and shop. They want to surround themselves with anything plush, lush, or beautiful. They are tied to the physical world. That means they notice it or experience it more intensely than some and they can suffer emotionally or psychologically if their environment is dirty, cheap, plastic, cheesy, or mismatched. Colors or surroundings that are garish, clashing, or asymmetrical are physically uncomfortable and create discord not only in the environment but also inside themselves. They yearn for luxury because luxury makes them feel rich, pampered, secure, and well taken care of.

Quality Affected by Hard Aspects to Earth or Lack of Earth Element

In a natal chart, this gives people confusion about what makes quality and why it should matter at all. When they shop, all they see is a bargain item with a low price and they snap it up. They end up with cheap, shoddy, or ill-constructed items that leave them wondering later why they didn't last. They don't care or invest time in grooming their home or grounds: their head is elsewhere. At the extreme, they have no taste, no pride of place, and can be known as "trailer trash."

Practicality

Where (earth house or planet Earth in a house) do you reject fad and fluff? Where do you look for something that is durable and applicable and real? Where are you a realist? Where are you going to be sensible and not take any guff? Where are you the best at cutting to the chase? Where and how do you look for things to make sense? What (Earth sign) do you have great common sense about? Even though luxury and cleanliness is important to earth people, there is also a practical side to be considered. Sometimes it is quite natural for surroundings to be dirty or messy because nature is sometimes dirty or messy. Deserts, farms, woods, beaches: these are not luxury locations, but they are natural and therefore embraced wholeheartedly by earth people. That said, practicality is also the art of forsaking what is seductive or attractive at the moment for that which makes the most sense and proves the most valuable in the long run. There is an art to facing reality. It is always hard to let go of a great idea you had or a path you are on, in the face of it. Sometimes there is just no help for it: whatever those plans may have been, there comes a time when we must revise them because everything is not as we thought it would be.

Our goal may still be obtainable, but we see that we are going the wrong way or something more is needed. Every once in a while, we even find out that what we want is not even possible. Practicality helps us to handle that information. Are we able to stop and shift according to the way things are or will we waste time clinging to a dead end? Practicality is also a way of sifting through distractions, excess or useless information, and getting to the heart of the matter.

Practicality Affected by Hard Aspects to Earth or Lack of Earth Element

This leaves the native shy of practicality. They are naive and vulnerable to manipulation. They cannot hone in on what is important and they get lost in a sea of extemporaneous junk. This also creates feelings of being overwhelmed by all that they must do because they can't break a task or a goal into logical steps or understand priorities and see only what they must do right now. They get grandiose ideas that can't fly or want things that aren't possible given the circumstances. They can't or won't see where they must either change their plans or put extra effort in to get where they want to go and ultimately, have trouble knowing how and when to apply earthly organization and requirements.

Patience and Persistence:

What (Earth sign) are you patient about? In what area (earth house or Earth in a house) of your life do you have endless patience? Where are you slow and steady? What kind of determination do you have? Where are you prone to stubbornness? How are you stubborn or what is likely to provoke or bring out your immovability? How and where are you strong and stalwart as a rock? Where will you never quit? If you have embraced practicality, another ingredient for success is patience or persistence. Earth people understand that possible happenings, just as in nature, have their own pace and time. They will be willing to wait for the right time to say or do something because it makes sense to. They know that nothing of lasting value happens overnight. As long as they can see the progress they are making, they have confidence that it will work out in the end, one step at a time. If they feel they are on the right track, they will persist, sometimes against all odds, as sometimes grinding away is the only way to truly get something accomplished. They aren't likely to give up until all hope is lost.

Patience and Persistence Affected by Hard Aspects to Earth or a Lack of Earth Element

In the chart, this means that the native does not have an inborn gift of persistence. When things don't go the way they think they should, they quickly get discouraged. Also easily distracted by the next big thing, they jump from one half-completed project to another; whatever happens to look more interesting at the moment. They get fired up by an idea and just can't get interested in process or practice to achieve their goal: they simply want it now.

Sensuality

Where (earth house or Earth in a house) are you tuned in to your senses? What (Earth sign) methods do you employ to connect with your senses? Where do you trust your senses? How do you trust your senses? Where are you likely to trust only what your five senses tell you and no more? How do you regard your senses? How do you please your senses with beauty? What thrills your senses? Where do you immerse yourself in sensuality? Where do you stop and "smell the roses"?

Sensuality Affected by Hard Aspects to Earth or a Lack of Earth Element

This would deprive the native of strong sense of the world. Our senses connect us physically to our reality; they deepen our experiences and keep us open to the many pathways of enjoying a rich palate of life. Sensual pleasures give us excitement about simply being alive. Lacking sensual connections, life could be dull and lifeless for them. They may be a workaholic because pleasure isn't high on their list of priorities or they may even be uncomfortable with the idea of indulging their senses. Sensual pleasure may be an embarrassment to these natives because it harkens back to the animal in them. Separated from strong sense input, they experience life mostly in their mind and not in their body, keeping the native from trusting physical experiences and ultimately the reality that is right outside their door. They are not invested in what is physically around them; they see no point in it. These are the people who throw trash out their window and leave old broken washing machines out in their yard. They have no pride of place. They can also go the other way and overcompensate with addictions to things like sex, adrenaline, or gambling because they can't get enough of the sensual or physical. They can't feel satiated, so they overload the senses, looking to fill that hole in their psyche.

Wealth, Value, and Ownership

What (Earth sign) do you value? How do you value something? What do you know the value of? Through what filter or lens (Earth sign) do you assign value? What brings money or material wealth to you? How do you go about bringing material goods to yourself? How do you feel about material goods? What do you collect or hoard? What do you consider wealth? How are you rich? Where (earth house or house planet Earth is in) do you need prosperity? What must you own? What do you possess or want to possess? What lengths will you go to in order to protect that wealth? What gets in the way of acquiring wealth and/or material goods?

Wealth, Value, and Ownership Affected by Hard Aspects to Earth or a Lack of Earth Element

This may remove the need to own or possess anything. The natives don't care if they ever get rich. They see no need to be physically rewarded for what they do. These are not necessarily negative things, unless they contribute to the native's difficulties of finding a home base, a center of operations that they may work from to accomplish or establish something of worth. They may not want to make something of themselves or their life and that may work out or not, depending. Their values may be warped or at least not in sync with their culture and therefore have psychological issues with values. They may have great difficulty hanging onto material wealth because of bad decisions or illogical spending habits. They also may not understand *what* to value or what is of value and why it is valuable, making it hard to understand what they should keep or throw away. Having no innate, inner knowledge in this area breeds confusion and overcompensation, lacking balance; they may go the other extreme and become hoarders or at least pack rats of worthless junk.

The Physical Body

If Earth is truly representative of the physical body in place of Saturn (and the jury is still out), then we would look to the Earth sign in the natal chart for answers to these questions:

What kind of body consciousness do you have? How (Earth sign) do you look at your body? How do you treat your body? How does your body treat you? What are your issues with the body or in what area of the body are you prone to problems? Feeling satisfied with the physical body is difficult today because our American culture insists on projecting impossible standards of perfection onto us. As a result, I think a lot of people just try to ignore their body. At any rate, people tend to take it for granted. Consciousness or at least, awareness of the body is necessary in order to work with it so you don't end up against your body or it against you because I think we would really like our bodies to be able to take us wherever we want to go. With strong earth placements in a natal chart, the native would have rational sense when it comes to their body. The body would naturally be strong and solid, with few health problems.

The Physical Body Affected by Hard Aspects to Earth or a Lack of Earth Element

This may indicate a lifelong struggle for satisfaction or health of the body. They don't like their body or their body's vitality is just not robust and they have to make constant adjustments to have the strength and energy that others with easier aspects take for granted.

Lack of earth here leaves a blind spot when it comes to the physical body; they just aren't in touch with it. There isn't any allowance for this entity and its care and feeding. They don't care to eat right or even give the body the rest it needs. They are also impractical with their physical limitations and may take heedless physical risks. This could escalate to someone who has no sense of danger, who doesn't understand that what they are doing could injure the body or even get them killed.

Green Living and Ecology

Lastly, where Earth is located in the chart is also where we are conscious of our Earth as a planet and as our home. How (Earth sign) do you feel about Earth? Planet Earth in a particular astrological house corresponds to where (earth house or Earth in a house) we are being asked to be conscious of our planet Earth in our life. This house is the area of life where you can contribute the most to the planet, where your true gifts for ecological awareness and working with the environment are. It is also the place where you are able to best communicate with and about the Earth in all its forms. How (Earth's sign) can you best work in harmony with the Earth? What kind of Earth consciousness do you have? What unique "green" contributions can you make to the environment?

Green Living and Ecology Affected by Hard Aspects to Earth or a Lack of Earth Element

In the chart, this leaves a gap or even animosity between a person and their earthly environment. Similar to what was said about nature, they may feel threatened by earth or in competition with it, so they must conquer it to have what they want: think real estate developers gone wild. People with difficult aspects to Earth, and Earth only, see the easy or cheap way to get what they want and aren't willing to work to preserve nature's balance and work it into the equation of what they want to do – ironic, since the Earth is the one ultimately providing for them and keeping them alive. The difficulties these people have around relating to the Earth go directly back to a lack of sensual input or experience. I feel that if a person isn't able to really enjoy the sensual pleasure of feeling the wind through their hair, the thrill of the color of a garden, or the smell of woodland, then why would they be that interested in saving the Earth? There is already a disconnect in our society between our reliance on the Earth for our sustenance. That, coupled with a lack of a sensual enjoyment of the planet, could leave any native wondering why they should care about this blue and green rock?

Summary

Adding planet Earth to any astrological chart and house creates a corresponding shift in our interpretation of the human condition/personality, incorporating a new sense of physical reality for us, one that is bound to help us get deeper in touch with earthly things, not the least of which is our own home world. Once we are able to truly relate to our planet, productivity will be more complete as we can easily take the Earth into account whenever we apply our considerable creativity to new technology, construction, and improvements. A higher consciousness in this area will insure that our actions do not adversely affect the natural processes that we and the other inhabitants here need to stay alive. This would be a big bonus and, perhaps, just in the nick of time.

The addition of our planet to a natal chart brings in a host of new expectations and characteristic traits not brought out to the forefront just yet: first and foremost, a supportive and nurturing relationship with our own physical bodies. This is becoming almost as crucial as saving our planet. We need to heal ourselves; more than that, like our planet, we need to *thrive*. This does not have to be the chore we think it is. We can now use the sign and house our Earth is in for hints as to how we, personally, can get this done. Some knowledge of medical astrology would come in handy here, too. As Earth is accepted and integrated, some expansion of Taurian traits is to be expected. Bereft of a true ruler, Taurus has never completely come into her own. As we learn more about our planet, we learn more about ourselves. A different (very non-Libran way) of using our creativity may surface. What we value and why, will undergo some shift.

Any way you look at it, the fact that we live on the Earth plane has to mean that both the planet Earth and the earth element play more crucial roles in our life than we (as astrologers) have yet to be completely aware of. They are certainly both very important for success in any venture we might undertake. Without the earth element, we haven't the wherewithal – money, resources, connections, know-how, or talent – to make our dreams into a reality. Indeed, without earth or Earth, our dreams do not have a good chance of coming true because we don't even know how to plan correctly or the plans we do make aren't incorporating the most essential element needed for manifestation: earth.

Chapter 10
The Psychology and Physiology of Sun/Earth Diametric

"Till now man has been up against Nature; from now on he will be up against his own nature." ~Dennis Gabor, Inventing the Future, 1963

The Opposition

I understand that the idea of confronting, studying, and finally integrating the Sun/Earth opposition in our natal charts is just as revolutionary as adding our planet Earth to the astrological chart. Why would we want to do that and how might that play out?

The opposition is just what it sounds like: two different kinds of energy locked together, in an endless battle of wills. In the astrological chart the opposition aspect is created when two planets, points, or house angles are in signs that are a hundred and eighty degrees apart from each other. They also have to be within orbital influence; that is, close enough to the same number of degrees in the chart. For example: If a planet is in the sign of Aries at 18 degrees in the chart, then a planet in Libra, Aries' opposite sign, has to be about 18 degrees (of Libra) to create the tension. I say "about" because the two planets are still having oppositional issues within a certain numerical or positional sphere of influence. Astrologers differ on just how far apart these two planets can get from each other before they lose interest in the altercation. This is like a couple kids having a heated argument in the living room and mom decides to separate them. If she puts them in their adjoining bedrooms, they could still see each other and fight from the doorway. If she puts one in the guest room and one in the kitchen, the problem might get solved through the old adage "out of sight, out of mind." So if Libra's planet is, say, at 15 degrees Libra, well, that is still pretty close numerically, which also means it is in sight of the planet in Aries at 18 degrees in the sky. The planet in Libra could also be moving away from the planet in Aries, at perhaps 20 degrees of Libra, and the opposition aspect would still be alive and kicking. Generally, astrologers will agree that after 4 or 5 degrees to either side (before 14 degrees and after 22 degrees approximately) of the, in this case, 18 degrees, the "tension"' between the planets begins to dissipate and the opposition wanes.

If someone has an opposition in their natal chart they have tension between two planets (or points or angles) in opposing signs. What kind of tension that is, what the argument is about, is represented by the astrological symbolism of the two opposing planets and signs. It might translate as a fight between the differences of a native's thoughts and their emotions, their personal philosophy and their country's philosophy, or their taste in clothes and their mother's. Any way you look at it, somewhere in their world, there exists two very different ideas about that life and how to live it.

The opposition in any astrology chart sets the owner on a path to search for some kind of middle ground between the two. One can't simply squash one side down and give all their time and attention to the other; at least not for very long. Both sides must be heard from or acknowledged more or less equally. Those of us who have played on teeter-totters remember that when each party stops pushing against the other, you can find a wonderful spot, parallel to the ground, where you both just hang in mid-air, achieving perfect balance. That is what you need to fix an opposition. The key word here is compromise: both sides working together despite their differences, to find that place of balance.

As any owner of a chart with a strong, or tightly orbed, opposition can tell you, it brings in a keen awareness of not only how truly diverse the world can be, but how to (or how not to) balance it. They are born with two opposing ideas competing for dominance in their lives. Of course, they can choose to ignore one side. The traits or symbolism of the side that has been dismissed will then fall into a category known as "shadow" energy, infiltrating and sabotaging on a subconscious level from the sidelines, any chance it gets. This shadow energy can also play out in their life by attracting in opposing people who challenge them or tricky situations that require the same kind of balance and compromise reflected in those two planets and opposing signs in their astrology chart.

Oppositions are not uncommon in astrology charts, although there are people who have none, or the few they do have aren't very strong. However, if we insert Earth in the natal chart, everyone will suddenly have an extremely powerful opposition prominent in their natal chart: Earth opposition their Sun. If it is so strong, how have we walked around all these years and not known it was there? We do know it's there. We deal with the shadow side of it almost every day. We deal with it in terms of a disconnect with our home planet, our own bodies, and a just plain pig-headed single-minded-ness.

More on the Earth/Sun Opposition in the Astrological Chart

Earth is a unique planet in astrology due to its permanent opposition to the Sun in every chart. This begs to be addressed when approaching a discussion on delineation. Earth in the natal chart will set us up on a journey to consider the other side of ourselves, that one-hundred-and-eighty-degree piece of ourselves that has always been difficult to understand and incorporate into our single Sun sign center of operations. This opposite ingredient is the very thing we need to find our psychological and physical balance. It unites us with a missing link in our personality and also marries consciousness with our physical body, making us whole.

Life on Earth is a dual plane of existence and because we live in a world of opposites, with Earth in our charts, taking note of the Earth-Sun opposition, we see our own reflection in that dual world and the challenges we face as a result. This dual planet configuration of Earth/Sun means that we are always sensing and responding to subtle divisions of the life force and its physical manifestation. The Sun is the receptacle of the spirit/mind/intention; it is home to our energetic essence. Earth is the physical receptacle of the Sun's life force, an anchor for it, grounding it and keeping it centered and focused, so that the native can function and work within the physical parameters of this earth plane. Thinking of our "centered selves" as a marriage of two planets rather than one may be a radical idea, but it seems to make sense in lieu of what we know of the human condition. We have anima and animus (male and female) halves within our minds. We have an apparent split between our body and our mind. We have to consider and work with both rational thought and irrational feeling every day of our lives.

Earth "signs" of Strength and Weakness in the Body

As stated in Chapter 6, Earth may rule the physical body. At the present time, general textbooks on astrological

Sun signs talk about the strengths and the weaknesses of the body due to the Sun in certain signs. When the Sun sign is supported by aspect or placement in the chart, it carries a stamp of strength for that sign's characteristics and the parts of the body under the rulership of that sign.

If the Sun sign is afflicted due to difficult placement and aspects, then it is said that health problems are associated with the parts of the body the Sun sign rules. For example, Sun in Aries is likely to have health issues with the head, such as headaches, bumps, or even brain disorders, or for Sun in Taurus, health issues or weaknesses with the neck and throat, etc. I still think that this would be true even if Earth does indeed rule the body. Then, of course, strength or weaknesses leading to health problems should also be noted for Earth in a sign just as for the Sun. This would be because adding Earth to the chart only confirms another reference to the Sun in that permanent opposition. They are a package deal and what happens to one almost always involves the other. There is a flow between the Earth and Sun in astrology, just as there is a flow between the planet Earth and that star named Sol in our sky. The flow between Sun and Earth in the chart is between the conscious center/will and manifestation/body.

The Earth (along with the 1st house) may also then describe in more detail the body type and build, perhaps even more the condition of the body than individual health issues, but that remains to be seen.

In Chapter 2, I talked about this opposition in global and societal terms. Here, we address a more personal side of it, as within a natal chart and what would happen if we could stop our personal teeter-totters and find balance.

The Aries/Libra Diametric
EXPECTATIONS

The oppositional diametric of Aries and Libra is always a quest for the balance of "me or you" and "us or them." It goes on to be about resolving conflict, when to assert yourself, who gets our way and why. It also addresses the balance of polite and/or assertive.

Sun-sign Libras (with Earth in Aries) are out of balance because subconsciously they want everything to be calm, nice, and beautiful, and this is not in keeping with the reality of life. They also want a large circle of friends to interact with. A busy social life actually centers and energizes them and adds a lot to their feeling of well-being. To keep a lot of friendships active, one has to be constantly supportive and even defer their ideas or wants to others on a regular basis. Libra is usually fine with that trade-off.

Aries is not. Sun-sign Aries (with Earth in Libra) are out of balance because they tend to place themselves at the center of everything and subconsciously feel that their needs should be everyone's needs. They get myopic and unconscious of others and their points of view. They actually relish an occasional clash of wills; they reaffirm themselves and what they stand for by pitting themselves against an opposing force.

HISTORY

While growing up, Librans were taught that other people are necessary and very important to a quality of life. Somehow, the very soul-survival of the Libra's family was predicated on the kindness of or interaction with others. Perhaps the family had a business that was dependent on keeping the customer satisfied at all costs. It could be that they were involved in politics and that, too, depended on acceptance from other people. However it came about, as children they were shown that you must do everything you can to keep other people around as active participants in your life, keep them happy, even giving up what you want if need be. They were also taught that life should be serene, even beautiful, and discord isn't at all nice. You don't want to cause problems or argue or people won't want to be around you.

Aries were taught that they are special and no one matters as much as they do. The family somehow revolved about this person. Either they were an only child or the favorite in the family. They were encouraged to reach, step up, face down their fears, stay strong, go after their dreams, and don't take no for an answer, that "where there is a will there is a way". In the Aries' family, dealings with other people rarely mattered. They enjoyed or desired independence and did not take charity. You made your decisions and, right or wrong, you lived with them. From the Aries' point of view, the family was an active and on-the-go one.

ARIES SPIRIT/LIBRA BODY CONFLICT

Sun in Aries and Earth in Libra, this body needs to relax. Go out and socialize with other bodies; whatever it is doesn't have to be done today. Hang out, have a drink, and listen to what others have to say, as it may ultimately help you with your own personal projects. Tension isn't healthy and Libra asks the Aries to let go of control on a regular basis. The Libran idea of physically kicking back and allowing or even embracing some passivity is very good for an Aries spirit. No demands and no conflict will lower their blood pressure and help the body rest and heal. Because of the possible Libran influence on the body, there can be problems keeping bodily chemicals in balance or kidney issues in the health department.

LIBRA SPIRIT/ARIES BODY CONFLICT

Libra's body sign is Aries. The opposition sets up a conflict that asks the native to be "me first" selfish where their body is concerned. Libra's physical survival must come from an uncompromising attitude when it comes to things like healthy food, enough sleep, and exercise. One example of this scenario could be a Libra's social calendar running their body down. After stopping every night after work for drinks or chit-chat, they would not want to cancel that dinner and a movie they were so looking forward to on the weekend, but their body might demand it. Earth in Aries would suggest that Libra is a sign that really needs a physical dynamic (like exercise) in their life to stay physically healthy. Librans would find themselves in a constant compromise between their instincts and desires on a mental level and their body's high demands of its physicality. Ignoring the "selfish" desires of their Aries body leads to physical exhaustion. Earth in Aries also calls anger issues into the Libran's life. They would be slow to show it but frustration could simmer a long time if they aren't dealing with it, making them feel worn out and sickly. Because of the possible Aries rulership of the body here, there could be chronic headaches as a health problem.

WHAT INTEGRATION AND BALANCE BRINGS

Aries with his Libra integration soon finds out that always putting yourself first gives you a party of one. Learning when to assert themselves and when to listen and give in to others means everything gets done without building resentments or sabotage. They learn there are times when compromise is the bravest thing one can do. Aries doesn't have to be the astrological overachiever anymore. They can stop micromanaging and realize that not only does the job still get done when others are allowed to pitch in, but they have time left over for fun and relaxation, too. It may be a good thing for Aries to discover that other people are kind of nice (and helpful) to have around.

With Libra energy integration, Aries can now see the softer side of life. Everything doesn't have to be a challenge to be worthy of their time, and life doesn't have to be such a struggle. They stop and smell the roses or actively pursue their creative side. Ultimately, they are allowed to be 'one of the fellows' at last and that feels kind of nice after all. The axis of Sun Aries and Earth Libra, if incorporated, gives Aries a marriage of self-motivated desire with an open attitude toward other people's input. They acquire an attitude of work hard, but play hard, too.

For Libra, there are times when anger is appropriate, even righteous, and where assertiveness may ultimately be the only way to really make everyone happy. With Aries integration, Libra begins to understand that they cannot be all that they could be if they are hiding their light out of a desire to please or avoid ruffling feathers. How can they fully develop what they have to offer with their unique talents if they always worry about what the other guy thinks?

Ideally, with a balance of Aries, Libra acquires assertive kindness. They know how and when to speak up without offending anyone. Confrontation is met head on, but with charm and efficiency. Society makes progressive leaps and achieves growth so much easier when everyone feels validated and accepted.

Libra holds a gentle, yet Aries-passion-firm allegiance to that which is beautiful, symmetrical, and peaceful while they now possess an inspiring way to ask (or even lead) everyone else to join them on their journey. They bear the message: "take action but remember to take everything around you (people, animals, or places) into consideration as you move forward."

The axis of Sun Libra and Earth Aries gives Libra self-assertion, firm decision-making married to tact, diplomacy and charm, and an ongoing respect for the different ways or ideas of others.

The Taurus/Scorpio Diametric
EXPECTATIONS

The opposition of Taurus and Scorpio was discussed in some detail in Chapter 7. This opposition is concerned with the collecting or deleting of everything, from material things and emotional baggage right on through to the extreme example of embracing life or allowing death. So the question here is: "What makes life worth living?" or "What do I keep (on every level of life) and what do I throw away and why?"

Subconsciously, Sun-sign Taurus is out of balance because they want constant physical affirmations of life's certainties and really, when you get down to it, there are none. However, they continue to covet and collect as insurance against any change that could lead to death and obliteration. Excess baggage is necessary because it is a comfort to have the familiar around you at all times. It helps the Taurus feel solid and safe.

Subconsciously, Sun-sign Scorpios are out of balance because they feel there no point in getting too attached to anything or owning anything if it's just going to turn ugly, leave them, decay, or die. They also fear that if they don't control and manipulate everyone, the awful truth (whatever it is) will be discovered about them and the Scorpio will be excommunicated from society. This would be devastating to the deeply emotional nature of this sign. They are always afraid they will lose what personal power they have managed to acquire. On the other hand, they are given the strongest psyche in the zodiac to withstand such calamites. For the Scorpio, death is a clean and refreshing slate to begin again with no extra or useless baggage holding you back.

HISTORY

Taurus's history is covered in more detail in Chapter 7. Growing up, the Taurus Sun native was taught that owning things is connected to who you are. Perhaps their family owned a store or had an extensive collection of something that was valuable and admired by all. There is pride (Sun) as well as identity (Sun) connected with the items. It is also what sustains that family and is something that is always there, serving as a backdrop that bestowed stability. They were encouraged to create but always warned to be careful of the darkness out there in the world, so stay safe.

Scorpio Suns know how raw and intense life can get. They were exposed to some kind of precarious fault-line in the life system at an early age, leaving them with a relentless emotional vertigo. This could have been as a result of raising and slaughtering farm animals, dealing with mental illness in the family, or being left on their own at age 13. Regardless of how it happened, they don't take anything for granted, since they got down to the essence of what life is and what it isn't pretty quickly. They have also seen that material things can be taken away and don't protect you from the inevitable.

TAURUS SPIRIT/SCORPIO BODY CONFLICT

Sun in Taurus spirit fights with its Earth in Scorpio body about how much it should eat and drink. In this case, the Scorpio energy body doesn't need as much as the Taurus spirit thinks it does. It could easily thrive on a lot less than it's given. The willpower for or against cravings or bad habits can be particularly strong but probably remains untested because of the Taurian tendency to indulge. The body is overwhelmed by the luxuries the Taurus wants to give it. The Taurus will feel stronger and healthier if they learn moderation and when less is more. With the possible

Scorpion rulership of the body here, health problems with elimination and the reproductive system could occur.

SCORPIO SPIRIT/TAURUS BODY CONFLICT

Scorpio Sun, Taurus Earth asks the Scorpio to see to their body's comfort even when it seems excessive. The Taurus body needs more sensation to be satiated than the Scorpio is completely comfortable with. The native may get disgusted with their natural body's impulses that seem so at odds with their mental philosophy. The Scorpio Sun may want to put its Taurus body on one of those calorie-restricted diets, but this body needs sustenance, not starvation. Scorpio will have to adjust to an understanding that their body can work hard like Scorpio wants, but only half as long as he'd like, and then there must be a soak in the tub and lots of pillows to rest on. With the possible Taurian rulership of the body, there can be health issues with the throat and thyroid.

With the fixed nature of both these signs, there will be a strong tendency toward habitual patterns in physical behavior.

WHAT INTEGRATION AND BALANCE BRINGS

Taurus is on a journey of discovery to find out that all that they truly own is already inside them and not outside of them and that includes the feeling of security. If they don't have it on the inside, then nothing they acquire outside themselves is going to give it to them. By tapping into and embracing the Sun/Earth, Taurus/Scorpio axis, a valuable lesson is learned. They face the reality (Earth Scorpio) that they want to avoid at all costs: that everything on Earth dies, matter is transitory, and change is inevitable.

If they can come around to another angle on their quest for constancy and remember that change is what you can count on and there is security in knowing that death always allows space for growth, if they can rest within that cycle of life and death, with that knowledge, then they have found the balance that the opposition offers. They will not have to have the reassurance and the physical proof of existence. Then they can become a fearless and powerful being.

To the Taurus Sun, ownership and release of ownership is not the only key of empowerment; the Taurus/Scorpio axis is also a treaty of what is or is not ownable. They can get pretty attached to all kinds of items, including people, and feel an entitlement or control over that item where there isn't any. They can hoard ideas until they become locked down with them and all forward mental motion ceases. This is in itself a death, although Taurus seldom realizes it.

Calling on their Earth sign and the natural opposition of Scorpio, they would feel (paradoxically) ever greater security in discharging excess or inappropriate material of any kind. When thrown off their center, a Taurus Sun needs to get to the source of it and clean things out (Earth in

Scorpio) to feel stable again. By taking the garbage out, either literally or figuratively, the native will always feel stronger and satisfied when they understand when it is good to own something and when to toss it away.

Scorpio's journey includes learning that just because people don't act the way you think they should doesn't make them wrong. There is Taurian value in everything just as it stands. Things don't always need to change, die, and transform. Scorpio needs to see the value in what "is." Their need for unencumbered, clean, crisp and clear channels of truthful feeling is a wonder, but sometimes life isn't about the truth, it's about a journey, and cutting to the chase (and truth) too soon cheats the process. The process is something necessary or even precious.

Scorpio understands that ownership is a risk, but Taurus says it is one we all have to take because what we possess helps reinforce who we are. If there is some representation of how we feel and who we are outside of ourselves, it helps us feel more substantial when life seems fleeting. Outside ownership of certain manifested things serves to remind us who we are becoming until we can hold that notion in our hearts all on our own. The Taurus Earth here helps Sun Scorpio to have and hold those things that are of value in their life and keep them long enough to make good use of them until they are no longer needed.

Scorpio Suns have a deep fascination with other people. They want to know how human emotional moods work and to understand the emotional body, that layer of energy just beyond the physical where feelings and emotions reside. This is something that motivates people and prods them to do what they do. Anyone who is in control of this becomes powerful. This power can also be wielded to maneuver people or situations to some coveted conclusion. Scorpios are learning about control, what it is, who has it, and why. But if Scorpio Suns are not careful, they can get caught fast in their experiments on other people and lose their way and their own personal power.

Taurus's counter-balance reminds Scorpio to keep things simple, to stick to the basics. It isn't necessary to always go to the depths or to worry about and analyze everyone's feelings and the inner motivations in every situation. You don't need to control others to have the things go your way. Taurus says just listen to your own heart and mind and ask yourself: "Who are you and where are you going?" Those are really the only answers you need to get you where you want to go. The only person you can truly control is you.

The Gemini/Sagittarius Diametric

EXPECTATIONS

The opposing energy of Gemini and Sagittarius asks the question: "What is more important in life: fact or personal truth?" or "Should I go through life being objective or subjective?"

The Sun-sign Gemini is out of balance because it only wants the facts in life and all choices open to it at all times. It craves the mental excitement of new ideas or shifting situations. Life is best in an observational mode without commitment or emotional entanglement. Facts and trivia are so stimulating and much easier to work with than more contemplative and complicated truths.

The Sun-sign Sagittarius is out of balance because it emphasizes its own subjective experiences in life so that its thoughts and feelings become more important than fact: "All that is true is what I feel is truth; how can anything be real if I don't relate to it?" "Principles are what count; they give you the best guidance to living this life."

HISTORY

As they were growing up, Gemini's household was a place of wonder or curiosity. Everyone sat around the dinner table and talked about anything and everything. The kids were asked about the day's events or quizzed on what they learned in school. Dad might ask what the state capital of North Dakota was as Mom reminisced about the way the world was when she was a girl. Current events were discussed in great detail with input encouraged from all on how those happenings could have gone better. A phrase of disapproval heard often was: "That doesn't make sense!" If the Gemini had a problem they were told to look at it rationally: everything could be understood better by using your head.

People in the Sagittarius household lived with or were governed by some kind of higher truth or law. There are many ways this could have played out. The family might have been deeply religious, spiritual, very scientific, or just every-day philosophers. At any rate, there was an expectation, an abstract code to be lived up to. Knowledge was meant to be expounded upon. Knowledge was important, but more important was the way you used it and applied it. People were encouraged to take something they had learned, form an opinion about it and make it theirs. Experimentation was expected within a certain framework, whether those structures were intellectual in nature, philosophical, or emotional.

GEMINI SPIRIT/SAGITTARIUS BODY CONFLICT

Sometimes Gemini is so busy thinking they forget they have a body. This body gets under stress due to the mind. The body needs lots of hiking or riding in the big outdoors to relax. Earth in Sag is an inconjunct and this misaligned Earth energy could produce a body that is confused in its proportions, making it a bit awkward or gawky. However, this body wants to move and Sun in Gemini lives much of their life in the mind. The key here would be the enticement of something new to experience that would pique Gemini's interest and satisfy the Sag needs of exploration. One outcome may be an adrenaline junkie looking for adventure outside while pushing and testing their physical gifts or stamina amidst nature's wonders: bungee jumping the Grand Canyon or rock climbing Mount McKinley. With the possible Sag rulership of the body here, there may be health issues with the hips.

SAGITTARIUS SPIRIT/GEMINI BODY CONFLICT

Like Gemini, Sun in Sag doesn't pay attention to the existence of the physical body much, either. They need to educate themselves on the best care of it and not be sidetracked by fads or personal beliefs. There is a tendency to override medical or nutritional advice, making claims that it is not for them, like Christian Scientists whose philosophy is sometimes at odds with what the body may need. They should get a good book on how the body truly functions and read it. Famous for traveling, they have been known to be caught up with the next big thing and push the body beyond its limits. They need to think about their body and do what the facts say to do for it. With the possible Gemini rulership of the body here, there may be health problems with the shoulders, arms, and hands.

WHAT INTEGRATION AND BALANCE BRING

The Gemini is on a journey to find meaning and depth in the facts and information he gathers. For Gemini, it's easier to stay objective, linear, and logical by avoiding the deeper meanings that might call into play more complicated and conflicting truths. Staying unemotional means they are uninvolved and unattached to outcomes as well. Their attitude is similar to some scientific methods that encourage conclusions to be made of what a life-form is all about by observation only: watching what it does, not what it thinks or feels. Gemini collects knowledge the way Taurus collects knick-knacks. They can live in their head quite easily and from that perspective things can look pretty straightforward and simplistic. Life is easier to interpret with superficial sound-bytes: good or bad, right or wrong, it is or it isn't. They embrace logic wholeheartedly, following a thought or idea to a compelling conclusion, the next most obvious step. The trouble is that life is not always logical. In fact, an even number of times it can be illogical. People live in their hearts and even their souls as well as their minds. Gemini will never really understand anything if they use logic alone. All the while, they think they have what they need to label the world around them when they are really missing vital pieces of information.

Sagittarius says to Gemini: "Information is great, but what are you going to do with it?" Facts describe, but they don't tell you what something truly is. Take your ideas to their conclusion and find out what they really mean to you and to the world at large, then use them or apply them. That is the point of knowledge.

Geminis are famous for their distractions: variety and choice. Their active minds want things to think about; that is what makes life worth living. They want to know everything about everything and they fear having to make a choice for one because this means an end to the other choices.

Sag explains to Gemini that when you make a choice, variety isn't lost. What are the properties of this choice, and how deep do you want go with it? There is still variety inherent in every single choice. The deep satisfactions of understanding this choice will more than make up for any loss the Gemini may still feel. With Sag figured into the equation, Gemini acquires meaning at last.

As the opposite of Gemini, Sagittarius stresses personal truth. Any information that comes their way must be at least partly integrated into what has come to them before. Their personal data bank is a framework of knowledgeable opinions forged by years of consideration and contemplation of the world and its workings. Higher truth is a pursuit, and here factual information is not always relished because it gets in the way of personal expansion. For Sag, the freedom of abstract thought and theory bestows a feeling of connection to a greater mindset, perhaps opening up spiritual pathways.

They wish to know the mind of God. Yet their knowledge is so based on emotional connections, personal experience, and formed opinions that any information they work with is way too subjective. They have a strong sense of knowing, but what is it that they know? Is it based on any real truth or reality at all? Gemini's balance brings the Sag back to the basics of fact. Gemini asks Sag to research his theories and give more rationalization to his abstract thought: "Don't get so buried in one or two ideas: be open to a variety of information, from a variety of sources, so you can stay open-minded and test your theories for facts."

Having a meaningful relationship with the knowledge acquired is a good thing. It leads to personal truths and a philosophy that can sustain someone throughout a lifetime. Still, one can't really come to any higher truth if they don't start with some facts. There must be a balance between objective and subjective thought, because without logic, true meaning will ultimately be lost.

The Cancer/Capricorn Diametric
EXPECTATIONS

The oppositional diametric of Cancer and Capricorn gives us a choice of home or career. It asks the question: "Will we be sustained by career or by our family?" Where do we owe our allegiance? A follow-up question that lurks in the background is: "Do we stay where we have been planted and nourished, or seek our destiny and fortune by taking our rightful place in the greater world around us?"

The Sun-sign Cancer is out of balance because they are too attached to their source, their true home. The most important thing is family or their close friends and their emotional connections to an ever-tighter knit group of people. Their sense of emotional stability is reinforced by their group's opinions and traditions.

The Sun-sign Capricorn prefers to set their emotional ties aside because they get in the way of getting things done. They are out of balance because they are too attached to outside things, like their career and reputation. Personal connections seem trivial and inconsequential to them. Being useful and feeling accomplished is too important, along with being rewarded with respect and material gain by their colleagues for what they have done.

HISTORY

Growing up in the Cancer household meant that a lot of affection was usually given out or at least emotional connections were somehow cultivated and maintained at all times. The family checked in with one another and temperatures read of the general feeling or mood whenever certain decisions were made, more than any full-out discussions of the topic. There were things that weren't questioned because a certain way of living and how everyone felt about that was understood and handed down by those that came before. Everyone knew where they stood and what was expected of them. Perhaps this is a family of doctors or miners whose ideologies were always an integral part of the outlook and attitude of the rest of the family. When there was a problem, everyone came running to connect with each other and then console or defend. Everyone in the family liked to feel secure on their joint path of where they are going, with whom, and why.

There may be a family business in the Capricorn household as well, but here either the attitude and beliefs from that business are not brought home to have much influence on the rest of the family or the business came first before the family. What is important is that the business (of the family) is prosperous, (not group hugs), because then the town will look upon this family as one they can trust. As a result, they may have become leaders of that community. On the other hand, the family may be dysfunctional when it comes to emotional support, with the children encouraged to take up responsibility at an early age and go out into the world before they are ready. They are shown that life can be hard and money makes it easier. No one is going to rescue you. Emotions can change; don't invest in them because they can't be trusted. What is better is to be master of your own fate.

CANCER SPIRIT/CAPRICORN BODY CONFLICT

Sun in Cancer is another case of the Spirit feeling

that it needs things that the body (Capricorn) really doesn't. Cancer reaches for the glass of wine or a Twinkie for emotional satisfaction and the Capricorn body would rather have a suitable dinner at the same time every day. The body gets cheated of regular, reliable, and substantial sustenance. The native has to use their body to the best of its abilities or it will lose its built-in endurance. The unnecessary overindulgence may prove to be indicative of a high rate of diabetes with this combination. With the possible Capricorn rulership of the body here, health issues may be chronic and have to do with the knees and joints.

CAPRICORN SPIRIT/CANCER BODY CONFLICT

Sun in Capricorn and Earth in Cancer fight over indulgence. Capricorn is too busy getting things done to stop for the substantial lunch their Cancer body not only craves but emotionally requires. They need to remember to take a break during the day, to delegate some of the workload to one of their peeps while they munch on a (hopefully healthy) treat or by the time they get home their body will be collapsing and shutting down in a sulk. The revenge is ulcers and digestive issues due to possible Cancer rulership of the body that will certainly ruin Capricorn's tight schedule and career goals.

WHAT INTEGRATION AND BALANCE BRING

A very successful astrologer and friend of mine has been seeing a contradictory trend in Cancerian Sun people for many years, one that has, over time, changed her mind about who the typical Cancer is. The most common astrological interpretations for Cancer Suns have always emphasized home, mothering, and family. In recent years, though, Cancers seem to be leaving home in droves and applying their considerable skills as entrepreneurs and even CEOs in the work-a-day world. They have found out something amazing: they are really good at it. Maybe this fact is only the result of no one really staying home anymore or maybe it turns out there isn't a lot of difference between organizing a home or an office, but I think there is even more going on here.

These are the Cancers who have discovered their other side, their built-in Sun/Earth opposition and the balancing power of their Capricorn Earth sign. As the human race evolves, our personal growth naturally involves filling in any blanks in our development. Human personalities tend to emphasize certain traits and when we arrive at birth with certain natural areas of expertise, it is usually at the expense of others. All Sun signs can look to their opposite sign or Earth sign to see what those areas are. This might explain Cancer's sudden success out in the world. Cancers are beginning to work toward a balance of outside success and a loving family. They don't mind a little power, but they are going to have a life while they get it. Cancers always empathize and understand how people feel about things. How can this not contribute to their success in many areas of business?

Capricorns have a little more work in front of them. They don't see what personal feelings have to do with anything. Emotions don't change the facts or the spreadsheets. They might think that a business that runs on mood and emotion is a very shaky one. Cancer reminds Capricorn that work is done by people and that they have feelings and emotions. To run a successful and strong company, one must address the morale issue at all times.

When people feel good about who and where they are, they give more energy and time to the company, there is less friction, and they are more inclined to help wherever they can. Items are better made and details attended to with more efficiency when workers have a good attitude because they believe the company cares about them. Understanding people's emotions and moods are absolutely crucial if you want to sell or market something, too.

Cancers and Capricorns are also learning how to become emotionally practical. Where and how are emotions handled in places and situations that traditionally have excluded them, like business affairs? They address the question of belonging: "Where and how do I fit in?" We need to fulfill our destinies but we need an anchor too, a support system sustaining us, as we do. We need our place in the family, but we also need our place in the world.

People's expectations outside the home are sometimes very different than inside the home. So C and C together ask when you begin to find your special place in the world: "How are your basic core beliefs challenged and how do you meet those challenges?" Capricorn reminds Cancer that working to be all they are meant to be means letting go of many family attitudes and traditions (Cancer) and the trick is doing it in such a way that the family isn't threatened by the move. Together, these two signs achieve a balance between upbringing and ambition.

The Leo/Aquarius Diametric
EXPECTATIONS

The Leo/Aquarius schism is somewhat similar to Aries and Libra but here it is less intimate or personal. Here the question goes beyond "me or you" and addresses the concept of individuality versus community, culture, or society. Leo and Aquarius together put forth the question: "What is more important: my own passion or my own species?" or "My desire or my tribe's desire?"

The Leo Sun sign is driven to produce something unique to portray their own take on things and distinguish themselves in order to stand above the faceless masses. They are out of balance because within their singular, passionate call to arms, they have forgotten that they are part of a group of people whose efforts ultimately influence, sustain, or reject the individual's creativity.

The Aquarius Sun sign is concerned with everyone around them. Who are these people and what do they want or need? Aquarius is out of balance because they feel the group is more important and forgets to acknowledge the value of more individual, personal skills and that to develop those skills means a more unique contribution to society.

HISTORY

In the Leo household, self-expression was everything. Members of the family were either creative individualists or had passionate, personal feelings about life. There was never pressure to conform; instead, Leo was expected to form their own ideas and defend them if necessary. Other members were very interested and invested in the Leo in some way. Attention was paid to him/her (good or bad) and praise was given for any of their efforts. They realized early on that they mattered more than the others around them and that they were somehow special.

The Aquarius household was always a little different from the rest of the neighborhood. Maybe they didn't mow their lawn or maybe they didn't even have a lawn. In a ritzy area, they were the ones with a tight budget and the kids wore clothes that (horrors!) came from the thrift shop. They were ridiculed or rejected, leaving them to ponder what it took to be a member of the masses. Or they were the ones with the

Victorian 6-bedroom with a swimming pool in an otherwise very modest housing tract. Somehow, their different ideas or different lifestyle gave them a profound awareness of living apart from others. At the same time, everyone might be welcomed over to swim in their pool when the days were hot. The family felt a need to share what they had with those less fortunate. Whatever the scenario, the Aquarius child soon realized that it wasn't all that fun to be distinguished and unique. It made them feel guilty or even caused trouble. They wanted a world where everyone belonged. Sympathy for all outcasts naturally gave way to the question of: what have you done for others today? They knew that when one person wins, then another has to lose, and this was never satisfying. What could be done so that everyone was a winner? What made groups of people happy, healthy, and successful?

LEO SPIRIT/AQUARIUS BODY CONFLICT

Sun in Leo with an Earth body in Aquarius may feel like a foreigner in their own body; they may have a hard time feeling any attachment to it. An extreme case of this may translate as something akin to apotemnophilia or Body Identity Disorder, when people want to remove perfectly good limbs. Some element of disjointed understanding of what the body can handle or endure is likely here because Earth in Aquarius is the astrological 'fall' of Earth and so is weakened or afflicted. They might consciously or unconsciously put themselves in dangerous situations, risking bodily harm. With the possible Aquarius rulership of the body, here there may be health issues with the shins and electrical system of the body.

AQUARIUS SPIRIT/LEO BODY CONFLICT

An Aquarius Sun with a Leo Earth means the body is caught between the physical need to stand out in any room and feel the attention and support emanating from others and a desire to detach from the body entirely to be rid of distractions that only get in the way of their plans and contributions. The Aquarian thinks that the body is merely a vehicle and nothing more. They tend to shun the physical contact their Leo physicality needs. After many years of living in the mind, their body, living with a lack of love, rebels and gives them heart trouble due to the Leo rulership of the body.

WHAT INTEGRATION AND BALANCE BRING

The duality of Leo and Aquarius asks us to simultaneously consider the importance of the individual and the community.

Leos need to share themselves or produce something that reflects who they are. They then need others to recognize either their skills as a leader or their products and to support or admire them. This gives Leo a reinforcement of who they are. So Leo, for all its individualistic tendencies, does need a connection to the masses because, ironically, without them, Leo loses their sense of self. The Aquarius balance reminds

Leo to stop and consider humanity and the impact their individuality has on it. Aquarius says to Leo: "Don't forget that you are a part of a larger whole" and "There is great power in camaraderie." When people think or work together, they can accomplish far more than any individual can achieve. A group also has the power to support and nurture individuals who create and help them contribute even more to the world, making everyone a winner.

Aquarius understands that we need society because we are a social species. Besides our craving for company and interaction, society plays a role in our cognitive development, helping us to develop many skills (like language) whose advancement would not be possible without the contributions of the larger group or tribe. People who live in the same area have much in common because they have shared experiences. This makes them brothers and sisters. We need each other and are beholden to each other. With Leo's help, Aquarius can be free to consider their own individual skills and what they alone have to offer the world. Without Leo's intervention, Aquarius would devalue their own power and miss developing it and utilizing it for the greater good.

Together, they can see that self-expression or single-minded creative pursuits affect everyone, creating stability or a schism. They also learn that single oddities (Leo) have the power to lead a group (Aquarius) beyond where they could have gone if they had all stuck together. Embracing invention and originality allows conditions in a society to improve, in turn leading to their health and progress, for that group or an individual.

Individual creativity and a strong, well-functioning community are both important in turn. This duo is also about passion and drive for self-aggrandizement while embracing their place and function within a group: preservation but also growth, passionate commitment and focus, together with spontaneous, open invention, and acceptance. Leo provides the leadership, passion, and reasons for the causes Aquarius takes up. Aquarius connects the Leo individual to their particular support group that gives them sustenance. Society needs leadership (Leo) but also connection and coherence (Aquarius). The individual is important to the group and the group is important to the individual.

In the 2010 movie The Bang Bang Club, there is a great example of the conflict between the human quest for rewarded creativity (Leo) and social contribution (Aquarius). It shows photojournalists that are passionate about their craft, determined to succeed, and a bit addicted to the advantages their activities bring them. After covering the fight for freedom in South Africa, they start questioning their ideals and intentions and chastising themselves for not realizing the influence they had in their hands and the help they could've afforded a group of people that needed it. They go from being special and separate to considering being comrades of the cause, just another important member of their own human race. Together, both Leo and Aquarius learn how they think and what they do is not only important to any individual, it can have a profound effect or impact on others as well.

The Virgo/Pisces Diametric
EXPECTATIONS

Our last diametric has some similarities to the Leo/Aquarius, but is farther reaching. It still compares the individual, but now we go beyond tribal society to the source of all life. The question Virgo and Pisces ask together is: "Am I of this world or all worlds?" "Am I God or one of its creations?" A follow-up question would be: "Should I live my life in a practical or spiritual way?"

The Sun-sign Virgo contemplates daily life with a magnifying glass. Each detail is scrutinized to see if it there could be an improvement made. They are out of balance because they feel that all that matters in life is how well you live it. Correcting and perfecting the steps on their path and those around them, occupy them constantly.

The Sun-sign Pisces closes their eyes on the world around them and reaches beyond the every-day to contemplate where life comes from. They need a connection to the largess of the universe. Pisces is out of balance because they forget to think about or attend to daily life on this planet.

HISTORY

The Virgo household was a place of order. Like life in suburbia, everything was done on time and with a kind of finesse. Problems were thought through and adversity was met, with logic and practicality, using a left-brain emphasis. There's no need for shouting, crying, and other silly emotional displays. Vulgar activities or maudlin displays were shunned. Life was a game of "get it right." Lists of "To Dos" were done daily and carried out in the most efficient way possible. "When you learn and follow proper procedures, things always go just the way you want them to." There was also an expectation here that one could always do even better, though.

There was also an element of distrust or discomfort that permeated the house. Worry or fear of losing something: control, wealth, status, decorum, organization, or intelligence, and not being able to get it back. Life was a challenge, and there was your role to play, and your job was to educate yourself and make the best of it. The family was probably successful and well respected as good, solid, down-to-earth people, "good eggs" that did their share and could be counted on to help out when the chips were down. On the material level, things usually worked out well and outsiders marveled at how together the family was, but inside, trust was decidedly lacking.

The Pisces household bore similarities to an ashram or a commune. Things worked out more by the grace of god than any real planning. The right brain and the creative side of life were embraced. Finding the essence of what it means to be alive and be human was an important part of living. Exploration of that idea through emotional experimentation, like spiritual studies, poetry, dream interpretation, music, or art, was encouraged.

Helping others out was an expected occurrence because there was an attitude of "we are all related, part of the same human family or the same planet." The idea was that those in need are just like us and as a result there was a complete and sometimes terribly misplaced trust in those they took in. The family always managed to recover, though with faith undaunted. Sometimes it seemed as if someone or something beyond their ken took care of them.

There was an element of uncertainty here regarding proper procedures. No one was ever quite sure what the result of their actions would be or there was a member of the family that interfered with order and brought havoc in. The outside world seemed to work in mysterious ways. The family made decisions emotionally, with imagination, and through intuition. Together with sympathetic connections in their neighborhood, most of the time, things just seemed to work out. Their mantra was "Be open to what could happen; dream big." Despite any difficulties, there was a great feeling of love, connection, and trust abounding.

VIRGO SPIRIT/PISCES BODY CONFLICT

While Sun Virgo worries about all the mental details of life, her body could use some emotional investment or physical contact. With the Sun-sign Virgo checking the mirror to see if there is anything out of place – hair, a zit, or a slip – showing on her way out the door, her Earth-in-Pisces body is gasping for some down time, away from the day-to-day demands. Earth in Pisces needs more internal space, time to be alone, rest, and contemplate. Pisces wants Virgo to consider the body as not just a physical machine that needs a few vitamins. For the Pisces, the body doesn't only exist in the physical plane. We have many other energetic bodies that cannot be seen. The astral, the ethereal, chakras, etc.: for the Pisces' presence, these are all valid bodies and directly contribute to what the physical body perceives, thrives on, or looks like. They might need something like a meditation on these other bodies. Their health as well as the manifested, physical body's health must be attended to in order to stay in perfect harmony. With the possible Pisces rulership of the body here, health issues with the feet can also occur.

WHAT INTEGRATION AND BALANCE BRING

Virgo is always busy dealing with the chores of every-day life: picking up the kids at soccer, getting the groceries, planning that farewell party, making a nutritious dinner, and serving on the town beautification committee. They know things aren't going to get done on their own and they are the best one to do it. They have plenty of know-how.

This makes Virgo feel that it has to micromanage everything or it won't get done right. "Never leave for tomorrow (or someone else less efficient to handle) the things that need doing today", but that kind of attitude is exhausting and stressful. All that worry over the correct way of doing things and yet, when it comes to life, is there only one way to live it? Pisces comes to Virgo's rescue by reminding them that there are a myriad of opportunities to dream up or imagine how things could work differently if you would just give yourself permission.

Virgo's expectations just run way too high. Perfectionism can actually prevent things from getting done. How can anything ever be released for public use with confidence, when it has to be flawless? Pisces says there is no doubt that life is messy and it's a mess you will never ever be able to clean up to your satisfaction. Wanting it to be otherwise just puts you in an endless frustration over what should be instead of just accepting what is. Work to make things just "good enough" and let go of the endless tinkering. Accept that no one is ever truly satisfied and move on: "We are not God."

Pisces' counterbalance to Virgo's fear and worry is: have a little faith in the universe. It will help you if you let it and may even send things your way, but if you're too busy pushing the river, you won't even notice when what you want shows up. A prayer is sometimes answered only when you let go of the circumstances around its arrival. Just because the universe works differently than how you think it should, doesn't mean it doesn't work. A Pisces phrase for the Virgo to study is: "Let go and let God."

Pisces lives on the spiritual side of life, embracing the shamanistic ebb and flow of the universal consciousness. They understand the plight of the humanity, living lives of quiet desperation. They receive emotional vibes or messages from life and its creatures and therefore have compassion for all. They've learned not to force their little will on the larger will of the world because there is a plan, a path they can't see but can walk to great satisfaction and success. They feel we're here to rise above our reality and connect with the source: God, or something like it. That is how we will understand what life is for, at last.

Virgo points out to Pisces that they take too much on faith and don't collect enough hard-nosed knowledge and experience to meet the demands of every-day life. If you want something to happen, you need to make some effort to get there. Remember too: "God helps those that help themselves."

Virgo explains to Pisces that understanding ahead of time what is involved or what to expect in situations, helps you to know whether you really want them or not. Then you aren't as likely to be disappointed in them or be taken for a ride in ignorance of them.

The balance of Virgo and Pisces produces a practical poet or a spiritual realist, someone who can feel connected to everything and yet function well as a separate entity. Life should be lived simultaneously on both the practical and spiritual levels. We can meditate and tune into our spiritual side in the morning and then study or work hard in the afternoon.

Whether God is within or without, we're all part of the world and, ultimately, the universe. Do what we can do when it's time to do it, but learn when to let go of the things we can't control or aren't in charge of. Let others do their part, but lend a hand when help is needed. We can always do better, but there is no need to go to extremes. Pay attention to details, but don't lose sight of the larger force at work within our lives.

Together, Virgo and Pisces ask us to see the spiritual side and find inspiration in even the most menial tasks of every-day life. They are busy finding ways to improve themselves, but at the same time are emotionally in tune with their species and their world: "I am one flowing into many and many flowing into one." We are separate beings with duties and obligations, but we are also part of something greater, something wonderfully imaginative: the human race, the planet, and, finally, the universe.

Summary

The idea of confronting, studying, and integrating the Sun/Earth axis in our personal natal charts could become a revolutionary act of power for our psyches. This union of opposites may ultimately incorporate the spirit (Sun) with the physical body (Earth) giving us a great potential for wholeness of body and soul. We have lost a meaningful connection with our own bodies and are not facing the reality of what they need. To begin to see our human condition as both a spiritual and a physical one, combined, opens the door for a new perspective on our overall health and the wholeness of life itself.

To create a balance of opposing energies has always been difficult for us a species, finding a way to live harmoniously with two different energies or opinions will resolve the constant duality that is naturally inherent in our universe. The dual nature of the opposition aspect will immediately help us be aware and focus in on many of our single Sun-Sign personality dilemmas we have been born into. In addition, it shows us how to complete the journey we are on for allowance and tolerance of those who are different from us.

When we confront the challenge of that part of us that is a little different, we will get used to accepting differences in each other. We will get to exercise our flexibility and our power of choice. We find compassion for the struggles of others and what it is to be human. I once heard the astrologer Isabel Hickey say: "Everyone is trying the best they can with what they have." When we see how everyone is coping with a fixed opposition in their chart, we will understand that statement well.

Chapter 11
Delineating Earth

"Life is not a problem to be solved but a reality to be experienced." ~Siren Kierkegaard

In astrology, there are favorable and unfavorable signs for certain planets to be in. The terms for the different levels of favorability are called: dignity, exaltation, detriment, and fall.

The dignity of a planet in a chart is when it happens to be in the sign it rules, like Pluto in Scorpio, for example. The exaltation of a planet is when it is in a sign that gives the planet its greatest strength. The detriment of a planet is when it is in the sign that is the opposite of its rulership and therefore the energy is awkward and thwarted to some degree. The fall sign is the most difficult assignment for a planet; it is in a sign that doesn't match or understand that planetary energy at all, leaving the planet very weak.

In any chapter on the delineation of a "new" planet there should be an attempt to assess the dignities and debilities of that body.

I proceed here with some caution.

Astrological Dignities and Debilities of Planet Earth

In classic astrology books, dignities and debilities of planets are clearly labeled and there is a formula used. It would be easy to just reassign the same traditional planetary dignities and debilities for Earth, swapping out Venus for rulership of Taurus and putting in Earth. This seems to work when we come to the detriment, which traditionally is the opposing sign of the rulership. Therefore, Earth in Scorpio would the detriment of planet Earth. This makes sense as Earth means life to us and Scorpio, as we all know, is representative of death. I also like the symmetry of the fact that Scorpio was once ruled by Mars and historically Mars in Taurus was the detriment. Perhaps it would follow that Pluto in Taurus would then be a detriment as well?

The moon is exalted in the sign of Taurus so traditionally speaking we could say the sign of Cancer is the exaltation for Earth. The opposing sign to Cancer is Capricorn. Considering then a "fall" position for Earth in Capricorn, we could point to the idea that Capricorn is the depth of winter and the closest the Earth comes to death every year, while, paradoxically, we could discuss how the Earth holds on through such a test of life-threatening temperatures, folding in on itself in slumber and preserving its life and strength until spring. In some ways, the "dead" of winter is *all* Earth: simple, basic, and no frills attached.

Now according to George Llewellyn in his book <u>A to Z Horoscope Maker and Delineator</u> Moon in Taurus is exalted and the planet Uranus's fall is in the sign of Taurus and not Capricorn.[1] I presume that he is pulling in the old rulership of Aquarius by Saturn (and Capricorn) and moving them around? In any case, Aquarius is a great match for the fall position of an Earth sign. Uranus also happens to be exalted in Scorpio.

In <u>The Astrologer's Handbook</u> by Frances Sakoian and Louis Acker, an exaltation is: "…the planet in its sign of exaltation is in the environment which according to *natural* law generates the basic principle of that planet. Therefore, a planet in its sign of exaltation is in the most powerful sign position for volume or intensity of energy."[2] (Italics and emphasis mine)

Cancer is a great match for this description. If we look at our planet Earth in June/July (midsummer in the Northern Hemisphere) we see absolute fertility and all living things at their peak of growth and strength. Cancer's position (4th house) on the natural wheel of the zodiac also supports the Earth scenario. We know that the ascendant-descendant axis of the chart wheel is symbolic of the division of the Earth and sky. From the ascendant upward we have the sky, and moving downward as we cross the descendant, we pass under the horizon of the Earth. Of course, the 2nd house of Taurus is below the horizon, giving it a base, a symbolic grounding, below the Earth. When we get to the house of Cancer, though, it is at the very bottom of the wheel, a very grounded position and the farthest point down in our psyches we can psychologically travel. It _is_ the base of the wheel. Now, the descriptions of the natural 4th house of Cancer are also very interesting and applicable. The 4th house begins with the angle known as the Imum Coeli or I.C. and it is known in chart interpretations as the root or source of whatever the chart is cast for. It is where the chart's energy is coming from. It provides the foundation for the native of the chart.

It would follow that planet Earth in its fall should be either Capricorn or Aquarius. Capricorn is certainly a good candidate, but in the end I feel that Aquarius makes the most sense here. The breakdown of structure and matter that is Aquarius, and the chaos that it brings, is the antithesis of Earthly stability. Aquarius would chafe at having to follow set directions step by step and adhere to tradition. Earth in Aquarius would be looking to tear apart or break out, not build up. February is also a very difficult month for the creatures of Earth. The last vestiges of winter are pounding the critters and they have to hold on through that last month until March.

Here are my suggestions for the D and D of Earth:

DIGNITY/RULERSHIP: Earth in Taurus

DETRIMENT: Earth in Scorpio

EXALTATION: Earth in Cancer

FALL: Earth in Aquarius

I should also like to give a little statement about the exaltation of Earth that might be a bit of a stretch. Looking at the fall sign of the Earth (Aquarius) and going backward to its classic opposite, another possible exaltation would be Leo. Earth exalted in Leo? Leo sits next to Cancer, and it's still summer for most of us on the planet. This is an interesting idea, given the fact that Leo is ruled by the Sun and the Sun is of central importance in the natal chart. The Sun rules the vitality of the native too. The sign of Leo and the Sun, may even rule the human race as a whole. If you consider this hypothesis, it would also bring the last fixed sign energy of Leo (in a round-about way) into an equation (Taurus + Scorpio + Aquarius + Leo) that would give us that symmetry of the four signs that may symbolically rule our reality mentioned in Chapter 2. However, the fire element of Leo isn't a good fit for Earth, not to mention the complication of the Earth and Sun in permanent opposition so, I think Cancer is the best fit for the exaltation of Earth over all.

The Influence of Aspects on Earth in Signs

In the natal chart, easy aspects to planet Earth will, of course, bring out the best that can be hoped for in that planet and sign. In an ideal chart situation with supporting aspects to Earth and Sun, there would be great opportunity for the balancing of both signs involved, a creative integration that would make for a very complete and powerful wholeness in body and spirit.

Challenging aspects to Earth (and of course Sun) in the chart would mean that Earth is afflicted in the natal chart. This would put a negative spin on planetary combinations, creating problems or issues with security, substance, grounding, money, productivity, and (theoretically) the physical body in combination with the traits of the sign Earth is in.

An important word about "good" and "bad" aspects: difficult aspects do not mean that the native is saddled with the negative side of any sign/planet combination for the rest of their life. It only means that the best of that energy must be worked for; it isn't handed out freely and easily. In fact, having positive aspects can sometimes be a curse because there is nothing being asked of them, there is no effort involved, and natives can be unconscious to the power in them or lazy in the use of them. Negative aspects can actually have quite the opposite effect. The native is keenly aware of what they don't have and are motivated to change their situation. With effort, they acquire full use of the benefits of that planetary combination later in life.

The Shadow Earth

In the last chapter I discussed what I call the diametric, or the axis, the marriage of two opposing planets (Earth and Sun), the opposing signs they will find themselves in, and how uniting them brings about a much needed balance in human nature. The single delineations of Earth in the various signs should be considered as a shadow side of the opposing Sun sign until we can integrate them. At this point, they will show their power most prominently in whatever houses they fall into or in a strong aspect with another planet in a native's astrological chart.

Planet Earth in Signs

FOR EASIER COMPREHENSION WORDS DESCRIBING EARTH ARE ITALICIZED

Earth in Aries

With planet Earth in Aries in the natal chart, the native would find *stability* by being physically active. The more on-the-go they are, the more *secure* they feel. To be in motion would be a *grounding* factor any time they need to key into their earth

They would find *security* by pushing up against something: an unmet desire, an adversary, a challenge, a mountain to climb, a wrong to be righted, or just a game to be won. This is the way their personal Earth in Aries is triggered when they need to feel *stable*. Anything that connects their body to its energetic source, like a sport, would engage their Earth. They could be a great athlete because they would find the *determination and dedication* to practice the moves of their body over and over to perfection. They would develop *stamina*.

The act of physical love would also clear their energy and help them to feel connected with a *concrete* whole. Expression of their physical desire would also give the native a feeling that any relationship is *real and permanent*, whether true or not.

Self-concern would be brought to the forefront with this combination. There would be *natural* inclination to 'know thyself' and develop whatever *personal resources* they were born with and cultivate more personal potential all the time.

Another angle to consider when Earth puts on an Aries jacket is the discomfort of feeling like she's being rushed. Earth never likes to hurry and Aries' fast pace makes Earth feel like it is going to miss important details or be tripped up by something it doesn't see coming. It's a struggle between "wait a minute, how is this going to work?" versus "let's just do it and see." There is a conflict of now versus *later* as well: "do I go for instant gratification or *plan* for a better future?" Hopefully, both.

In an astrological house, natives would *value* activity of any kind and admire movers and shakers in all walks of life, people who know how to get things done that really count. Earth in Aries would admire or even worship people of either physical or mental *strength*. Earth in Aries would make good foremen/women themselves for any company, understanding both the reason for a fast production of goods but also exactly how much *quality* that might sacrifice.

They would feel grounded by taking action, being on the go, sex, exercising, challenges, or seeing any progress being made.

EARTH-CONSCIOUSNES/ECOLOGICAL LEANINGS

Earth in Aries can create a leader when it comes to living *green* or working for the Earth. The Sun-Libra (its opposite) qualities these individuals possess may be at odds with their Earthy Aries' latent aggression, but their unique Aries/Libra axis, the personal assignment to find a balance between what they want and what others want, especially in terms of *physical, material* goods, can give them great insight as to how the rest of us can deal with the challenges of living green. The art of compromise can be accomplished and they can show us how. They are born with a feeling that the Earth is a dynamic (Aries) and even demanding entity, sometimes even a bit overwhelming in its energetic force. The idea that we must take more and more from it seems one-sided, base, and even selfish, a "gimme" attitude that goes against the (Sun) Libra grain. They have trouble justifying taking so much from planet Earth unless they also champion it in some way as a road to restore balance. Of course, Aries is a doer, so they want to know what is being done about pollution. Their creed would be: "Stop sitting around talking about it, it's time to fight for cleaner air and water." They may spontaneously join an *ecological* protest but avoid any *long term commitment* to it. "Waste to Energy" plants would make their hearts beat faster.

NEGATIVE

Afflicted Earth in Aries generates someone who doesn't even consider the environment. They are too caught up in their own lives and have way too much on their plate to think about what they consider too far in the future. "Worry about future generations? I'm too busy worrying about mine!"

AFFLICTED EARTH IN ARIES

In this area, the negatives of Earth in Aries would be trouble gained by jumping into action before all the factors have been considered. In the back of their mind they might have a thinking process that goes something like this: "My plans or ideas must be right or *solid* because I am taking action on them." This is the old 'jumping into the pool before checking to see if there is water in it' scenario. The free-wheeling action Aries enjoys keeps getting bogged down in the idea of *conservation or proper process*. Action becomes all herky-jerky first fast and then slow, resulting in mistakes to the project or accidents to their body.

Aries and anger go hand in hand, the result of a blockage of action. With Earth in Aries, it is more likely to manifest in frustration rather than fisticuffs. This anger/frustration is likely to build for some time before an expression of it and this may in the long run, help the native to develop and call on their *endurance, determination, and sheer will* to see their idea through, *resolve* an issue, or *complete* a task. This would result in courage. Earth in Aries could be more than brave. They have the courage of their *convictions*. Of course, it could also make for anger that is terribly and unreasonably long-lasting and enduring, a *grudge lasting* a lifetime.

Another negative side would be a tendency to crave *permanence* or *quality* and not be in the mood to work for it *step by step*. They want it now and would tend to think that something *solid and lasting* can be had quickly. No need to carefully *plan and execute*.

With Earth in Aries, they have a strong drive to *build* something, but it is crippled, because they can't have it when they want it. This frustrates and thwarts their desire to the point that they may just want to forget the whole thing and move on. The *patience* that is needed to construct from the *ground up* isn't there and the "cut to the chase" attitude doesn't allow real *stability*. When tested, the native's projects may crumble and collapse because the proper *foundation* wasn't *carefully* laid. This would be akin to a *gardener* that is always pulling the vegetables up by the roots to see how far they have grown – "can I eat it *now*?" – thereby stunting or even killing the chance for a good harvest.

There are potential problems and security issues over their strength, physical abilities, impatience, distrust, grudges, being defensive, and selfishness.

Earth in Taurus (Ruler/Dignity)

Taking Earth as the ruler of Taurus, this placement would have to be pretty ideal. The native is aware of what they have to offer the world, that is, what their *resources* are, and know when and how to *use* them, in the same way they understand what is *valuable* or what gives something *value* and seek to *surround* their selves with that. They would be good at getting things *done*, knowing just how much effort is needed, the order and timing of the steps involved, and how to *organize* the tools, people, or resources. They would have great *perseverance*, working until the job is done. They are *reliable* and *responsible* because they know that is what it takes to be successful.

In an astrological house, Earth-in-Taurus people would find *security* in following a *routine* that has been *carefully built* over time. They would *trust* what has been *tested* and found to work in a *predictable* way. They look for *assurance* and buy a lot of *insurance*, that way they are always *prepared* for any eventuality. They would also seek out their own personal connection with the *natural world*, such as planning vacations to the Grand Canyon, talking a walk through the park at lunch time, or signing petitions to save the polar bears.

When Earth puts on Taurus' jacket, it's a perfect fit, so comfortable that it never wants to take it off. Natives would have a drive to create something *solid* out of *well-researched ideas* or at least increasing in *value* or *volume* what already exists. *Stability and consistency* in life comes easily because *good planning* and *patience* come naturally to the native. They would also gravitate toward anything that gives them a *sensual* thrill: art, nature, bubble baths, music, gourmet food, or attractive people. Their senses are keenly developed and they like to use them. For their experiences, the more senses they can engage the better. They won't waste time on hollow joy-rides, but, paradoxically, they have no problem sitting in the sun – recharging – for hours either. For them, there is a difference between the pointless action of one and the feeling of need for the other.

They would feel grounded by literally feeling the earth under their feet, being outside in nature, gardening, building something, saving money, as well as any routine ideas or actions.

EARTH-CONSCIOUSNESS/ECOLOGICAL LEANINGS

The native would be conscious of the planet and have an instinct for using the resources of Earth well. Having a concern for the health of the Earth would be so natural to Earth in Taurus that they would be surprised to find others aren't thinking about it. The *practicality* of *preserving* a planet that is ultimately *preserving* them would be just plain *common sense*. Their love for the *beauty* of the Earth would also be a big inspiration for keeping it clean. Being at times passionately (for Taurus) against development and "improvements," they want the *natural* state of the seashore or the mountains to remain unspoiled. They are the first on their block to start composting and would enjoy growing their own food to avoid putting unnatural things in their body. Their recycling mantra would go something like this: "Money for returning useless, empty bottles? Count me in!"

NEGATIVE

Afflicted Earth in Taurus gives us someone too self-concerned or lazy to bother. Washing out bottles that could more easily be thrown away seems dumb: "Recycling? That's too much trouble. I wonder what's on T.V.?"

AFFLICTED EARTH IN TAURUS

Resistance is a problem for Earth in Taurus; the degree of the *resistance* would depend on aspects and the house placement. Shifts in social customs would be looked on with grave suspicion. However, life is change and Taurus has always had trouble catching up to it. They are the last ones in town to get that new cell phone or a hybrid car. They *hold* themselves to a course of action that has given them *satisfaction* in the *past* because making changes requires a good imagination and that is not usually something they give any free rein to, so, while they are clutching the *familiar*, good opportunities are missed. The world can pass them by while they are waiting for *proof and certainties.* Another naturally negative aspect of Taurus is *saturation*. This is a road that runs parallel to *resistance*. It is in the nature of Taurus to gather in and *hold on* to what they find, to *collect* or *acquire* whatever they can. It is part of knowing what the *security* of *possession* feels like. It helps them to counter their *fears* of death and chaos. It is easy for them to take *hoarding* or even eating to extreme, *weighing down* their life and trapping them in one place both physically and mentally. Add to this a dash of Taurian *self-concern or selfishness* and you have someone who can get really stuck.

There are potential problems and *security* issues over: *safety*, body image, *personal resources, money, ownership, possessions, nature, laziness, unyielding persistence, narrow views*

Earth in Gemini

Earth in Gemini would find *stability* in the availability of endless information. Books of all sorts would be the *physical* representation of information and so *collectable* too! This is a potential bibliophile if there ever was one. Lack of information would have them scrambling to the library or the internet. To "know" anything would help them to feel *connected* and *grounded*. When they want to know something, they would be very *determined* to find the answer. They have a great interest in *building* up a pool of knowledge that they could *rely* upon. They might have filing cabinets (*physical proof*) to keep track of all the *acquired* paperwork. Here, Earth wants knowledge to be *useful,* as in: "That's nice to know, but what can you do with it?" *Practical "How-To"* books would be a favorite. Because of this Earthly concern with *usability* and the Gemini penchant for cold logic, this placement might produce more than its share of cynics too.

In an astrological house, choices are also important to their *security*. Knowing that they always have a choice in life would help them to feel *safe*. At its most positive, Earth in the Gemini jacket slows Gemini down, allowing it to methodically sort through possibilities and eliminate them *one step at a time* until the right path is determined. The natives study habits would be good, reading and talking more focused, and research *thoroughly* done. This placement would make for a great teacher because they would understand the importance of *waiting* for the student to catch on before moving on to the next level. They would have *patience* with the *process* and *progression* of knowledge and how the brain needs time to *absorb* what is being explained. The Earth in Gemini's love of knowledge, *patience* to teach it, and their enthusiasm for it, would always make learning fun and interesting.

Here, mixed with Earth, the famous Geminian sense of humor would tend to the *bawdy or slapstick (physical humor)* and even be a bit base. Life seems lighter-hearted, but also less *sure* and *substantial* with this position, so, to get a better bead on things, they will (uncharacteristically for Earth) want to talk it over with someone, hopefully an *expert* or at least someone more experienced, someone who has been through "it" before them.

They would have the drive to communicate as any typical Gemini would, but talk *slower* and prefer more *traditional, reliable* methods like snail mail and land-line telephones. They would expect *results* from their communication. They would not excuse others who do not return their calls or send a Thank You card when appropriate. Their attitude would be: "I made the effort, now what about you?" As far as Gemini's attraction to advanced technology, they would need to see the *sense* in it. Hype wouldn't interest them; they need proof that this new *tool* is *tested* to be *worth* the claims and *indispensable to daily life* before they will hand over their *money*. They may not be able to resist owning an iPod, though; having their *music* right in the palm of their hand would be very *attractive* indeed.

Another perfect profession for Earth in Gemini would be a disc jockey, a marriage of the *soothing or musical voice* of Earth with the Geminian love of communication. Any kind of writing or voice recording would be coveted, as they are *physical manifestations* of the intangible spoken word. They would be interested in the way words *capture and keep* in our minds the *physical things* they describe. How words are *used for all time*, as representations of the *physical* items we have named. They would love the idea that words can be *tracked* or studied through etymology: a discipline that offers *proof* or *tangible evidence* of a step-by-step *progression* or history of the source of our words.

Earth in Gemini would understand how to adapt earth-ruled items to a variety of changing or challenging conditions.

They would feel grounded by being busy, by variety, having an escape hatch, learning new things, possessing knowledge, talking, reading, writing, and filing cabinets.

EARTH-CONSCIOUSNESS/ECOLOGICAL LEANINGS

Their attitude toward ecology is to learn about it, talk about it, get the facts, and then spread the word. They would enjoy collecting information and organizing it. Journalistic research and fact-gathering for the cause would fall in the Earth/Gemini's lap. They would enjoy traveling around town and teaching others how easy it is to recycle. They might even enjoy driving the recycle truck, that way they get to have first dibs on collecting anything that looks interesting!

NEGATIVE

Afflicted Earth in Gemini might start out with the fervor of the converted, saying: "Hey, going green, what a neat idea!" but soon be bored with the *day-to-day effort* it takes to carry it out. The interesting part for Gemini is always the idea itself, not the tasks associated with it, which can quickly become a dull *routine*.

AFFLICTED EARTH IN GEMINI

An Earthly Gemini gets ahead of itself. It never feels that it is covering all the bases and those not half fast enough. They see too many paths to take and get a pervasive feeling of being overwhelmed, undermining their ability to proceed in their usual, earthly, *straight-forward*, confident manner. Too many choices to be made can stymie Earth or cause it to freeze up and take no action at all. The attitude would be: "If I make a choice, all other choices are removed and I can't decide anymore, so I better not move at all."

A *comfort* level is hard to come by because it's difficult to know for sure which choice or answer is right and which is wrong until it is made. Life doesn't hold the absolutes Earth would like, just no clear black or white and way too many grey areas to think about for them. They have to find a way to get comfortable with that.

Learning disabilities or problems may crop up because of the schism of rhythm or pace: Earth's slow and deliberate against Gemini's light and fast pace. One example of this would be learning to read. To begin sounding out words takes patience and focus, and Gemini would see a word and jump on it, pronouncing it the way he thinks it should sound, too eager to move on and already bored with procedure. This might incur a stubborn test of wills with an educator.

There are potential problems and *security* issues over: early schooling or learning new things, intelligence, focus, communication abilities, the power of choice, speech.

Earth in Cancer (Exaltation)

In Cancer, we have the (theoretical) exaltation of Earth. Cancer is a folding-inward energy that seeks to *preserve* and protect whatever is of *value* to it. Earth's instincts are similar. They both reach for the *things* or people they admire, to *own* or belong to, and, in that having, they have a *secure tether* to this world. *Having more* is of great concern to them. They surround themselves with whatever makes them *calm and comfortable* as much as they can. A good home is extremely important to the well-being of this combination, and Earth-plus-Cancer makes a queen of "cozy" in décor department.

In an astrological house, Cancer works their will and looks for *security* on an emotional level, and Earth always works through *physical representation* of some kind. When it comes to Cancerian family belonging and *loyalty*, they both want *proof* that they have their proper place and are *appreciated*. Earth needs proof in the physical, such as *money* spent on them, *gifts or other stuff*, phone calls, and invitations to dinner; something they can point to and say: "See? That's how I know they care." Cancer's need for reassurance is more intangible but just as ingrained and monitored, for example, how did the family react to them today? Who is supporting them this week with encouraging words? Did everyone say: "I love you" when they said goodbye? With both the emotional and the physical *connection* important here, any *bonding* they make would be almost unbreakable.

Of course, there is also the well-documented Cancerian need to give care and support as well as they get. Cancer and Earth both love to feel *needed*, even essential, by their friends and family. Cancer's attitude in this regard always reminds me of the line from Shakespeare's Romeo and Juliet: "The more I give to thee, the more I have." Here, the Earth energy has more of a limit to how much time and effort they will spend before they decide it is costing them too much. Earth tempers Cancer's penchant to give everything. Earth in Cancer also never makes promises they can't keep. They show up when they say they are going to, always remember your birthday, and they never take cheap shots at your expense. Sensitive, easy going, helpful, and *down to earth*, this combination produces the very best friend or family-member to have.

When Earth puts on a Cancer jacket, tradition and loyalty to the past is emphasized together with the need to *solidify* it in some way. What creates *stability* for them are pictures of ancestors on the wall, antique *collecting*, or *traditional* or annual celebrations that they would *organize* to help them feel more *connected* to their sense of self and to those they love. Their love and ability to sacrifice for family would be boundless and they may (if afflicted) be easily *taken for granted*. It all becomes part of their own growing legacy that they feel will live on after their death. At these gatherings, they like to be able to sit back and have their personal circle (*collection*) of special people all around them and observe the arc of their life, each person representing something significant to the native Earth in Cancer. This is their idea of *comfort, safety, and security*.

They would feel grounded by investing in a home, being surrounded by family, collecting something, studying history, or caring for someone or something.

EARTH-CONSCIOUSNESS/ECOLOGICAL LEANINGS

A combination of Earth and Cancer stresses the *conservation* side of any ecology movement. They look to *preserve* Earth and most likely give *money* to organizations that buy land to protect it, like "The Nature Conservancy." Natives will also crave their own piece of land or body of water so they may keep it *natural* and protect it from harm. By *holding land in trust* they feel they are contributing, doing their part to *preserve and* nurture a world they love for their children and their children's children.

NEGATIVE

Earth in Cancer's way of life is more like a legacy than a lifestyle, and to change that would be like wiping out a childhood that is sacrosanct. Living the way their parents did comforts them and gives them a feeling of continuity. Going green might seem like an affront to mom, dad, and apple pie. They won't see the need because their other needs take precedent.

AFFLICTED EARTH IN CANCER

The *collecting and acquiring* penchant of Earth/Taurus when married to the holding and protecting element of Cancer could really produce a hoarder extraordinaire. Cancer adds a deep emotional attachment to things and with Earth/Taurus's desire to *collect and hold* onto things for *familiar reassurance*, Earth would go along all too willingly. This tour de force may not be able to let go of anything.

When afflicted, *any* kind of change would hardly be looked on with a friendly eye. When they've found something that works for them, they aren't likely to give it up. Even if others show them something better, they can talk all day: if it rocks Earth in Cancers emotional boat in any way, they aren't listening and it won't make a difference.

The *possessive* element in these two energies includes people, too. Holding family and friends hostage through emotional blackmail can be a problem. Irrational and childish arguments break out when they feel they are not being given *their due,* sending them into their rooms for a long dose of the *silent* treatment for days if not years. Forgiveness may be difficult as they have a hard time *letting go* of the hurt and moving on. Their human circle is like a *shield* sheltering them from life's more difficult events, with co-dependency as the result.

There are potential problems and *security* issues over: home, security, patriotism security, sacrifice, possessiveness, emotional attachments, and living in the past.

Earth in Leo

Leo lends spark-age to the *steady* and *steadfast nature* of both these fixed energies. Leo energizes Earth's *plans* and supports her *creative* side beautifully. They both need to express themselves; it's why, what they create, and who they are ultimately working for, that can cause a kafuffle. Earth tends toward *building beautiful* but *useful* items and Leo wants more "wow" factor in their need for self-expression. Leo wants to make an impression on the masses, not necessarily be of *use* to them. Leo wants to move people, to fire them up. Earth wants to *calm* them down and allow them to experience *quality* and *tranquility.*

Leo would surely help Earth find more energy for everything they want to do but with the stipulation that recognition is around the corner. Earth never sees any real point to that unless it gets them *paid* a little more. If *money* is involved, then this match-up might indeed be Kismet. Good *taste* would probably follow this combination around like a dog. Leo would be an embracing and initializing energy and Earth would be busy *organizing and smoothing* the creases out of any endeavor.

Devotion is a keyword for both these energies; with Leo's motivational powers they can really get something done under the right circumstances. Both parties have a strong will and would want things done their way. Having great pride in their accomplishments, they wouldn't take kindly, (a distinct understatement) to an interloper wanting to tinker with their "baby."

In an astrological house, *self-reliance* is brought to the forefront with Earth in Leo. With a Leo jacket on, Earth is encouraged to step into the light (instead of hovering in the background) and be noticed a lot more than usual. A certain haughty, yet vibrant attitude is manifested. With Leo wanting to feel good about who they are and Earth wanting to be *attractive*, their ever-increasing *magnetism* could render any member of the opposite sex, or anyone for that matter, totally helpless.

Earth isn't very comfortable in Leo's leadership role, but if there is logic in it, or if things just aren't running right, this combination would be glad to step in and inject some *dependability*, *reliability*, and *quality control* into the process even if it's just for the interim. They would be very qualified. This combination would lead with *creativity* and with *patience*. Their ego is kept in check by *common sense* dictating a desire to have a *workable and productive* outcome. With Earth being symbolic of life and Leo always looking for fun, this combination would surely have a zest for life!

They would feel grounded by being admired, creating, being in love, having children or projects going, and taking charge.

EARTH-CONSCIOUNESS/ECOLOGICAL LEANINGS

Earth in Leo would want to be a part of something that really made a difference in the world. They would want to see their organization's name splashed across the headlines even if it was negative publicity. They want to stir people to action, to get them fired up. Not content to sit at a desk on a phone tree campaign, they want to be out at the front lines carrying signs and marching, even leading the parade for change and a healthy environment.

NEGATIVE

Afflicted Earth in Leo has all the arrogance that always puts people first and any other form of life on Earth, a pale second. Other life forms are inferior and just don't qualify for much attention.

AFFLICTED EARTH IN LEO

When afflicted, fiery Leo becomes an uncomfortable fit for *undemonstrative* and *safety- minded* Earth. Leo's ardent love nature could also put Earth into some awkward situations, such as latching on tight to whoever showered them with gratification or attention by flowery words and large gems. When they are tempted with *sensual* treats and the promise of fun, Leo may lead Earth down an ill-conceived or careless path to a most uncomfortable and more time-consuming affair than she had planned for. They may find themselves in *repeated* situations where being magnanimous means spending too much *money* to keep people happy or to *preserve* a cherished reputation. Leo's penchant for melodrama plus Earth's *self-concern* and *tenacity* could mean over-the-top displays of self-righteousness or anger over what they perceive as *personal* injustices in their world. With afflicted energy, these scenes are potentially *selfish* in nature, aimed at nothing more than gaining attention and ego gratification. *Money* will also be spent on a lot of *personal beautification* remedies to impress people who probably aren't worth the trouble.

The fixed or steady energy of both Earth/Taurus and Leo make it hard for this combination to get out of their own way to change and grow when they have faults they need to work on. By the time they realize some habit isn't working for them, the *repetition* of it has gotten them dug in pretty deep.

Earth and Leo is a *self-concerned* combination that could create quite a *selfish* and *self-centered* angle to a person, a "How does this affect *me*?" attribute. Along with their need for show and drama, this would have them taking actions that appall a part of themselves, triggering self-loathing. It may take a lot longer for this combination to reach a decent maturity level. They may consistently get *reined in* by outside forces, by *reality checks,* or even stomped on by authority figures that, over time, kill their spark and enthusiasm or burn them out in a fiery blaze of *self-indulgence.* They end up as has-been performers, shadows of their former self.

There are potential problems and *security* issues over: popularity, attention, play, romance, leadership, creativity, willpower, and self-reliance.

Earth in Virgo

Here are a few words about Earth in Virgo: productivity, productivity, productivity. Earth loves getting things *done* in a *consistent* and *common sense* manner and Virgo understands the most efficient way to *accomplish* anything, so she's just the gal to do it. The sign of Virgo seems like a good place for Earth to hang its hat. They have the same energy signature in the element earth. The sign of Virgo sits on the threshold between the inner signs: those concerned with personal and private issues, and public signs: those interested in issues and interactions with people or the environment. This place of transition gives Virgo a unique perspective, and with this split emphasis, a bit of a psychic inferiority complex too. Earth in Virgo knows how to take care of *herself* but she also cares what other people think and tends to measure herself by their yardstick as well as her own.

Virgo enjoys time *alone*, but also craves time interacting outside the home. In the case of Earth in Virgo, Earth could probably use an excuse to venture out and "being of service" is a good one, one that makes a lot of *sense*. Service would be combined with *safety* in this placement and one thing that goes on in the work place is *safe* socializing. In a work (and service) environment, there are not as many social expectations or need to fill awkward silences, we are just thrown together with our colleagues and it's natural and easy to have things in common with them almost immediately. On top of all that, this camaraderie only improves cooperation and increases *productivity*! It's an *affordable* and *reliable* dream come true for both Earth and Virgo.

When Earth puts on a Virgo jacket, she moves *cautiously* yet confidently, checking her answers with the data she is getting along the way. When in uncharted territory, she gets her *bearings* by being needed or, more importantly, indispensable. Virgo loves to learn and so she learns all she can about any situation or operation she is involved in and with each piece of information, her *comfort* level goes up. *Patiently, step by step*, she achieves her goal: to be the number one go-to person on the scene with all the answers when anything goes wrong. This creates a *secure* niche for her in any environment, one she can stretch out in and keep growing into. Meanwhile, it ticks off most of the goal boxes of an earthly vibration, making her: *reliable, dependable, and practical*.

In an astrological house, small events and day- to-day life are always looked at as important, *worthy* of notice, and they are *invested* in. Everyday life is lived with *firm* goals in mind and *sensible* ideas to meet them. They have an innate sense of how to do a great many things even before they've tried them.

With Earth's natural affinity for determining *worth* and Virgo's *attachment* to perfectionism, good *value* would be very highly emphasized and strongly desired with this placement. Nothing less than the best will do and don't try and fast-talk her, since she's surely done her homework. The best that can be attained in both *form* and function are important and this creates an innate and amazing sense of refinement.

If Earth is connected to the body and Virgo is concerned with health, then this combination steps up the healthcare issues, too. A common sense approach will be evident, though. They aren't likely to go on the banana diet anytime soon. They would only read literature from trusted sources like medical universities or first-rate doctors implementing whatever seemed sensible after they've had time to consider it.

They would feel grounded by fact-checking or finding and correcting errors, being indispensable, having the answers, refinement, being on a health regime or program, cleaning, dealing with the details, worrying, and criticizing.

EARTH-CONSCIOUSNESS/ECOLOGICAL LEANINGS

Virgo would be interested in doing their part for the environment; their approach would be to integrate *ecological* ideas and actions into their daily routines. They would be the ones to go around the house with a checklist, changing all the light bulbs to energy- savers, tying up newspapers, turning down the water heater, and turning off the lights. They would also love the *money* they save. Recycling and composting are also high on the list. They might even do their part by volunteering at the recycling center.

NEGATIVE

When afflicted, Earth in Virgo would feel that nothing they do would be good enough or be a complete enough solution for a problem this complex, so what good would it do to attend to silly details like composting or recycling, The Earth can never be made perfectly right or whole again.

AFFLICTED EARTH IN VIRGO

Once Earth in Virgo finds that most of their dual needs of productivity and camaraderie occur in tandem through a job situation, the work environment might become so stimulating and satisfying they may just want to stay there, setting things up for a first-class workaholic.

Even though Earth and Virgo knows better, she can't help but take outside opinions or (god forbid) criticism about herself to heart and that can easily throw her off her game. This sets her up for a loss of trust in her abilities and once that worry begins, she can't think straight. Making one mistake is enough to lay out all her wounds around the imperfections she's tried to ignore in herself, *grounding* her in an attitude of "It's too hard: I can't do it well enough." A great fear of failure resides in this sign placement and getting points for "making the *effort*" just isn't enough. Calling in an expert tutor, someone who can assess the *reality* of the situation might be enough to make her right as rain again.

Conversely, busy monitoring her own potential for errors makes her overly sensitive to the failings of others until she sees flaws everywhere and with the *tenacity* of Earth to goad her on, she'll be a *dog with a bone*, riding people about every little slip-up. People might start calling her a Nazi or at least a bore. With her *security* tied up in being right or correct, letting go of this bad *habit* will not be an easy thing to do.

This same energy marker can also turn against the body, making them extremely picky about everything their body does or incorporates. They could spend too much time in front of the mirror making sure every hair is in place or monitor every type of food and vitamin consumed, take their blood pressure daily, keep a log of every type of exercise they get, and, in the end, create a deeply hypochondriacally-hampered personality.

There are potential problems and *security* issues over: old wounds, money, sense of propriety, health, perfectionism, errors, service, wellness, and wholeness.

Earth in Libra

With Earth in Libra, a native would find *stability* in the pursuit of ease, equilibrium, and a partnership of some kind. The sensitivity of Libra to harmony pushes them to seek that *sensibility* in *creating* things or *creating* relationships that inspire peace of mind. With Earth in Libra, their relationships need to have *practical applications*. They would excel at creating relationships that give them some kind of *advantage*. Relationships are something they must *have* as well, because when they are in a relationship they feel *grounded and safe*. They look for people and partners who provide a mental, emotional, or physical *tether* to *reality* for them.

When Earth puts on the Libra jacket, she feels her energy shift from *physical* to mental activity and from *practical reality* to a place that is just a little too light and mellow. There is a frustration of working through an impractical attitude when it comes to their *drive* or *making an effort*. On one hand, they want nice *things*, and on the other, they don't think they should have to overexert themselves to get them. Instead, what they *"work"* on is becoming more *attractive* to potential supporters of their ideas. Their need for social advancement and *financial* support becomes a *good reason* for socializing and partying. They gather people to them with great charm, smoothness, and *efficiency* and are so fun that their partners in any future endeavor do not mind taking on more of their share. I do not mean to imply that Earth in Libra doesn't rightfully earn their success, but they do it in a more mental or ethereal manner, in the form of an attractive/famous figurehead or representative, a coordinator, a spokesperson, or public relations person. Some position whose *worth* or *contributions* to the company are not easily *assessed* in the *ledger books.* From another angle, in business they would be more the *practical* idea person, the coordinator or the contractor, rather than the person doing the labor.

In an astrological house, Earth's potential *sensory* addictions coupled with Libra's need for nice-ness makes this combination pursue all forms of pleasure. Here is a position that would really appreciate *abundance* and *luxury*. Growth would be measured and *money* spent on cultural *acquisitions, material* or otherwise. The finest paintings, the most beautiful music, or simply *giving themselves* an air of refined appreciation for the finer *things* in life could lead them to become a bit of a social snob or maybe even hedonistic.

Even if they do work hard, they would require frequent vacations or down time with no interruptions by cell phone or other clever technologies designed to keep them in the loop. They need freedom from that stress and when they are out of the office, they are OUT.

Whether the Earth in Libra's special sensitivity is to their environment or an emotional sensitivity they have when around other people, it raises their awareness to an acute or unusual level. With Earth here, that awareness is brought down to *solid, useable form,* creating the potential for a brilliant artist through an innate ability to translate what they are seeing or feeling into a striking *form*.

An earthly pursuit of balance means developing *practical applications* for their diplomatic tendencies. They would be actively involved in settling disputes because it is *practical* to do so; it makes for smoother operations and better *productivity* in any environment. They would want to *form* grievance committees, pursue law degrees, or learn more about psychology for a better understanding of that contradictory thing called the human mind. *Gathering* more (and better) *tools* and honing their considerable skills for working with others of their species are *attractive* pursuits. *Growth* for them would be measured in the ease of their interaction and influence with people.

They would feel grounded by socializing/visiting, creating something of beauty, settling disputes, dispensing justice, being married, sharing what they have, visiting a spa or a salon, or taking a vacation.

EARTH-CONSCIOUSNESS/ECOLOGICAL LEANINGS

Earth in Libra would gladly take on any beautification projects, whether they are local or global, and they would be excel at it. Just don't put them on duty picking up road trash; it's not for them and is a waste of their talents. They are all for preserving natural areas; their beauty alone is enough to warrant saving them.

Their tact and *down-to-earth* diplomacy would be vital to *ground floor* discussions with the green movement opposition. They would understand opposing viewpoints and be able to lead debates, making sure everyone had their say and was treated fairly. Don't be surprised if all parties leave the meeting feeling satisfied and more open and contemplative.

NEGATIVE

"I don't want to know how bad it is out there: I shudder to think. Besides, going green just takes too much effort."

AFFLICTED EARTH IN LIBRA

For an afflicted Earth in Libra, work is a four-letter word and hard, *physical* work definitely looks, well, too hard. Intense, *consistent effort* is difficult to make on any behalf and working from the *ground up* does not interest them at all. They also hate having to *plan* too far ahead; there must be an easier way to succeed. Here would be the right position for a classic marriage of *convenience*, a union with another for some kind of *physical gain.* They want to skirt any *sweat* and stress involved. For them, this becomes a very *practical* thing to do and if it works, then well, why not?

The Libran tendency to go along with what is popular would be rooted in their *security issues*. They might be willing to give up a lot of their freedom of choice to get along with others and avoid rocking their beloved *routines*. Their talent for ideas gets squashed under the *weight* of earthly *requirements* like *consistency* and *practicality* in their work. Before they take any steps that *cost* them, they may want unrealistic *assurances*. This may also be the position of the starving artist, *stubbornly* suffering for the sake of aesthetics when they could compromise by taking a commission now and then or even flipping burgers for a few hours each day for rent *money*.

There are potential problems and *security* issues over: artistic integrity, social issues, popularity, being alone, energy loss, gold-digging, glitter and glamour rather than effort, partnership, resistance to getting hands dirty, diplomacy applications, and beauty.

Earth in Scorpio (Detriment)

This is the sign farthest away from Earth's natural home of Taurus; its opposition is therefore the detriment of the planet. When we look at the month and time of year assigned to Scorpio, it becomes obvious why this sign would be the detriment of Earth. November is 180 degrees from May. The month of May is a time of steady root deepening and forward *growth* of all (northern hemisphere) Earthly things, but come November it is a time for much of that life to let go, power down, and even die. A pattern of energy taken from this scenario that can be applied to the human populace is: whatever is *collected* in a time of growth must be released without hesitation during a "harvest." On Earth there is always a dance of *acquisition* (Earth/Taurus) and then release (Pluto/Scorpio).

In astrology (as elsewhere on this planet), opposites have things in common because they are the same energy taken to the two extreme ends. Both Earth and Scorpio are willing to look at hard *reality* with no denial or prejudice. They rarely judge *what is*, they just try and *work* with it. They carry around a protective mindset, guarding their psyche against any attacks or injury. They watch for *security* breaches and don't take kindly to people crossing certain lines of familiarity in their business affairs or personal life. Don't tell them what is what; they know, so don't push them. They can hold out forever on anything if they want to.

When Earth puts on the Scorpio jacket, her feelings about the world are deepened and intensified. Everything is more serious because death (Scorpio) is suddenly very *real* and *solidified*. *Responsibilities* weigh heavier and life is a test of wills or even a matter of life and death. It's them against the world. Where is the blow going to come from? They shore up their emotional defenses and silently study humanity and the world at large, ever adding to their knowledge, intuition, and their power over their life. *Security issues* become very important. A constant reconnaissance gives this combination an internal power structure that is *unshakable* and could be harnessed in so many fortuitous ways.

In an astrological house, all the senses are intensified to the point of almost having an extra one (like intuition or even E.S.P.) that goes beyond the five, and what they perceive with it they take *seriously*, even if other people discount it. They believe nothing of *value* comes easily anyway.

Behind their bid for power is a vulnerability that is difficult to see. Now as you know, here we have a Sun in Taurus/Earth in Scorpio combination, a combination that has a keen awareness of both the highest highs and the lowest lows; *life* in all its glory and death: the final curtain that at any time erases it forever. It's a lot to live with. How can they feel very powerful when they know there is something far greater than they are, out there? They don't delude themselves. However, the one place they might have a shot at control is their own *personal* power, the rulership over their own life and the people in it. It's all they have. They *value* power, the *strength* to make a difference.

This combination needs to feel *strength* and energy flowing from their very core. They can't abide weakness because it's an insult to the vitality of *life* and the reverence they have for it. They will always pitch in if the cause is *worthy* enough, no matter how hard or lowly the chore. They can be both incredibly kind and incredibly selfish.

They also dislike waste, pettiness, small talk, and superficiality. Being *real* is what they are after, at least on their terms, or more precisely, right up to the point of having to crack open those well-guarded bunkers of personal subconscious fear and loathing they carry around. They will at times conveniently pass those by, but only if they haven't acknowledged them or they don't know what to do about them yet. Once their awareness has been raised (and it almost always is), the need to dig into a toxic waste dump to clean it up or to transmute dark into light, always makes *sense* to them. Scorpio *invests* in the process of discarding or letting go of whatever isn't adding to the *quality* of *life* for both themselves and the world at large. Possessing a singular power of choice between dark and light makes for a great innate sense of ethics; the awareness of what is right or *life-affirming*. One might even call it *natural* law. They wish to *collect* trust.

Earth in Scorpio *consistently* understands that pieces or parts of something do not count as much separately as they do when they are part of a whole. In other words: "a whole is more than the sum of its parts." Earth in Scorpio likes to stand in the background and *collect* or *connect* people or things, joining them together for the purpose of *building* something with more impact, like an organization or a new building. For them, there is a psychological satisfaction in merging, becoming part of something that produces more, the more parts that are added. When they find something worthy, they dive in with their whole heart, whether that is a cause or a relationship. They will also want to know on an emotional level everything there is to know about it

They would feel *grounded* by staying behind the scenes, researching and gathering information not generally known by others, gaining trust, cultivating integrity, being in a committed relationship or cause, working with transformation, being ethical, creating a power base, or managing others' resources or money.

EARTH-CONSCIOUSNESS/ECOLOGICAL LEANINGS

Earth in Scorpio would tend to be pretty passionate about the *environment* and might even go as far as joining some radical group like Earth First. To deny that the *environment* doesn't have problems would be silly to Earth and Scorpio. They would see devastation occurring with clear eyes and not be afraid to walk up to it, discuss it and clean it up. They would ask others to give up their sacred cows of *neediness* (like the amount of material possessions they buy or oil they consume), transforming the old, outmoded, and highly impractical ways they have always lived to embrace a truer, simpler, cleaner way of living for the greater good.

NEGATIVE

Their *realism* goes to the extreme, creating a pessimistic attitude that cannot believe anything we do now is going to make a difference in the damage. The time of the human being is over: we should just accept that it is too late to reverse the effects we have had on this planet, wait to die, and be replaced by a species much more in tune with the planet.

AFFLICTED EARTH IN SCORPIO

Their constant need for both *stability* and transformation leads to confusion regarding what is *valuable* enough to keep and what is not. This can translate into a couple, seemingly, contrary, ways: either they never *hold* onto anything - the old: "throws the baby out with the bath water" syndrome - or they *hold* onto everything. When it goes awry, Scorpios strong desire for control gives them a great fear of losing anything (emotional and *material* connections) they have *acquired* or worse, having someone take it away from them. They are ever vigilant. The Scorpio energy in human form, likes to keep their motivations hidden anyway. When they're feeling threatened, they tend to go in for psychological manipulation, losing the *trust* of people around them. This triggers anger and resentment in others which, ironically, sets Scorpios up for one of their worst-case scenarios: falling prey to other people negative reactions and possible unscrupulous, behavior.

With an afflicted Earth in Scorpio, the *sensual* input here can be so magnified and intense, that there is a danger of becoming overly *sensual*, sexual, or *hedonistic*. The *self-generating* intensity of feeling that is Scorpio, when married to Earth's *attainment and possession,* makes it really hard for natives to let go of any emotional issues. It takes them a long time to get over something.

When afflicted, the great need for power is undermined, they feel weak and make lots of errors in judgment, trying too hard and taking things too *seriously.* Power-grabbing by needing to be right or righteous all the time is frustrating and wearying both to themselves and others.

Earth solidifies or makes real a soul's darkness that Scorpio usually only *senses* is there. Of course, everyone carries some psychological darkness around, but Scorpio is the one who faces it and works with it. Remember though, that this darkness is only something that has been denied, isn't being used correctly, or hasn't been fully integrated into the whole. Earth creates more *responsibility* for it and this can weigh heavily on the Earth in Scorpio's mind or spirit. If they aren't strong enough, they may feel terribly inadequate or even downright bad and may look to blame or project it onto others. This coupled with those control issues creates paranoia and a walled-up or closed-off personality who sees threats to their *security* everywhere, prompting them to lash out and become known as too intense, *didactic*, *dogmatic,* and *selfish.*

There are potential problems and *security* issues over: manipulation, temptations, power plays, ownership, paranoia, resistance, death, purging, transformation, other people's money or investments, as well as control and who has it.

Earth in Sagittarius

Earth in Sagittarius is about making that which is foreign or untried *safe* and *secure*. Sag wants to explore anything that hasn't been known or experienced before; they want the thrill of feeling new feelings and witnessing the world in a whole new way. It's what helps them feel alive. Earth wants *routine* and *familiarity*. Here we have a *practical* or *productive* traveler or a very *grounded* travel agent who has a knack for keeping people *safe* when they are on challenging trips or abroad. They may *work* in a foreign embassy, *steadily building* up to a position of *trust* with people from all walks of life.

All the same, Earth in Sagittarius wants *routine* newness, *consistency* in their explorations. Another way Sagittarius expands their horizons is through the mental realm of ideas and learning. They would find *safety and security* by seeking out any kind of higher education. Learning new things is fine, but Earth in Sag always wants to go *deeper* than that. They want to understand and contemplate whatever they learn and develop it further into *usefulness*. They enjoy integrating what they learn into their way of thinking, even making it a part of their life. This helps them to feel *centered*, giving them a *tether* to a world that seems to hold so many contradictions and oddities. They *solidify* their experiences into a personal philosophy and to Earth in Sagittarius it would be absolutely essential to *possess* a *usable* philosophy, one that was *sensible* and could be *applied* anywhere under any circumstances. This is their code, something that guides them in their actions as well as their thinking. Very commonly, this is also a religion. There is another code that belongs to any society they live in: what is accepted in that culture and what is not. This becomes the law of the land. The *grounding* of any philosophy into the *physical reality* can *naturally* lead to the passing of it into laws. Earth in Sag understands where law comes from and relates to it, and even with their love of freedom they would still respect and revere the law as long as it made good *sense* to them.

In an astrological house, Sagittarius would push the *boundaries* of all earthly ideas of *reality* to the limit, whether in their mind or with their body. Sag spends so much time scouting for the 'hill beyond yon hill' that it develops a hopeful and optimistic attitude. Surely the next place will be better, or why bother to go at all? A sense of humor naturally tags along. *Serious matters* must have some levity in them so that one may always *push* on through. It gives them *assurance*. Otherwise, when things get dicey, they would run for the closet and stay there. There would be no adventures taken at all. Earth in Sagittarius *collects* humor and incorporates laughter, and if they can't laugh at the absurdity of life, they laugh at themselves trying to live it.

Still, there is some discomfort when Earth puts on a Sagittarius jacket. She is a little afraid that she won't be taken *seriously* if she jokes around too much. She might lose her *credibility*. She likes the *luxury* of that *persistently* hopeful attitude she has gained together with the great wide perspective she now holds, stemming from an ability to look beyond what is right in front of her. She just isn't sure where it all will end. What is the point of constantly moving the horizon? Earth is sure that true *growth and productivity* has to have roots, but Sagittarius argues the point. This is not a confident position for Earth, but knowing Sag, he will make the best of it.

Earth in Sagittarius would feel grounded by travel, exploration, freedom, higher education, making people laugh, inspiration confidence, teaching, and developing and living by their own philosophy or religion.

EARTH-CONSCIOUSNESS ECOLOGICAL LEANINGS

Sag would be inclined to explore *nature* from all sides and, having gained first-hand knowledge of what is going on out there, Earth in Sag would be more than glad to travel the world to report on the health of the Earth, lecturing and giving presentations to raise awareness and *money* for a cleaner, more *stable* environment.

NEGATIVE

Earth in Sag may have developed or been given a philosophy that doesn't include or even contradicts the ecological movement. Their personal and subjective experiences haven't prepared them to be open to it.

AFFLICTED EARTH IN SAGITTARIUS

Both Earth and the sign of Sagittarius are known for innocence: Earth because it is concerned with *basics and efficiency* and cannot see why anyone would want to expend energy making trouble and Sag because it is a trusting, generous soul with an optimistic, breezy attitude. This makes Earth in Sag somewhat stupid when it comes to being taken for a ride. People could take them for granted, especially in the *money* department. They end up giving *money* to the wrong causes. Investment opportunities and sob stories alike should be investigated thoroughly by this combination. The sense of humor becomes *physical, base,* and even gross or insulting when Earth is afflicted in Sag. It may be that few find their jokes funny.

They could also get into trouble in their travels by an absence of *common sense or reality checks* while in foreign places. Thoughtless remarks or actions or just being in the wrong place at the wrong time break *rules* or cause scandal and bring brushes with angry natives or even the law.

Their philosophical ideas are *abundant* and run contrary to the society they live in, setting them up for a lot of counter-*productivity* and quelling any chance at *consistent success* in their endeavors. They can also be *dogmatic*, didactic, and *unyielding* in their religious beliefs.

There are potential problems and *security* issues over higher education, a sense of humor, travel and explorations, generosity, religion and philosophy, exaggeration, teaching, and pushing established boundaries.

Earth in Capricorn (Source Energy of the Element Earth)

Here, planet Earth stands face to face with her source, the most spiritual level of earth she will ever encounter. It is the wellspring from which she flows, the root of all that she is. This native is not as concerned with *building up* as much as in laying down the very best plans. They are the planners and dreamers of *earth*. With these natives, there is an inner understanding of the way this *reality* works and that translates to being able to get anything done *physically* in the most *efficient* way possible. They can answer all kinds of questions like: "what's the best way to *make*…" and "how do I make *money* from…"? They know how to tie together theory or ideas with the *physical* fabric of Earth. *Structures or rules* that would hinder or crimp another's style Earth in Capricorn sees as opportunity. They embrace principles and they respect authority. They put their faith in that which has been done or thought of already and they take it from there, finding a more *efficient* way to be *productive*, how to branch out, how to take a little *money* and make it much more, how to create *felicity* and *abundance*. They have the tools and they have the talent to take everything to the next level.

When Earth puts on a Capricorn jacket, she feels connected to the source of her power. She doesn't fear taking on something that has deteriorated: as long as there is a clear *plan* with logical *guidelines* to *follow*, she has all the confidence that a little brainstorming and hard *work* will yield the *necessary* and satisfying improvements.

Earth in Capricorn finds *safety* and *security* following *tried* and true techniques and obeying *rules*. They are on a path to find something of *quality* and when they get it they *invest* their time and talent into it, becoming duty-bound to it. Coming up against a well-conceived and well-built set of *structures* they can work with restores their faith in humanity and even the world.

Earth in Capricorn is a mature placement, meaning they simply *possess* knowledge that is usually only reserved for people who have had that experience. They understand the uses of time. They have an innate knowledge of how long anything will take without having done it. They know the *value* of time, how to use it to their advantage, how to manipulate it, and, lastly, how to sell it.

They are *result*-conscious and there better be an equal *payment* of some kind for the effort they've made. Any endeavor that doesn't pan out will be ruthlessly dropped or scheduled for a renovation on the spot. They are *stubborn* about the correct compensation for their *work* whether it be the physical (*money/items*), emotional (alliance/allegiance), or mental (knowledge/expertise) kind.

In an astrological house, Earth in Capricorn always has the ability to do what needs to be done while others are cowed by the emotional burden of what that might entail. For Capricorn, it doesn't make *sense* to put off taking action simply because it is hard to do: do it now and get it over with and everyone will be better off.

Responsible is a word that is used a lot for Capricorn, and Earth only lays out more *ground* for it to cover. One meaning of the word we don't often think about is "the ability to respond." With Capricorn it isn't just an ability: it is a quest. They feel *required* to step up, take charge, make decisions, coordinate, and keep the train moving in the right direction and on time. They feel the pressure of being "out there" in the public eye whether they truly are or not. They understand that intangible as well as *physical* rewards have great *worth,* such as credibility and reputation. Credibility and reputation are sometimes all you have to sell an idea and start a company, all you have when others are accusing you of some wrong-doing, all you have when you are looking to get hired, incorporated, or accepted, all you have to ensure your success and popularity. When you have a good reputation, you have status you can *spend*. That is a key that lets one in while others are locked out. Earth in Cap would work *diligently and patiently* for that kind of *quality* in their life. This gives them their version of power.

They would feel grounded by having the legal documents, following the rules and staying within the boundaries, getting an A on the test, having an investment pay off, getting well paid, getting a promotion, organizing or coordinating a project, dreaming up new ways to make money or start a business, or being in charge of a company or even a family.

EARTH-CONSCIOUSNESS/ECOLOGICAL LEANINGS

Here, Earth in Capricorn would understand the precious *resources* that planet Earth possesses and would *invest* heavily in her, gladly giving *money* to whomever or whatever was *improving* conditions and making her *strong* again. They would excel at taking on a leadership role in rescue *projects* themselves, either in the community or worldwide. They know how to make *progress* in these areas. Their knack at working *within the rules*, the law, or politics could make them a great lobbyist in Washington.

NEGATIVE

All that would matter to them is the bottom line of *profit* at the present time and adjusting any process for the good of the environment, in that business would cost too much in time and money. "Who cares about the future problems, I only need to get mine or I have what I need right now."

AFFLICTED EARTH IN CAPRICORN

Here, Earth in Capricorn can feel the weight of the world on her shoulders. Feeling too *responsible* for everyone and everything can mean no *peace* of mind or time to spend on themselves. *Duties* must be attended to or crushing guilt follows. They see the world as a serious place of lack: lack of organization, lack of *abundance*, lack of warmth, etc. They feel sullen and *serious* and can rarely lighten up. When they do take on *projects* they never feel they are *rewarded* enough and get a reputation as a hard guy. They may get to a point where they barely answer a question without a charge card or some other exchange for it in their hand.

In an astrological house, Earth in Cap doesn't understand why emotions so often get in the way of *efficiency*. There can be a social awkwardness or incorrect social expectations by the native. Discomfort around the illogical and irrational feelings of other people leads them to escape into any place or situation that is run by *rules and regiment*. In that situation, everyone knows where they stand and what is expected of them. There is no need to cajole or compromise.

In this house, instead of possessing good timing, time gets out of joint. Their instinct for a proper give-and-take *rhythm* is thrown off, but their confidence isn't. They can make outrageous and undoable demands, such as "Why can't things run according to my timetable or schedule?"

There are potential problems and *security* issues over community cooperation, reputation, status, time, their place in the world, responsibility, authority, planning, failure, and success.

Earth in Aquarius (Fall)

Earth in Aquarius is in the fall position for Earth, so Aquarius here would feel their *safety and security* in ways that for the rest of us, look quite the opposite. They *trust* instability because they know that *growth* comes from it. When thoughts, feelings, and situations stay in the same old *pattern,* there is no hope of progress. For Earth in Aquarius, every time they break out of the old and into something new they catch their own brand of excitement and download their way of *connecting* to the world. In this house, risk-taking is a way of feeling alive, locked and loaded into the *physical* world.

When Earth puts on the Aquarius jacket, she gets a little scared. There isn't much here in the way of *consistency* or *solid ground* for her. Here is a jolt of raw truth: that the world is not *stable* and the unusual is more *commonplace* than she ever dreamed of. The idea of *trusting* in chaos is not easy for her to *relax* into, yet she must seek out those shifts in perception that have to occur to create a new and better *reality*. Once she sees the *strength* of the new paradigm, she comes to see the *sense* in it. She learns that seismic activity often happens just before a new *equilibrium* kicks in. All she has to do is lash herself to the mast and ride the waves. It isn't comfortable, but it is *predictable,* she can take some comfort in that.

Earth in Aquarius *invests* in the future; she has a way of *sensing* how the world could be, and she *cultivates* vision. She looks for *reliable* solutions to what she perceives as unnecessary *structure or rules* that serve only to keep us all downtrodden. This leads to invention. In this case though, her inventions will be *useful and practical and applicable*, not usually attached to untried or theoretical ideas. She would know instinctively, where and when to cut the cords of *reliance* others may cling to.

Aquarius likes to experiment and in this case the experiment would be on her personal *reality* or even (like a physics professor) *reality* in general, testing it to see which *rules* really apply and which don't. Hopefully her *senses* would tell her how far to go before everything in her life implodes or falls apart.

Earth in Aquarius would be *stubbornly* unconventional and individualistic. Don't tell her that people just don't do what she wants to do or even that she isn't capable of it. It will only help her *dig in her heels*. With Aquarius it isn't just about her personal rights, it is outrage for anyone she encounters who isn't living up to their full potential, who isn't getting *"real"* in their lives. She is too aware of the *value* of individualism. The deeper people are allowed to sink into themselves and become everything they can be, the more unique skills they develop and those special skills are an incredible *resource* all of us can use. As far as she is concerned, individualism is the ultimate in *efficiency* and *productivity*.

They would feel grounded by not being grounded, risk-taking, getting to the truth, freshness, new things, having vision, creating community, making friends, fighting for individual rights or equality, and experimentation.

EARTH-CONSCIOUSNESS/ECOLOGICAL LEANINGS

Earth in Aquarius knows exactly why we are in this ecological dilemma and what the fix should be: we are stuck in old, comfortable habits and routines that are destroying the planet and we need to break out and be open to new ideas and experimentation. She would love to encourage us to lose our fear of the unknown and untried and cultivate a new vision of how green the future could be before it's too late. She would make a great consultant if we're willing to let her try rerouting our old, conventional ways of doing things into something a lot more green-efficient.

NEGATIVE

She probably wouldn't care whether the planet is saved for us or not. We goofed it up and it's time to let some other life-form have at it. She feels that the Earth will go on without us and we deserve what's coming.

AFFLICTED EARTH IN AQUARIUS

In an astrological house, Earth in Aquarius would be *determined* to shock or shake up people, places, or things on a *regular* basis. Her *dogged allegiance* to instability hampers any chance of true progress *or growth* within this sphere. She uses the qualities of earth to make others (and herself) uncomfortable for the purpose of further development. Her attitude is that her idea of rights and equality are the only ideas *worth* thinking about or taking action on.

She *continually* goes after those ideas and *routines* that give people the most *reassurance*, seeking to rip them away. For her, this is the way to *make* everyone change to her satisfaction. Her popularity is *always* shaky because she cannot compromise her cold logic. It's the only thing that makes *sense* to her. The future is all that matters and she won't have any *patience* with *rules, traditional* ways, etiquette, or even ethics if they threaten to prevent her future goal from being reached. Needless to say, the sensitive feelings of others are an illogical and unnecessary concern when the *result* will be a better world for them anyway. Another area of affliction for Earth in Aquarius would be a disconnect with the physical body.

There are potential problems and *security* issues over change, future planning, society or cultural expectations, traditions or rules, community, convention, independence, shock value, and bodily harm.

Earth in Pisces

Earth in Pisces would feel *stability and security* in going just beyond *ordinary reality* or in that mindset or place that is not quite of the Earth, a will to connect with the creator of Earth, whomever that might be. They also seek to make their dreams or daydreams *real*.

This is a very creative placement because Earth in Pisces has the *patience*, the *ability,* to contemplate *earthly mechanisms* and then rise above them. To let go of any unnecessary earthly *restrictions* while still *maintaining* an instinctual *attachment to* what is necessary for anything of the earth plane to be *strong* and vital.

Unlike Aquarius, they aren't restless and they don't go to extremes, so they have that advantage of gentler, deeper considerations of any *process,* to pick and choose what to leave in and what to take out of any *earthly equation* for the purposes of *growth or* progress.

They have an innate *natural* understanding of the emotional cost of living life on Earth. For them, emotional connections are what make things *real*. They *own* their feelings and seek emotional *safety, reliability*, and *productivity* from themselves and from others. They don't see feelings as irrational but as a *basic* part of the scheme of things. Emotions are *productive* because they add another layer or dimension to what is being *planned or constructed*.

The energy of the sign of Pisces always seems as if it is looking to pull something out from the ethers that isn't ready or able to *manifest* here in the *physical* yet. Sometimes it succeeds and then there is a kind of magic, at other times it falls flat and there is delusion and defeat. This position would have them trying even harder to integrate those "magical" things into the earth plane, to make the unreal *real*. They can bring back *down to earth* insights that have escaped our notice or promising ideas long forgotten by the rest of humanity. They are the archivists and they *value* holding all the thoughts and feelings of humankind in trust until they are required again. They have a long and accurate memory, capturing for us those fleeting emotional connections between the human heart and all the rest of the world. They *work* to *conserve* and *preserve* all that makes us human.

Their *sensory* input is their highway to grace: putting themselves in alignment with the spirit of Earth, craving a spiritual union with the *earth* plane. This would translate as a *strong*, personal, connection with *nature* that would also provide *peace* of mind and provide a *tether* to their *reality*. With the placement of Earth in Pisces, they want *tangible proof* in God, too. Anything that could show them that other side of life would be a source of *attraction* for them. Who or what is truly in charge of this plane? How can I emotionally connect with it and experience it? They long to have it touch all their *senses*, to know it is *real*. How can they *use* it and then make it *useable* and helpful for everyone else as well? How does one make *sense* of the mysterious? These folks would know.

In an astrological house, Earth in Pisces would look for *practical applications* of their dreams and *creativity*. They *invest* in them and *work* to *manifest* them. Dreaming is never a waste of time, just a vital part of any *planning* process. Nothing can even begin without a dream. They could have a knack of making all their dreams, day or otherwise, come *true*.

With one *stable* foot on this Earth and one over on the "other side," artistic is their middle name. They reach out and capture the essence of life and then some, in any creative *manifestation*. They infuse their work with haunting ideas and dizzying *sensations*, which, when in the presence of their performance, would then create a kind of out-of-body experience for the rest of us.

They would feel *grounded* by the grace of "God", trusting in their connections to spirit or things they cannot see but surely sense. Meditation, dreaming, creativity, intuition, emotional awareness and insight, humanity, and communing with nature would also help them keep their *balance*.

EARTH-CONSCIOUSNESS/ECOLOGICAL LEANINGS

Piscean empathy is of course, legendary, but this would include great empathy for the planet as well. Earth in Pisces isn't elitist in their sympathies: they would extend them to all life and its creatures. They would remind us to think globally at all times and include any non-human populations. They are the Shamans, arguing that there is no line between animals, plants, humans, and even minerals. Earth in Pisces would probably prefer to write a poem of inspiration rather than get involved in neighborhood can collecting.

NEGATIVE

Earth in Pisces could choose to live in their own world where there is no need to live ecologically because pollution isn't really happening or they may have the attitude "let go, let God" and don't think anything is up to them.

AFFLICTED EARTH IN PISCES

Here is a position that needs to make extra sure her friends and associates are trustworthy and have her best interests at heart and in mind. Earth/Taurus has a tendency to be a bit gullible and Pisces is famous for it. With an idealistic attitude and a love of *ease*, this combination just doesn't understand why anyone would take the trouble to go out of their way to *plan* ways to be mean or inhumane to them. They know those things never *pay off* and probably come back karmically to bite you in the end, so they don't suspect others of wrong-doing. Needless to say, this is a set-up for vulnerability and victimization, big-time. When bad things happen to them, it would also seem to give them some kind of odd *proof* that, as they suspected, they don't deserve better, finding *grounds* again and again for their disappointments, sacrifices, and heartache and feeding their *insecurity* issues.

They have a tendency to harbor illusion and confusion about earthly things, like dreaming up the perfect *garden*, holding that image in their mind, and sending good vibes out for it, all the while forgetting to water or weed. The actual *work* is too *coarse*, too *raw*, and they may balk at it.

Any Pisces can have trouble with the concept of *reality*, but in this case Earth in Pisces thinks they really have some kind of unique inside track on a *reality* that is totally alternate. Then they are *stubbornly* convinced that it is real. In other words, there is a danger with disconnect when they think they are connecting. Like a video game fanatic who becomes so involved in that holographic universe, they start to forget the *real* world doesn't work like that. This could be inconvenient, frustrating, and even downright dangerous.

Earth in Pisces could get so overwhelmed by the *necessities* of life on Earth and the demands of constantly having to face *reality* that they just want to lock themselves in the closet and refuse to come out. They may begin to look at addictions as a *grounding* mechanism, one that gives them a *sense of security*.

There are potential problems and *security* issues over their emotional responses, intuition, spirituality, God, nature, other people, gullibility, escapism, addiction, creativity, reality, dreams, passivity, unrealistic ideas, and ignorance.

Planet Earth in Houses

Chapter 4 dealt with the element earth or the various earth signs on house cusps. This section is about the actual planet Earth in each house of the natal chart. To me, astrological house energy is a more subtle experience for us than planets or signs. It is as if the planet that is in that house, that part of yourself that that planet represents, is living inside a structure containing certain rules, and it is quite possible for the planet to "get away" with not noticing the environment in which it resides for periods of time. I look at the houses in astrology as if they are asking something of us. It is like the planet in that house getting a constant tap on the shoulder to do something with this house energy. The planet of the native can choose to ignore the house's insistence, but the native won't be as happy as they could be. They won't be using the energy they've been given in the best way possible, so a deep satisfaction in that area of life isn't there. Also, the native feels the annoying "tap, tap, tapping" and there is psychological stress in avoiding the house question being asked. When activated by tight orb aspect or transit, all bets are off though and that part of life will react with or without the native's cooperation, and they can assume that the outside world is barging into their life, feeling (incorrectly) they don't have a choice in directing that house energy.

Planet Earth in the 1st House

Planet Earth in the 1st house asks that the native take Earth and all it represents into consideration in every aspect of their waking life. The environment and environmental issues are noticed or at least they are being asked to be noticed by the individual. If the native is not yet fully conscious of this, they may have problems in their environment until they see it. It is in their face somehow. They attract into their lives things or people of substance and value. They want to see the methods and mechanisms of earth working and thriving at all times in their surroundings; they want consistency in their life. Negatively aspected, nature takes on an aggressive tendency for the native and could deliver a scenario like Salvatore Dali's: fear or loathing of the natural world. Earth in the 1st would also provide a greater awareness of the native's physical body. Since this position puts the Sun in the chart near the Descendant, the sense of self is difficult to hold onto and is somewhat eroded. In response, they would invest heavily in their body as a substitute, focusing on what it needs and catering to it one way or another on a day-to-day basis. Their longing to "put themselves out there" is slowed down to studying which way would make the most sense or be the most advantageous for them. They want assurances about the safety and comfort of any immediate environment. They have a common-sense approach to life and they would be determined to achieve something, looking to build or attract a solid, quality base of operations for functional, steady growth. Their body, their strength of a physical connection to earth, and a reliable outlook would be a grounding mechanism for this native.

Planet Earth in the 2nd House

Earth in the 2nd house asks the native to be ever-more methodical and steady in their acquisitions. In the natural house of Earth, earth qualities are intensified and natives carefully accrue money (or other valuables) and will not risk them but will gladly look for any and all ways to acquire more. The key words for Earth here are: "insurance and investments." They are always on the lookout for what can be acquired, collected, or gathered in to give them the advantage. They consistently build on whatever resources they have (education, savings, stocks, skills, talents) until they are assured of success. They work toward building a personal set of values to live their lives by. Things are measured against this very real but unseen personal ledger and everything is considered and evaluated for the purpose of guidance in life but also any investment of time and money the native may undertake on their behalf.

The natural world is also essential to their wellbeing. It recharges or refreshes the native. They have an eye for the reproduction of anything valuable and the patience to see it through. Stability and security are paramount, and, if afflicted, they would be very inflexible when it comes to them. Adding to their resources, their sense of values, possession, or owning and collecting things would be the grounding mechanism for this native.

Planet Earth in the 3rd House

The house of communications and ideas gets a healthy dose of "does this make sense and is it reliable information?" This house would ask Earth to speak up. What would earth want to talk about? Resources and money, sure, but also anything that helps the native feel more attached and grounded in their situation. Communication is the grounding mechanism for this native.

Their ideas could be all about the natural world as they mentally feel a connection to it. The good news with Earth placement in this area of life is that it helps Earth loosen up and not take things so seriously. The bad news is the 3rd house longing for variety and its desire to contemplate things on a purely theoretical level undermine Earth's confidence and scatters its energy. Earth slows communication down and asks the native to really think about what they are going to say, to check their facts, and that can really be a bore when this house wants to go on to the next thing of interest. The physicality of Earth in an air house may manifest as someone who, when it comes to communication, is better at writing than talking. They think more clearly when they are feeling the deliberate and physical connection of their hands making the words on a keyboard or with pen and paper.

Planet Earth in the 4th House

This house asks Earth to own a home or property. Extra acreage is even better. Lucky for the native with a 4th house Earth, it's probably already in the family and they simply inherit it. The psychological roots they've acquired ask that the native always run everything they think and do against the traditional views or upbringing they had. The family is/was rock-solid, reliable, and of course, acquisitive in some way. So a question that has been planted in the subconscious is: "What will be gained by this activity?" The native is coming from a psychological place of stability and safety that has bred self-confidence. If afflicted, the place of stability is a detriment but stubbornness and ignorance make it difficult for him/her to shift and move beyond. They will use both family and the feel of the Earth beneath their feet as a grounding mechanism, going back to the farm or family home or talking a walk in the woods when they need to get back on track.

Planet Earth in the 5th House

In the 5th house, Earth is looking to create something of lasting value. It is never "art for art's sake;" they want to see something is gained by their efforts, hopefully in the financial department. Art is practical here, too, i.e., making furniture or designing houses or businesses. There is a need here to be a real individual, to activate and develop the self in a plain, sensible, but powerful manner. The value of the self and all that it can be is, in some sense, worshipped with this position. Self-concern and consequently stubborn resistance is "amped" up here.

Recreation is also taken seriously. There is no real sense in working yourself to death. Recharging is necessary and anyway it increases production in the long run. Children are considered a big responsibility and brought up properly with respect to their culture and their elders, but also themselves. Children are expected to behave, but also explore their talents and resources to see how they might best support themselves in their later years. The parents invest in their children, stocking them up with lessons or experience for future dividends. If Earth is afflicted here, a parent might look at the child as their retirement program, a way of supporting the parent in later life. Having children or being a true individual is the grounding mechanism for this native.

Planet Earth in the 6th House:

The 6th house is a very comfortable residence for Earth, as Taurus's sister Virgo owns the property. In regard to ecology and Chiron (Virgo's possible new ruling planet), a native with Earth in this house would ask: "What exactly is wrong with Earth? Give me the details." They have an extreme consciousness of all that is wrong with Earth. How do we fix this environmental mess and make Earth whole again? This native instinctually knows. How is the health of the planet connected to health of individuals on it? If the Earth is sick, then we are sick. This position would also bring awareness of all the other life-forms on Earth that stand to be affected by an unhealthy planet. They are willing to work, sacrifice, and do what is necessary to serve the Earth and the community.

Personally, they are persistent and determined to live healthy. Down to earth in regard to their health, they take care of their health as a practical necessity. Physical safety is cultivated. They have much willpower when it comes to diet and exercise.

Their approach to every-day life is humble, methodical, plodding, and reasonable. Slow and steady wins the race. They are willing to wait and plan by degrees for a better life. They can use their perfectionistic tendencies to real advantage, applying them to fixing those little annoyances that drive us all crazy.

They invest in every-day life. They value common things and do not see them as trivial. They are unimpressed with the "grandiose" in other people's lives. They are not into keeping up with the Joneses. Doing every-day chores, attending to health issues, fixing problems, and just plain, solid work are the grounding mechanism for this native.

Planet Earth in the 7th House

They want harmony at the most basic level with their partner. Who they select to live with must agree with the native on what the practical necessities of life are and also how they will work for them and apply them together. The native can overlook a lot in a relationship if the partner is stable and reliable and helps the native to feel safe. The partner's resources are scrutinized for their potential advantages in the match and the native will be encouraging to his or her partner to add to them throughout their life.

The basic idea, premise, or rule of long-term relationships stays in the forefront of the native's mind, with the idea to work on and build it up from there. They want to feel that they have collected all the right pieces for the slow, steady construction of a lasting relationship. Assurance of some emotional, physical, or mental match-up of another person with the native's personality or way of life, is obtained before they say yes to commitment. As long as the aspects are good, they probably pick well and have few divorces. It may also be likely that their relationships, while having an overabundance of stability, could also get stale becoming too routine or boring as well. The partner may also hold the native back due to some necessity (like money) or because they expect the native to stay the same and never change.

With this position, the natives want practical partners with know-how, logic, and loyalty, and consistency is a must. The more pampered a partner makes them feel, the more trust and devotion they will give to them. Having a significant other in their life is a grounding mechanism to the native.

Planet Earth in the 8th House

Here in the 8th, Earth looks to make sense of the metaphysical properties of the earth plane. Practical applications of some of our more mysterious happenings here on Earth may be addressed; ghost-busting, for example. Earth will want not only proof, but usability of such things, or, if afflicted, may choose to spend time and money denying such things even exist. They make great investigators; they will research until they drop as they don't want to look foolish. On the more mundane side, this is the house of the banker, good at handling other people's money or resources, since they look at it as quite their own. They have an ability to understand what other people's worth may be and how to increase such gains, gifts, and talents. If un-afflicted, they should definitely be handling their partner's money. They will be prudent and careful.

The issue of power, personal, political, and otherwise, is addressed here. What makes something powerful? What increases power and makes it last?

If afflicted, the natives of this position will consistently find themselves in power struggles or feel that the underside or the darkness of life is always too real or being solidified in some way. In either case, they will work to cultivate integrity and trustworthiness and long to bring light into the darkness they see in themselves and those around them. Working for another's gain, researching and explaining the unseen levels of earthly life, releasing material attachments, and building personal power are the grounding mechanisms for Earth in the 8th house.

Planet Earth in the 9th House

Earth in the 9th house will want to invest in a philosophy or personal belief system or religion. They are looking to explain life and have it make some kind of sense. They want a solid connection to the largess of the universe, everything that life may hold. They acquire that by exploring and traveling to places they do not yet understand. They know that by placing themselves there, they will discover and absorb what they don't know. In this way, they collect foreign experiences to build a system of security and/or investment for themselves. This gives them the feeling of abundance and comfort. They want to use all the experiences they have in some practical way, perhaps through travel writing or self-help books.

They are productive and reliable when they are free to go where they choose and believe what they choose. They may wish to teach or at least share their philosophy with the world, where they can see it coming alive and taking root in the mind and heart of their students. That would make any system they've invested in seem more real and solid. They may feel drawn to the priesthood, believing that natural processes (nature) are a reflection of God or Quantum Physics is a peek behind the scenes of the mechanics of the universe. They understand cultural motivations and the laws that come out of those attitudes. They may choose to produce those laws, defend those laws, or even be an enforcer of those laws. They would like the feeling of a reliable framework of expectations for others to adhere to, even if they may not entirely subscribe to it themselves. Travel, exploration, understanding foreign concepts, personal philosophy, and/or religion are the grounding mechanisms for the Earth in the 9th.

Planet Earth in the 10th House

Earth in the 10th obviously seeks a career with some concrete power that guarantees a comfortable living wage to support a home life that is very important to a Sun-in-the-fourth kind of person. They also wish to see, in solid, manifested form, the idea of a special place in the world just for them; to be a very necessary part of the world. People see them as dependable individuals, stalwart and steady. They see the public as something to organize and invest in. In addition, these natives search out what is wanted or needed in today's world and put themselves right there in the middle of it. By selecting those identities and/or locations in society that are always in great demand, they assure themselves sustainable job security. Expert planners, they are ready for any and all that may come their way. They nest in time; it is their friend and their guidepost. They understand what is needed for any task to be completed well and on schedule. They know the value of a good reputation and they know just when and how to use it. The outside world is about productivity and usability. They gather in from that world whatever enhances and builds up not only their character and their skill level, but their family and home base as well. If afflicted, though, their uncompromising attitude with the realities of the outside world, public opinion, or authority threaten to destroy their home and their reputation. Being in the public eye, feeling they belong, leading their community, and having a productive career are grounding mechanism for Earth in the 10th.

Planet Earth in the 11th House

This is the house of Aquarius/Uranus and not the best place for the planet because Earth isn't about vision; it's more about the work to be done after the vision. Still, this house asks the native to be visionary when it comes to Earth or earthly things. Where are we trying to go with our Earth? What will the future of Earth look like? These people instinctually know. Their vision of Earth will ultimately be a practical one, but the process of arriving at this practicality will certainly raise a lot of eyebrows, of course. They want to be part of the construction and maintenance of their community and would excel at a position on the planning and zoning committee. Earth here will want to make a concrete difference in improving social attitudes of any society and not fall back too much on what was done before.

They will want to be inventive when it comes to Earth and earth, so they will ask themselves what needs to be invented to achieve our earthly goals. They work with practical applications of unusual things or unusual applications of the common place. If afflicted, they may struggle mightily with being inventive at all because of the demand Earth is making to keep it real in this area of life. Invention must be free of the tried and true restrictions during the process of inventing. One must "cut loose" all manner of convention in order to invent and Earth is sitting there like a big, wet blanket, saying that idea will never fly and inhibiting the native's confidence.

Their friends and acquaintances need to be "real." Phonies and flirts need not apply. They will want even their casual friends to be practical, down-to-earth people who can take care of themselves and they better not ask for a loan. Their crowd may be a quirky bunch but they and their friends, will be loyal and trustworthy in friendship.

The groups and organizations the native may look to join better have workable ideas, a level head in charge, good understanding of their goals, organized execution, and practical application. This native would be a great treasurer of such an organization, knowing what is valuable there and what isn't and how to get more for the group. They are creative and original in practical ways for any group or organization they are a member of.

They may be a bit of loner in their own community and, as such, they become an outside evaluator of community, a spokesperson with a good perspective.

They may easily go their own way and keep their own counsel in any of these 11th -house matters, too, not needing (or getting) support or assurance from others.

The native is asking: What is the value and/or application of 11th house things? How does vision have value? What is the reason for hope or wishing? How do you secure it and build on it? Of what value are friends, organizations, or community?

Original thinking, creating workable goals, solidifying the future, bringing vision down to earth, helping to run organizations, and collecting friendships is the grounding mechanism for Earth in the 11th.

Planet Earth in the 12th House

I think the workability of this position of Earth would depend more on the sign and aspects here than other placements. At any rate, Earth in the 12th house is looking for proof of God/Goddess/Great Spirit or whatever it is that is running the world.

They are ready to work with something that isn't really here, yet.

They would need to feel a concrete connection to the source of all life. The source might be experienced as some kind of living mechanism that functions in some usable way, like physics. They would need to have some kind of solid sense that such a thing exists. This is a no-nonsense planet in a house that does not always make practical sense. If they can't see any reason for other-worldly connections, they might dismiss them entirely until such time as some proof of their influence is provided.

The house and the planet have two different functions, yet they have a tandem relationship. Here we have an area of life that, for the native, signifies the source of all life and a planet sitting in that place that symbolically embodies manifested life, the source, and the material that comes from that source.

The house would be asking Earth to let go of her fixed boundaries and float within the primordial soup of non-existence. Earth would be busy trying to manifest what it is able to perceive as possible to manifest. It gropes in the dark, looking for handholds.

If Earth is the physical center of any chart, the native's place of reality, then what does that say about its residence in a house of non-reality? This placement tries to make reality of non-reality. This could transpire in very different ways, depending on the aspects. Negatively, the native doesn't have a very good tether on what is real, the "it sure looked different in the brochure" syndrome. Their judgment is impaired. The things the native sets out to do, build, grow, or enhance do not turn out the way they thought they would. They are unrealistic in their most definitive opinions or ideas. They try and manifest things without some basic information, the correct tools, or even taking the time to lay a proper foundation.

With a positive spin, this could work out as someone who becomes a powerful translator of the spirit world to the material world, taking that which is confusing, nebulous, and altogether missed and talking or writing it out in a way that finally makes sense and is useable for everyone. The collective unconscious would be at their disposal to sift through, such archival information that in the past, was slighted by our species and now needs to be understood or integrated. When sign and aspects are in sympathy, they would be a true co-creator, aligning themselves with the God energy and tapping into the collective to bring forth a workable spiritual plan. At the very least, they would infuse anything they do with an essence, an influence that revs up our imagination and gives us all something more to contemplate. If the native is successful in marrying the two worlds they would have great creativity at their disposal, becoming a mesmerizing artist, musician, poet, or something more physical, like a great architect. Anything they talk about or make might be infused with spirit.

The body is in the spirit source house here, so there is a bit of a disconnect between this most tangible aspect of being human. In a house that erodes physical matter, this threatens to undermine the health of the body. The native may have a delicate constitution, have chronic conditions, be prone to disease, or, like Neptune in the 6th, have trouble getting a proper diagnosis from doctors. With its companion planet the Sun in the 6th health would already be a big part of their consciousness.

Nature would be a religious experience to this native. They would find a tangible connection to their god there.

Attending church services or spiritual retreats also help to make the intangible tangible. When rigidity rears its head, the safety and security issues of the native prompts them to join a spiritual group or religion that (in their mind) has a handle on difficult and ethereal concepts. Taken to an extreme, this could lead the native to become a cult follower, investing a lot of energy in a leader that can guide and explain everything that feels nebulous to the native.

Meditation, attending church, spiritual studies, going on rides at an amusement park, walking in the woods, gardening, artistic pursuits, swimming, and day-dreaming would all be grounding mechanisms for Earth in the 12th house.

Aspects to Earth

Conjunctions

Always the strongest aspect, Earth in a conjunction grabs the planet or point involved and asks that its characteristics take root in the now. Earth says show me the tangible results of your energy, produce something relevant here and make it count. Security is tied up with this point or planet. It is part of what energy the native falls back on for a reboot when life gets too unpredictable for comfort. The native works hard to manifest the point or planet's symbolism that is in the conjunct.

Sextiles

Earth has a charmed life when it comes to making things happen with the other planet or point it is touching. It also lends a secure and supportive feel to the signs involved. Here are two planetary energies in a very friendly dance of "anything you can do, I can do better." The water sign keeps the earth sign in balance and in tune, emotionally connected, and the earth sign guides the water sign with rationality and sensibility. The fire sign infuses the air sign with energy and drive, and the air sign gives the fire sign inspiration and meaning. Together, all signs in this aspect are energized and ready to roll.

Squares

Internally, the native's idea about how to ground themselves seems to feel wrong, like they are out of step with the rest of the world. They were never given the tools or the education to understand how to make things happen. Reality is sometimes just too raw for them. They also get weary feelings, like they have to fight for every acquisition and opportunity to get ahead in life. When they are given a project, it's an uphill battle of trial and error that feels like trying to reinvent the wheel. This precious, missing piece of practicality in their psyche pushes them to strive harder than most people and eventually they establish their own provable methods they can rely on for stability and sustainability.

Trines

This aspect bestows great ability to make the most of any resources and earthly skills. However, they must first understand what they have here. Many people with trines assume that the ease they have in working with the planetary energies involved is something that everyone else has, too. They don't value, or, consequently, use, what comes too easily. Study those trines and embrace inherent gifts wholeheartedly. With an Earth trine, they would be able to construct, manifest, and make anything happen that the other planet or point is symbolizing. They understand its value, how much effort is involved, what they need to complete the tasks, and exactly how it will look when it's done.

Inconjuncts or Quincunxes

The native's ideas about the planet that Earth is touching are skewed. They don't really understand the functionality of the other planet or how to work with it properly. Their assumptions are incorrect and get in the way of seeing or feeling what is truly going on. They have to be able to confront and accept their baggage or issues concerning this duo and stay pretty loose and open to alternatives to handle the inconjunct. It requires them to study reality from a distance without getting too emotionally invested in the scene; to take a lot of notes. When they see the difference between their wants or ideas and what keeps happening instead, they will know what adjustments they need to make. It isn't easy.

Oppositions

Ideas about what is practical or sensible are continually challenged by other people or situations. Projects or people the native takes up always seem to have a bit of a "Wright Brother" syndrome embedded in them: critics on the sidelines yelling: "it won't fly!" This leads the native to believe that either they are wrong or the other people are, and there is always a feeling of uncertainty that undermines their self-confidence. They don't trust themselves. The tendency is to downgrade what they thought or did in favor of the naysayers or blindly challenge the naysayers in a rash manner and have the whole thing implode. The native always feels they have to choose. If they choose their own ideas with no thought to others, they find out that they are wrong in some respects, and if they choose the other's way of doing things, they feel frustrated, ignored, and held back because the other side is not entirely correct either. The object of this aspect is to find out how both sides are right (and wrong). They must incorporate both sides of the planet and sign energies involved, learn to listen to others and also respect and revere what they personally feel and think. Balancing the opposing signs' energies becomes a life-long journey.

Transits with Earth

When we face the problems inside our own psyches and fix or release them, we usually don't have to experience something like them in the form of negative experiences in the outside world. Earth transits, for the time being, are going to resemble what we know of Saturn transits until Earth is integrated and its characteristics are separated from Saturn by many more astrologers studying planet Earth in natal charts and transits. This means that an Earth transit would be a solidifying action, manifesting something, giving it a physical embodiment, or making more real whatever house/area of life, planetary idea, or symbolic sign it touches. We are able to see the reality of a situation now, add on to, grow, or improve it and make it more reliable or sustainable. We understand what it is worth. We know why we value it or what value it may have or not have. We become persistent or determined with it. We want security with it. We look for ways to use it. We want to use our senses to enjoy it. We have more patience with it. We want to build upon it or invest in it. We take comfort in it.

Another important consideration is that the Sun in the natal chart will likely be impacted in any Earth transit as well, so most of the time this is a double transit: the Sun dealing with its own aspect and set of problems simultaneously.

Earth in Horary Charts

IDEAS AND SUGGESTIONS FOR USING EARTH IN HORARY CHARTS

Depending on the aspects, house placements, and general overview, Earth in a horary chart would:

-Lend stability and solidarity to the item in question

-Reinforce ideas or situations

-Illustrate or call for practical applications

-Slow down or ground to a halt any action

-Hamstring efforts to progress beyond what is already known or accepted

-Increase resistance to ideas or change

-Block progress or change

-Increase resolve, create persistence, and determination

-Add sensual elements, perceptions through the senses, or fulfillment through senses

-Dismiss anything that has ambiguity or isn't provable at the time

-Add or support practical creativity

-Delay action until foundational needs are addressed or met

-Ask for the acquisition or application of basic skills

-Use practical common sense thought or application

-Pull in to the question the consideration or use of the physical body

-Gather or collect or hold onto something or someone

-Ask that things be done in a "step-by-step," tried and true manner
-Ask that planning and organization be incorporated or supported
-Emphasize acquisitions
-Involve or need money
-Assess or need value
-Emphasize Nature or the nature of something
-Involve ecology and environmental issues
-Involve saturation or satiation
-Involve solitude, single-mindedness, or selfishness

    The earth correspondence information in this chapter must still be considered speculative at this time. The information is supposition, based on the many writings of astrological symbolism by those that have come before me, years of study on my part, chart readings and client discussions, contemplation and the simple, logical conclusions that could be made if Earth is assigned to Taurus and Taurus is separated from Venus. Still, if Earth takes its rightful place in astrology, as with any new addition to the zodiac, we will only then *begin* the process of studying and learning what Earth really means to us in our discipline and our charts. It is not up to me alone to determine the exact outcome of what a transfer of this magnitude would entail and I wouldn't begin to say that my conclusions are all correct and without question. Astrologers spend years on their observations and day-to-day chart studies when these kinds of changes ask to be considered or impose themselves on us. It is my hope that I have done a decent job of rendering these delineations, based on the proposed premise of Earth in the chart, as faithfully as possible.

[1]Llewellyn, George. *A to Z Horoscope Maker and Delineator*. 41st. Saint Paul, Mn: Llewellyn Publishing, 1978. 50. Print.
[2]Sakoian, Frances. *The Astrologer's Handbook*. New York, N.Y.: Harper and Row Publishing, 1973. 242. Print.
[3]Mazzotta, Marilyn. E-mail Interview. 14 Jun 2005. 19 Apr 2011

Chapter 12
Summary

Like so many authors before me, when I began this adventure I had but one idea in mind: placing Earth in the astrological chart and studying it and that seemed simple enough, but of course, I found out it wasn't simple at all. More complications grew from that one single seed than weeds in my garden! Each had to be thoroughly thought through without deviating from the structure and discipline that makes astrology so unique among the soft sciences. I did not want to betray the integrity of my discipline and I admit there were days when I laid my head down on my desk and whimpered like a little girl. However, anyone who has studied astrology can tell you that "magic happens" and as fate or fortune would have it, there came flooding in (when I was lucky) a lot of fresh ideas, detouring me to possible new destinations of human insight. The wisdom of some of my solutions must be put to the test by other professionals. There may be other, better ways, of working with Earth, than I have been able to come up with here.

As far as inserting and studying Earth in the astrological chart, I felt and still feel, very passionate about this for reasons stated in Chapter one and two. There is a feeling of import for me here, that every once in a while reaches a crescendo of outright agitation. Whether we're talking about corporations, governments or every-day-Joes and Josephines unconsciously flushing their lawn fertilizer down the city street, we simply cannot afford to ignore Earth anymore, on any level. Astrologers can do their part for the environment just by deciding to use Earth in the any chart. The discussions that follow this action, whether with clients or other astrologers, will result in a deeper consciousness, of our world.

I am not asking for anyone to believe anything here. I am only asking, (more like imploring) people, to give it a try. Punch the button on their computer program and place the Earth glyph in their charts, see what happens for them, detail what they observe, put my theories and then theirs, to the test and enrich not only our discipline, but our mindfulness. This isn't the end of a discussion but rather, the beginning of it. I even look forward to someone running away with these ideas and hatching something completely new from it!

After all, Earth is our home world and I am always in awe of where we have landed. Everyday our planet provides us with the beauty of mountains majesty or the wonder of a spider's web. It gives us water for our thirst and nourishment for our bodies. Beyond that, it is our tie to solid matter, the thing that allows us to occupy a slice of time and space, connect us with our soul's vehicle, the human body, and explore a seemingly endless environment of ideas and experiences. Earth represents and contains all we perceive reality to be.

For us, Earth is undeniably the most important planet in our solar system and it deserves a more significant place in the study of astrology than it presently has.

The astrological house wheel of the astrological chart is, at the moment, our only reference to Earth in astrological charts. This wheel does not give Earth a real planetary power in our field of study and is therefore far too simplistic a symbol for what this planet and its symbology has to share with us.

We are moving into a time in our evolution when we are leaving our planet and spending more time in space. These cases, though rare and few at the moment, nonetheless foretell a time when a group of people will no longer reside on Earth. Then the use of our planetary glyph in astrology charts will be a must.

In the past, without any reason to take our own planet into consideration, astrologers placed many of Earth's traits onto the planet Saturn. As a result, the astrological symbology of Saturn may be somewhat skewed or obscured within this over-coated layer of substituted Earthly traits. We now know astronomically, that the planet Saturn bears no resemblance to Earth's solid mass at all but is composed of almost pure gas. With all we are learning about our planetary neighbor it might be time to take another look at some of our traditional beliefs about Saturn in astrology to see if some updates are in order.

If Chiron becomes Virgo's official planetary ruler the only sign without a ruler will be Taurus. This is ironic in lieu of the fact that Taurus is the most stable and consistent of the signs, the most like our home world itself. We have plenty of newly discovered planets out there to choose from: Ceres, Eris, Sedna, etc. and yet there is little talk about assigning Taurus to one of them. The time for picking a planetary ruler for Taurus is long, long, overdue. A synchronicity is occurring within this time and place, even within the symbology itself. The obviousness of Taurian indicators bearing such a close relationship to Earth is almost not worth mentioning. There is something shocking in the fact that there hasn't been more written about it.

The social (and other) leanings of Libra continue to match its ruler Venus, while the Quincunx aspect between the signs of Libra and Taurus should drive a final nail in the wall of separation between the two.

As a species of Earth we have a past relationship with our planet that is rich and complex, but over millennia: buildings, air conditioners, paved roads and ever higher technology has served to separate us from the natural environment. The power of Earth and any connection we may have had to it in the human arena has been downgraded, trivialized, and subsequently lost to many of us. We now take it for granted or ignore it completely and this attitude has become perilous to our race. We continue to struggle with even the most basic ideas and understanding when it comes to living within our Earthly means. For all the progress we've made as a species we're still polluting and destroying our own habitat and the rest of the animals and plants here as well.

As astrologers we may hold one of the keys to helping the Earth at a most fundamental level: awareness. Just the addition of our planetary symbol to our astrological charts speaks volumes about what we are willing to look at and accept into our hearts and minds. Astrologers have a very unique opportunity here, to put Earth on the map so to speak. To bring human awareness back to our planet, one client at a time. Indeed, just by inserting the glyph in the wheel an esoteric energy source is set in motion, one that will open a portal for a new consciousness of this earth plane, what it's about, and how we can help it (and us) to thrive. The symbolism of astrology is, as we know, a reflection of our "as above so below" reality. We all know what "leaving something out" symbolizes. When we put it in, whether it comes from our discussions of Earth placements in charts or the simple act of acknowledging Earth as part of our ongoing consciousness, we will be contributing to the reinstatement of Earth as a revered and respected power in the universe. We are an incredible and creative race, and we can be well on our way to figuring out not only how to be the best we can be, but better caretakers of our world.

There may be other ways than I have presented, to reconcile the permanent Sun/Earth opposition in the astrological natal chart but that symbolic representation of the duality in our lives on this plane is intriguing and too important not to consider.

The Sun/Earth opposition shows us a good place to begin to understand our history with Earth and also holds many more mundane, yet very exciting, opportunities for self-understanding and growth. From re-embracing the importance of physical health for our bodies, to working with and balancing a world full of opposites that have always confused us as a species, causing much pain in our Earthly lives.

As we study our "new" planet we will discover many things we didn't know, have a deeper understanding of those we did, clarify questionable ideas we might have acquired and begin a better integration of earth knowledge and its symbolism on so many levels. We will not only contribute to ecological solutions, but add to our symbolic resources in astrology and even address old and stagnated problems within our psyches.

I know that many of the concepts presented in this book are in conflict with, or at least challenge, some of our traditional ideas. One of the things I love about astrology is that it is incredibly complex, as boundless as the universe itself. There is always more to learn. With that in mind, my hope is that this book opens up yet another vista and gives suggestions for further study both on paper and in our everyday lives. I want to encourage astrologers to do their own investigations, ask their clients about Earth in their charts and come to even greater conclusions than I have about the ideas presented in this book. These ideas are not meant to be conclusive or as that nice earthly phrase states: "written in stone." Rather they are here to start some experimentation and open up a dialog. Within the astrological community it is my fondest hope that this book will be the start of our own "Earth Rise!"

About the Author

Cynthia Wood was minding her own business one night in 1968, when a friend of her mother's started telling her she was born under the sign of the bull. She was 13 years old and had no idea what the woman was talking about, but by the end of the evening, she did know one thing: she was hooked. She has spent the rest of her life studying and living with astrology.

She has been a professional astrologer, reader, lecturer, teacher, radio show host, a very slow blogger, and at last, a writer. In addition to astrology, she has studied and/or been actively engaged in: metaphysics, physics, Wicca, Tarot, and shamanism.

Cynthia has been published in The Mountain Astrologer magazine, a columnist in the alternative weekly The Sandpoint Reader, and the host of the astrological show "All About Us" on Panhandle Community Radio 88.5 KRFY. This is her first book.

Website: www.livingdeeper.com

www.ingramcontent.com/pod-product-compliance
Lightning Source LLC
Chambersburg PA
CBHW071642160426
43195CB00012B/1327